General Editor: Robert Rietti

LUIGI PIRANDELLO

Collected Plays

Volume Four

AS YOU DESIRE ME
THINK IT OVER, GIACOMINO!
THIS TIME IT WILL BE DIFFERENT
THE IMBECILE

This edition first published in Great Britain in 1996 by
Calder Publications Limited
179 Kings Cross Road, London WC1X 9BZ

and in the United States of America in 1996 by
Riverrun Press Inc
1170 Broadway, New York, NY 10001

British Library Cataloguing-in-Publication Data
A catalogue record for this book is available from The British Library

Library of Congress Cataloging-in-Publication Data
A catalog record for this book is available from The Library of Congress

ISBN 0 7145 4271 7

Typeset in 10 on 11 pt Times by Pure Tech India Ltd., Pondicherry.
Printed in Great Britain by Redwood Books Ltd, Trowbridge, Wiltshire.

CONTENTS

CONTENTS

INTRODUCTION

Surprisingly little seems to be known in England about Luigi Pirandello who died in 1936, and of whom *The Times* said: 'It is largely to him that the theatre owes its liberation, for good or ill, from what Desmond MacCarthy called "the inevitable limitations of the modern drama, the falsifications which result from cramming scenes into acts and tying incidents down to times and places." ' Only a few of his major works have been published in English to date and as a result there is a tendency to classify Pirandello as a purely intellectual writer, prone to 'cerebral gymnastics' and most difficult for an actor to interpret. Those who find him so might first study a little the life of the man and in so doing they may reach a better understanding of Pirandello the dramatist.

Pirandello was born at Caos in Sicily in 1867. He studied letters at Palermo University and later in Rome. For many years he taught at a girls' school, living in comparative poverty and growing steadily unhappier in his work. His marriage ended in disaster when his wife became mentally unbalanced and had to be sent to a mental institution. His literary efforts began with poems, short stories and later he wrote novels; he did not start writing seriously for the theatre until 1915 at the age of forty-eight, after which he gave to the stage no fewer than forty-three plays in Italian and several in Sicilian.

For a number of years he was in charge of his own theatrical company, which had as its leaders Ruggero Ruggeri and Marta Abba, and many of his plays were written as tailor-made articles for them and for the rest of his group. Despite the severe lack of finance, he never succumbed to writing plays which conformed to the style and idiom of the more successful dramatists of his time. He deliberately created anti-heroes. His protagonists are like 'soldiers who have been beaten in their first battle and have no belief in the future!'

Having lost a considerable sum of money with his own company, and become greatly disillusioned because his native Italy considered him 'too original for the box office', (often his plays were translated and performed abroad long before they saw the footlights in their own language) and already almost seventy, Pirandello suddenly announced that Europe had grown too old for him, that it could boast of only one other young brain (Bernard Shaw), and that he would take himself off to a country of new ideas—and then journeyed to America.

Pirandello was a fiery, passionate man who had reached his own particular outlook on life through adversity and years of tortured wondering at the true significance of reality. His primary concern was with the illusions and self-deceptions of mankind and the nature of identity. His works grew—as Eric Bentley points out—'from his own torment, and through his genius they came to speak for all the tormented and potentially to all the tormented, that is, to all men.' He delighted in creating an unusual but logistical situation—developing it seemingly illogically—and by continually tossing the coin until both sides have been clearly revealed, managing to convince his audience that his unconventional and not very credible treatment was in fact wholly logical and convincing.

Many of his plays were written in the style known to the Italians as 'grottesco': comedies developed tragically or tragedies developed comically. Nearly all spring from intensely dramatic situations—situations in which passion, love and tragedy make their presence strongly felt.

In England theatre productions of his works have been few and far between, and this may be due partly to the fact that producers and actors, when faced with a play of his, sometimes assume: 'he is going to be far too difficult for the audience so it will be up to us to put that right!' By approaching the text with the preconceived notion that a particular interpretation must shine like a beacon between author and audience in order to elucidate matters, one often succeeds merely in confusing the issue further. There have been examples of this author's brilliantly cynical humour, behind whose mask we are meant to see our own selves, being deliberately distorted to the level of unacceptable farce in an attempt to 'clarify'.

If Pirandello's plays were approached more simply, were permitted to play *themselves* more, and did not have the Latin sentiment and human compassion ironed out by their interpreters, perhaps the fear that one may not be able to follow him would be removed from the minds of many of our theatregoers. It would be found that his comedies, as Kenneth Tynan wrote: 'wear their fifty-odd years as if they were swaddling clothes', and his works might then find themselves a niche in our commercial theatre.

In presenting the complete dramatic works of Luigi Pirandello, we have attempted to hold to the line of simplicity in translation, avoiding the temptation of so many adaptors to reconstruct the author's statements in the light in which they themselves see them. Many translations offered to us have been by people with little or no knowledge of Italian, who have relied on a commissioned literal translation which they have rephrased in their own style. This is a method which should be severely frowned upon.

Pirandello's plays often leave the audience with an uneasy feeling that the situation is not concluded and that we have not wholly understood all we have seen. We feel the need to discuss the play and search for the real truth among the various aspects of it which have been depicted for us.

In many of his plays, events do not take place before our eyes: they have already occurred before the rise of the curtain. It is as though we are aware of an immutable past awaiting judgment . . . it weighs on the minds of the characters in the drama and they cannot abandon or dismiss it. They are caught up in a 'prison of fact'. As Leône Gala says in *The Rules of the Game*: 'When a fact has happened, it stands there, like a prison, shutting you in.'

Pirandello seems determined never to allow his audience to be satisfied. For him, the spectators are no inert mass which revives and becomes articulate only after the curtain has fallen. No—they have to be awakened, shaken up and agitated while in their seats and made to become involved with the actors. The auditorium is to be part of the stage and the listener to take part in the discussion; to be filled with doubt and uncertainty.

Pirandello constantly reverses the coin, revolves the situation. He never intervenes to clarify: 'the enigma must remain an enigma, and at the end there is to be no conclusion, rather a question mark.' As Giovanni Macchia, an eminent authority on the maestro, says: 'it is impossible to love Pirandello, but then the destiny of all artistes today is not to make themselves loved, but to be oppressed and tortured. And among the tortured, the spectator is not to be spared.' As to his protagonists, they are not tragic heroes, but miserable sad objects worthy only of pity, derision or commiseration.

The plot of *As You Desire Me* ('Come tu mi vuoi') was criticized as being far-fetched, yet it was very similar to a true case of mistaken identity (the Bruneri-Canetti case in the Italian courts in 1929, two years before the play was written.)

Cia, the protagonist of the play, is abducted by invading Austrian troops and completely disappears. Everyone believes her to be dead. Ten years later, she seems to have been discovered in Berlin where, under the name of Elma, she is a cabaret performer and the mistress of a mediocre writer called Carl Salter whom she loathes, despite the fact that she continues to live with him. Elma is a restless, tormented being, hating 'modern life' and all human beings whom she calls beasts; with the difference that 'beasts at least are endowed with the wisdom of instinct, and are natural, whereas when man tries to be natural, he becomes a destructive fool.'

What would happen if man were not gifted with reason as a strait-jacket?

The characters in the play are divided between those who believe she really is Cia and those who fear she is party to a masquerade. The audience too is likely to be divided until the final twist when Cia rebels against the mistrust of her 'family' as she realizes that her attempts to start a new life have proved futile.

In preparing this version of 'Come tu mi vuoi' thanks are due to Timothy Holme for some phrases suggested by him.

Think it Over, Giacomino! ('Pensaci Giacomino!') is Pirandello in a lighter vein; nevertheless it is typical of his queer logic and ability to turn the irrational into an acceptable argument. Professor Toti, an elderly teacher in a small Sicilian town, has patiently borne his underpaid situation for many years, unable to afford a wife and family. He finally revolts and decides to take a very young wife, thereby forcing the government to pay his pension to his widow for many years to come. He chooses Lillina, the daughter of the school janitor . . . only to discover that she is pregnant by one of his ex-pupils who is out of work and unable to provide for her and the expected child. Undeterred, the professor argues that this may be all for the best. He goes ahead with his plan, but once they are married and living a *ménage à trois* Giacomino finds he can no longer face the gossip and scandal in the Sicilian village, and succumbs to the pressure of his sister and the local priest to abandon Lillina and his child, and to affiance himself to another girl of their choice. But the professor convinces Giacomino to return to Lillina.

We are left powerless before the old professor's logic. We are convinced he is right to act as he does. He is no longer the ridiculous figure of the earlier scenes, he now captures our sympathy and the 'harsh satirical laugh dies on our lips.'

Pirandello's claim to have 'converted the intellect into passion' is given startlingly dramatic vindication in the play,

This Time it will be Different ('Come prima, meglio di prima') of 1920. The piece is dominated by Fulvia, a passionate rebellious woman who challenges all social norms. Her fiery spirit is signalled by her name, her flowing hair, and in the first two Acts by her *déshabillé*. It has found its outlet before the play begins in thirteen years of desperate living and promiscuity, culminating in a violent and bloody attempt at suicide. Her former husband, Silvio Gelli, as wooden and frozen as his name suggests, has rushed to her aid some days before the action opens and has saved her life. While Fulvia's whole nature tends towards darkness and dissolution, Silvio Gelli is rigidly conventional, rational and disciplined, a surgeon whose life's work is the restoration of order to broken lives and bodies. The play comes over as a dramatic rendering of the archetypal tension between these two opposed and often-classified kinds of temperment. Nietzsche's distinction in the *Birth of Tragedy* between Apollionian and Dionysiac being perhaps the most apposite in this case.

Fulvia seeks fulfilment for her ecstatic yearnings not through sex or the senses as one might expect, but through motherhood, which seems to hold out to her the promise of some kind of redemption or liberation. The play explores the emotional workings of parenthood from a relativistic viewpoint, and by extension demonstrates the subjectivity of all relationships. As in *All for the Best* and *The Other Son*, Pirandello is insisting that the blood-tie does not in itself constitute a significant bond. Fulvia longs for acceptance by her biological daughter Livia, who for thirteen years has been led to believe that her mother is dead, and whose mind is obsessed with ghostly images of a different, idealized Fulvia, firmly lodged with the saints in Heaven. Damaged, fierce and frustrated, sixteen-year-old Livia is the saddest figure in the play. Her name, too, resounds with phonetic associations (*livore*: spite, and *livido*: bruised, also pale and colourless). She seems a shadow, drained of life-blood, dreaming of phantoms and physically repelled by Fulvia, emblem of plenitude, overflowing with life and secret knowledge. She returns her mother's offers of affection with silent fury or with outbursts of virulent scorn.

Marco Mauri the mad lover completes the quartet of protagonists. As a personality he is inadequate and ridiculous, but as a madman he represents the angels of darkness and the forces of unreason. He is out of his mind with passion, and can scarcely be aware of the Dionysian resonance of his insistence on recognition (here I am, and I have to be considered). Even his name contains dark echoes, stemming from *mauros, maurus*: 'black' in Greek and Latin.

The central action is witnessed by a chorus of more or less grotesque onlookers. Those in Act I appear to be strangely peripheral, though the embittered bond between the Widow Nàccheri and her daughter Judith provides a sinister reminder of the death-trap which the mother-daughter relationship can become. As in many of Pirandello's plays the presence of caricatural figures punctuates the story with random and discordant detail, moments of bathos and hilarity, sharp-edged, cooling the melodrama, and keeping constantly before the audience the Pirandellian vision of the anarchic arbitrary quality of life.

The Imbecile ('L'Imbecille') is in the tradition of the *beffa*, a trick or practical joke, which forms a favourite basis for plots throughout Italian literature, from the stories of Boccaccio, via Renaissance comedy and the *commedia dell'arte*, to the plays of Dario Fo in our own time. A recurrent formula is that of the *beffatore* (or would-be *beffatore*) *beffato*, in which the trick backfires on the trickster, a variant of which Pirandello gives us here. It would be a pity to give away the plot, the sting in the tail which gives the play its point and its title. It must suffice to say that in Pirandello's hands the device takes on a deeply menacing complexion, its plot no longer determined by motives of deception and adultery, but by those of bitterness, anger and despair.

At the same time the play is a parable of evanescence, of the passingness of all human devices and desires, including the 'personal antagonisms and idiotic rivalries' of politics. It contains the unforgettable exchange:

COMMERCIAL TRAVELLER: What's going on?

LUCA: . . . So you don't live here in Costanova?

COMMERCIAL TRAVELLER: No. I'm just passing through.

LUCA: My dear good sir, we are all of us just passing through.

Like *The Man with the Flower in his Mouth* the play presents the microcosmic view of life which only a keen awareness of human mortality can bestow, but whereas the imminence of death inspires the man with the flower with a fierce delight in life (the often-quoted '*gusto della vita*'), it arouses in Luca Fazio nothing but an overwhelming sense of futility, pity and disgust.

ROBERT RIETTI
FELICITY FIRTH

AS YOU DESIRE ME

Come tu mi vuoi

1930

Translated by
Robert Rietti

CHARACTERS

THE WOMAN
CARL SALTER, a writer
GRETA, his daughter, known as MOP
BRUNO PIERI
BOFFI
AUNT LENA CUCCHI
UNCLE SALESIO NOBILI
INEZ MASPERI, wife of:-
SILVIO MASPERI, a laywer
BARBARA, Bruno's sister
THE MADWOMAN
A DOCTOR
A NURSE
FOUR YOUNG MEN IN EVENING DRESS
A PORTER

The first Act takes place in Berlin, in the home of Carl Salter; Acts Two and Three take place in a villa near Udine, ten years after the First World War.

ACT I

The living-room of CARL SALTER's *flat in Berlin, furnished with bizarre magnificence. Through an archway on the right, part of the study is visible. It is night, and both living-room and study are lamplit. The various coloured shades set off the strangeness of the furnishing and decoration, giving the whole a sense of mysterious 'set-apartness'.* SALTER's *daughter,* MOP, *is huddled in an armchair, her face hidden. She might be asleep, but in fact, she is crying. Her hair is cut in a boyish fashion and her face bears a strange, disturbing, expression which makes one think she must have suffered much.* CARL SALTER *comes in from the study. He is a man of fifty with a swollen whitish face and dark bags under his pale eyes. He is wearing a rich dressing-gown and keeps his hands in the pockets.*

SALTER (*excited, upset*): She's back with them again. I've just seen her from the window. (*Almost involuntarily he draws one hand out of his pocket—it is clutching a small revolver.*)

MOP (*seeing it at once*): What have you got in your pocket? It's a gun . . .

SALTER (*putting his hand back immediately—with irritation*): Nothing. Look, if she brings them up here, you're not to stay with them.

MOP: What are you going to do?

SALTER: I don't know. But I will not have these idiotic drunks from the night-club following her here. It's got to be stopped somehow.

MOP: Somehow? Are you mad?

SALTER: Go and listen at the door. See if she's coming up alone. (MOP *moves towards the corridor*.) Wait a moment. (*He holds her back, listening*.) I can hear her shouting. (*Distant and confused voices are heard echoing on the stairs below*.)

MOP: Perhaps she's getting rid of them . . .

SALTER: They're all drunk. And there was someone else following them.

MOP: Give me the gun.

SALTER: (*moving away, angrily*): Oh, don't be stupid— I'm not going to use it. It's just here—in my pocket— that's all.

MOP: Give it to me!

SALTER: Leave me alone! (*The voices are louder and nearer*.)

SALTER: Listen!

MOP: They're quarrelling . . . Quick, we must let her in. She may need help.

The front door opens. THE WOMAN, *the* YOUTHS *and* BOFFI *surge in. The men are in evening dress and very drunk. They are swirling round* BOFFI *and* THE WOMAN. MOP *attempts to rescue her while her father*, SALTER *endeavours to push the men out.*

One young man is fat with a ruddy complexion, another is bald, another is very effiminate and has dyed hair. They look to us like battered marionettes as they whirl their arms about meaninglessly. THE WOMAN *is in her thirties and very beautiful. She is also a little tipsy and cannot quite manage her usual dark frown which masks her contempt for every-thing and everyone, her despair and abandon in which—if she were to let herself go—she would lose complete control of herself after all she has been through. She wears a most elegant cloak beneath which she has a fanciful costume she dons when dancing at the Club.*

BOFFI *manages to look out of place wherever he is. He is convinced that life is one great gamble—he is intent on not losing a single trick. He tries hard to make an impression on others, but it is only a mask to hide a simple and naïve nature. From a habit of jerking up his head as though he were suffocating, he has contracted a twitching in his neck muscles which causes him at times to stick out his chin and draw in the corners of his mouth. He often laughs at this habit, and mutters—more to himself—'Let's be serious!'*

THE WOMAN: Stop it! Shut up! I'm sick of you all! Go away! It's not a joke any more!

1ST YOUTH: Won't you do just one last dance for us— the one with the broken glasses?

2ND YOUTH: Give us a drink first, one for the road! Do the 'Champagne Bubbles' dance!

3RD YOUTH: We'll sing you the music. All together now . . .

4TH YOUTH (*singing drunkenly*): Cloo—dovee—o—(*He is singing the name 'Clodoveo'.*)

1ST YOUTH: No! It should be sad! Sad as death!

THE WOMAN: Oh, leave me alone!

BOFFI: That's enough now! Off you go! (4TH YOUTH *breaks into song again.*)

BOFFI: It sounds lovely, but can't you see she's had enough?

SALTER: Get out of my house!

1ST YOUTH: A charming host, I must say! Give us a drink first!

2ND YOUTH (*to* SALTER): She invited us in for one herself, so you can't refuse.

3RD YOUTH (*confidentially*): And we're all going to get undressed!

3RD YOUTH (*singing*): Clooo—dovee—o . . . (*Then as* SALTER *hits him.*) Oh, you beast!

MOP: This is disgusting! It's an invasion! (*Then to* THE WOMAN, *embracing her protectively and at the same time pulling her into the living-room.*) Come away from them, Elma, darling!

THE WOMAN (*freeing herself and entering the living-room*): Oh, for heaven's sake, Mop, no—now you have to start mauling me—that's the last straw!

SALTER (*in the corridor with* BOFFI, *keeping the youths out*): I warn you, if you don't get out, I'll shoot!

BOFFI (*pushing them out*): Go on—get out! That's enough! Get out!

1ST YOUTH (*before the door closes in his face*): Elma! Come and caress me! Just one little cuddle!

2ND YOUTH: For you bow-wow!

MOP: They make me sick!

The FOUR YOUTHS *are out now and the door is closed. But they can still be heard making an uproar on the stairs. The* 3RD YOUTH *continues singing 'Clooo—dovee—o . . . .'*

SALTER: What did they want?

THE WOMAN: What do they always want? Bastards . . . And they made me drink so much . . .

SALTER: It's outrageous! And now the neighbours 'll be complaining again.

THE WOMAN: All right, then, turn me out! I've always told you to!

MOP: Elma—no!

THE WOMAN: Well, listen to him—he says it's out-rageous.

SALTER: It's quite simple—all you have to do is stop going with them.

THE WOMAN: I won't stop—I'll join them now. (*She makes a quick move towards the door.*) I'll soon catch them up!

BOFFI (*stopping her*): Lucia!

THE WOMAN (*turning to him*): Who the Hell *are* you?

SALTER (*to* BOFFI): Right! And what are you doing here?

BOFFI: I came to help her.

SALTER: He was following them—I saw him.

THE WOMAN: For so many evenings—like a sheepdog—he's always with me.

MOP: And you don't know who he is?

BOFFI: She knows perfectly well who I am. (*He twitches.*) Let's be see—erious! (*Then, as though to tempt her into surrender he calls her again.*) Lucia . . .

MOP (*worried*): Lucia?

THE WOMAN: That's right—just like that—in every tone of voice he calls me—'Lucia'—'Lucia'—following me everywhere . . .

BOFFI: And you always turn round.

THE WOMAN: Only because . . .

BOFFI (*interrupting*): Because you are Lucia . . .

THE WOMAN: No!

BOFFI: I say yes—every time I called her by her name, she started and went pale.

THE WOMAN: Well, of course—hearing someone call out like that . . .

BOFFI: Hearing your past call out, Lucia.

THE WOMAN (*to* MOP): At night, too, Mop—well, I mean—and then you turn and see that devil's face . . .

BOFFI: Oh, it's not really a devil's face—it's a trick of the light.

THE WOMAN: It's a trick of the trade!

BOFFI: All right, then—just as it's a trick of your trade to play God knows what part before these people—when you are Lucia.

MOP: What is all this about?

THE WOMAN: He really believes it, you see—he really believes it.

BOFFI: I'd stake my life on it.

THE WOMAN: That I am Lucia?

BOFFI: Lucia Pieri.

THE WOMAN: What?

BOFFI: Don't pretend you don't understand!

THE WOMAN: I didn't hear the name!

BOFFI (*turning to* SALTER—*a denunciation and a challenge*): I said Pieri. Her husband's name is Pieri.

THE WOMAN (*falling into a chair—worried*): My husband?

BOFFI: Your husband, Bruno. And he's here.

THE WOMAN: What do you mean? Here, where?

SALTER: This is crazy!

BOFFI: I called him here.

THE WOMAN: You really *are* mad!

BOFFI: He arrived this evening.

SALTER: Her husband has been dead for four years.

THE WOMAN (*turning on* SALTER, *spontaneously and involuntarily*): No...

SALTER (*stopped*): No?

BOFFI: I sent for him. He arrived this morning. He's at the Eden Hotel. Just round the corner.

THE WOMAN (*to* BOFFI, *very wrought up*): Stop this joke about a husband. I have no husband. Who did you send for?

BOFFI: Look how upset she gets.

SALTER (*to* THE WOMAN): So he's still alive?

BOFFI (*answering for her*): I tell you he's just round the corner. (*To* THE WOMAN.) If you like... (*He looks round.*) ... you can phone him. (THE WOMAN *breaks into hysterical laughter.*)

SALTER: What is all this?

THE WOMAN: I've got a husband just round the corner. You hear? I can call him whenever I like.

SALTER (*to* BOFFI, *to cut the matter short*): Look, you—whatever your name is—we neither of us feel like going on with this idiotic game...

THE WOMAN (*to* SALTER—*jokingly, but at the same time as a challenge*): No—wait a moment, Salter. What if I really were...?

SALTER: If you really were...?

THE WOMAN: Lucia. The person he's so sure he can see in me. What would you say?

SALTER: I've already told you—I called it an idiotic game.

THE WOMAN: All right, then—an idiotic game. But if I'm not Lucia—who am I?

SALTER: Who are you?

THE WOMAN: That's what I said. Do you know me any better than he does?

SALTER: I know you better than you know yourself.

THE WOMAN: Oh, no, my darling. Do you imagine that if I wanted to know myself—if I wanted to be a real person even in my own eyes—(*turning to* SALTER) this gentleman's Lucia, for example—(*taking* BOFFI's *arm*)—I could bear to go on living here with you? (*She leaves* BOFFI *and turns to* MOP, *capricious now*.) You tell them, Mop—what is my name?

MOP: Elma!

THE WOMAN: You see? It's an Arabic name. And you know what it means? Water . . . Water . . . (*And she stretches out her hands, rippling her fingers as though she were illustrating the deliberate inconsistency of her life now. Then with a sudden change of tone*.) Oh, God, they made me drink so much! Five cocktails and then champagne. (*To* MOP.) Give me something to eat!

MOP: Yes, of course. What do you want?

THE WOMAN: I don't know . . . I don't know . . . I'm all burnt up inside!

MOP: I'll go and see . . .

THE WOMAN: Don't do anything complicated, darling.

MOP: Some sandwiches?

THE WOMAN: A piece of bread'll do—anything to stop my head spinning.

MOP: I'll get it right away. (*She runs off, right*.)

SALTER (*to* BOFFI): Now, Herr what's your name . . . will you please admit you've made a mistake . . . and go.

THE WOMAN: Oh, leave him alone . . . he's a friend of mine . . .

BOFFI: She knows that I haven't made a mistake.

THE WOMAN: Providing you don't make me speak to my husband on the telephone—I draw the line at that.

BOFFI (*firmly*): Your husband has waited . . .

SALTER (*interrupting violently*): Shut up about this husband! (*Turning to* THE WOMAN.) You told me he died four years ago.

BOFFI (*louder, determined*): She told you a lie.

THE WOMAN (*rises and goes to shake hands with* BOFFI): I did . . . and I'm delighted to hear you say so.

BOFFI· Thank God!

SALTER: You did lie?

THE WOMAN: Yes! (*Then to* BOFFI.) But, don't thank God too soon! I only said I was delighted because you—affirmed my right to lie—under these circumstances. (*To* SALTER.) Shall I tell you all the lies I've told you, Salter, and you tell me yours?

SALTER: I've never lied!

THE WOMAN: No? But we never do anything but lie—all of us!

SALTER: I've never lied to you!

THE WOMAN: You even lie to yourself! With your own revolting sincerity, you lie—because you're not really as nasty as you make out. But don't worry—nobody really lies completely—we just tell tall stories—to other people and to ourselves. (*To* BOFFI.) Four years ago someone *did* die for me—even if he wasn't my husband! But that doesn't mean that my husband's alive and here—not for me. (*Deliberately mysterious, as though she were making up a poem.*) At the very most—he's the husband of someone—who no longer exists—a poor widower, which is like saying that . . . as a husband . . . he too is dead! But tell us your story just the same. It must be interesting if you've come all the way here. So we'll learn something at last about his Lucia—who you think I am.

BOFFI (*having made up his mind—moving to her*): May I speak to you alone for a moment?

THE WOMAN: Oh, no . . . not alone. Here in front of Salter—I want him to know. (*She lies down.*) Besides, there are no secrets any longer today—there's no modesty. (*To* MOP *who enters with a sandwich.*) Ah, clever Mop, you've found me something. (*She draws herself up on one elbow.*) Excuse me. (*She bites the sandwich.*) Oh, God, I'm hungry.

MOP: Look—your sleeve . . .

THE WOMAN: Torn? It must have been those bastards . . .

MOP: No, I think it's just come unsewn.

THE WOMAN: D'you know I couldn't knock the bottle down this evening—perhaps I was too far away. (*She playfully kicks off her slippers, and with the grace of a dancer, runs over on her toes to* BOFFI, *and takes his opera hat from under his arm.*) May I borrow that a moment? (*She snaps it open and places it on the floor in the centre of the stage: then she pulls her skirt up as far as her knees and, balancing on one foot, she lifts the other as if to knock over a bottle of champagne represented by the opera hat. She hums under her breath, accompanying the movement.*) Tairirari . . . tairirari . . . (*Twice she lifts her foot and gracefully kicks at the hat, missing it each time.*) You see? I was too far off! (*She picks up the hat, closes it against her chest and gives it back to* BOFFI.) Thanks. Did you know that Lucia—let's hope it won't offend her husband—Lucia dances in a night-club. The 'Lari-Fari'? Did you know that?

BOFFI: The more you go on like that, the more you convince me that you are she. Besides, how could I fail to recognize you? I've known you since you were a baby.

THE WOMAN: Really? Since I was a baby? Well, well . . . And have I changed much since then?

BOFFI: Everybody changes. But you've changed very little considering all you must have gone through!

THE WOMAN (*she looks at him for a moment*): You know you interest me? I've got all sorts of pasts. Even now— look at these two, father and daughter. (*She indicates* SALTER *and* MOP.) Such things—if only you knew!

SALTER (*shaking—he can't stand much more*): Be quiet! Aren't you ashamed?

MOP (*rallying to* THE WOMAN—*moved*): No, poor girl, she's right . . . (*She makes to embrace her.*)

THE WOMAN (*irritated, escaping from* MOP): Oh, Mop, for heaven's sake!

SALTER (*taking advantage of* THE WOMAN's *irritation—to* MOP *furiously*): Leave her alone! And stop playing around in those ridiculous pyjamas! Go to bed!

MOP (*tragically, moving towards her father*): It's you who should be ashamed of yourself, Father—not she.

THE WOMAN (*holding her back, with weary exasperation*): Oh, for God's sake don't start again!

SALTER (*to* MOP): I told you to get out—go to bed!

THE WOMAN: Yes, darling, go, go, go—go and make me another sandwich, eh?

MOP: You'll come and eat it in the kitchen?

THE WOMAN: All right . . . on condition that you don't kiss me, you know I can't stand it when you kiss me. (SALTER *laughs ferociously.*)

MOP: You pig!

THE WOMAN (*a sudden burst at* SALTER): Stop laughing! (*Then turning to* BOFFI.) It's the sort of thing that only happens to me! They're jealous of each other!

MOP (*hurt—begging her*): Elma—no! Don't say that, darling!

THE WOMAN: There we are, 'darling'—I only wish it weren't true, but just look at him. (*She indicates* SALTER.)

SALTER (*fuming, his hands in his pockets*): I can't stand much more of this!

THE WOMAN (*deliberately provoking, cruel, turning to* BOFFI): His wife won't divorce him, you see. So she sends her daughter to get him away from me. And what happens? I get landed with the daughter as well. (*To* MOP.) And she's worse than he! He may be old, but at least . . . (*She intends to say 'he is a man'.*)

MOP (*moving forward, looks first at her father, then at* THE WOMAN. *A clear denunciation*): I warn you—there's a revolver in his pocket—and it's intended for you.

THE WOMAN (*turning to look at* SALTER, *cold*): Is that so?

SALTER (*does not reply, sneers with tightly-closed lips, takes the revolver out of his pocket and goes to put it on the table by* THE WOMAN.) There you are—there it is—help yourself. (*He moves back.*)

THE WOMAN (*smiling*): Thanks. Loaded?

SALTER: Loaded.

THE WOMAN (*picks it up*): For whom?

SALTER: Whoever you like.

BOFFI (*as she raises it*): Let's be see—e—rious! Put it down! Lucia, are you crazy?

THE WOMAN (*lowering the revolver, then putting it down—to* BOFFI): You see? Nothing but tragedies.

SALTER (*once more holding himself back with difficulty*): Stop talking to him all the time—he's an outsider. It's me you should be talking to. You've got to decide about us, this evening. Don't pretend you've forgotten that? I haven't.

THE WOMAN: All right, then—let's decide. With the gun? (*She looks at the revolver.*)

SALTER: I'm ready.

THE WOMAN (*jumps up, pale, decided, picks up the gun and points it at him*): You really want me to kill you? I could do it, you know. (*She relaxes, lowers the gun.*) Oh God, I'm so tired of it all. (*She moves to him.*) Suppose instead of killing you—I give you—one kiss— here on your forehead. (*She kisses him.*) You might say thank you . . . (*She gives him the revolver.*) There's your pistol, sweetheart—go on—you kill me now, if you want.

MOP (*jumping up*): No! Look out—he'll do it!

THE WOMAN: Let him! After all, when you can't bear it any longer—I really do wish he had the courage . . . (*Going back to where she was before, to* BOFFI, *with desolate sincerity—it seems as though her own tiredness is talking.*) It's true, you know, I simply can't bear it any longer . . . (*Then rallying.*) I'm half dead with hunger—I ask for a bit of bread and he gives me a revolver—you keep calling me 'Lucia'—it really is a gorgeous evening . . .

SALTER (*jumping up—going to face* BOFFI): Look here, once and for all, this is my house—and I'm asking you to leave!

BOFFI: No. I'm here for the lady—not for you.

SALTER: The lady is in my house. She's my guest!

BOFFI: Are you in the habit of receiving guests with a revolver?

THE WOMAN: And can't I invite someone who says he knows me, if I want to?

SALTER: No, not at this moment, when an understanding must be reached between us. (*To* BOFFI.) Now, will you go?

BOFFI: Yes,—with the lady.

THE WOMAN (*rising unexpectedly, firm*): Very well! I'll come with you!

SALTER (*fierce, he springs over to her and grips her wrist*): You shan't move from here!

THE WOMAN (*unsuccessfully trying to free herself*): You can't stop me going out if I want!

SALTER: Oh yes, I can!

THE WOMAN: By force?

SALTER: If necessary—if you insist on taking up with anybody who comes . . .

BOFFI: Ah, but I'm not just anybody who comes.

SALTER: You're not wanted here—and she doesn't know you!

BOFFI: She doesn't want to know me. My name is Boffi.

THE WOMAN (*quickly*): The photographer?

BOFFI (*to* SALTER, *triumphant*): You see? She does know me!

SALTER: Boffi? (*Remembering*) Yes, course I've heard of you—you had an exhibition here . . .

MOP: We saw those pictures of his in the paper . . .

THE WOMAN (*determined, having taken a dramatic decision, gambling all in one throw*): I've been lying! I do know him! I do know him! He's a friend of my husband! (*Wrenching herself free.*) Let me go!

SALTER: But you laughed at the idea!

THE WOMAN: Because I didn't want to let him see it was me!

BOFFI: At last! But how could you imagine your husband doesn't know everything that happened to you?

THE WOMAN: No—he can't know! He can't!

BOFFI: He knows everything. Why, they collected all the evidence there.

THE WOMAN (*bewildered, instinctively*): Where?

BOFFI: At the villa, where you lived . . .

SALTER (*seeing her bewilderment—a challenge*): Villa? What villa?

THE WOMAN (*immediately—proud*): My villa! (*Turning to* BOFFI.) Tell Salter what it was—the evidence they collected! He took advantage of the position I was in—now throw that in his face!

BOFFI: She was heard screaming by the old gardener—Filippo—he died a little while ago.

THE WOMAN: That's right—Filippo!

BOFFI: How could she defend herself alone? When we came back, it was enough to see the ruin of the invaded countryside, to know how . . .

THE WOMAN (*as though struck by the sudden memory of something which had really happened*): The occupation! (*Triumphantly, to* SALTER.) You see, Salter, I told you!

SALTER (*taken aback; he is forced to admit this*): Yes, you did say something about the occupation . . .

THE WOMAN: And I lived there—near Venice!

BOFFI: We all know what the enemy was like. (*To* SALTER, *with dignity, as though to blame him for the barbarity of the one-time enemy*.) You see, Bruno Pieri, a gallant Italian officer, came back to the villa which had been reduced to rubble, he could find no trace of the young wife he had married just a year before . . .

THE WOMAN: Bruno . . .

BOFFI: He called you Cia . . .

THE WOMAN: That's right—he called me Cia . . . Cia . . .

BOFFI: He could only imagine what they had done to her . . . the officers who had seized the villa and he went

mad. He was mad for more than a year! If you only knew
how he searched for you at the beginning—he thought
you'd been carried away by the flood of the retreating
enemy.

THE WOMAN: I was! I was carried away on the flood!

SALTER (*to* BOFFI): Wait a moment . . . Wait a moment!
(*Searching his memory.*) I read that story somewhere . . .

BOFFI: In the newspapers.

SALTER: Of course . . . years ago . . .

BOFFI: Her husband had it printed.

THE WOMAN: I never read it!

SALTER (*to* THE WOMAN): You're a fake! (*To* BOFFI.)
I know exactly what she's doing of course. It was a friend
of mine, a psychiatrist in Vienna . . . (*Turning back to*
THE WOMAN, *with contempt.*) You're deliberately mix-
ing up two stories—yours and the one in the papers—and
you're trying to pass yours off as hers.

BOFFI: It's impossible—she is Lucia!

SALTER (*to* THE WOMAN, *with even greater contempt*):
You!

THE WOMAN (*calm*): He says so—and he's known me
since I was a child.

BOFFI: And I can't be wrong!

THE WOMAN (*to* SALTER): You've known me only a
few months.

SALTER (*disturbed*): I've ruined my whole life because of
you!

THE WOMAN: Not because of me—because you were
crazy about me!

SALTER: And who made me crazy?

THE WOMAN: You think I did? You wanted me so badly
. . . that's why you took me in!

SALTER: You tempted me!

THE WOMAN: Oh, temptation! That's a woman's trade,
sweetheart. Besides, after what life has done to me—you
heard what he said?

SALTER: Once and for all, will you stop hiding behind
this ridiculous fraud!

BOFFI: This is no fraud!

THE WOMAN: And anyway, why shouldn't I hide behind it? (*To* BOFFI.) You might have been sent by the gods to help me this evening, Boffi. My saviour, that's what you are. Tell me about when I was a child. I was so different then, that when I think about it, it seems like a dream . . .

BOFFI: Childhood seems like that to everybody, Cia.

THE WOMAN: Do you call me Cia, too? Does everybody call me Cia? Oh, what a pity—I thought it was only *he*.

SALTER (*unable to hold himself back*): Don't think you can get rid of me just like that—after the way you picked me up!

THE WOMAN: I—picked you up?

SALTER: Yes, you did.

THE WOMAN: Then why did you let yourself be picked up? You should have looked after yourself better. All right then, in a sense it's true. But you tricked me just the same.

SALTER: You've got no pity.

THE WOMAN: You've got the face to say that? I've shown you such pity—and your daughter will bear witness to it . . . (*To* BOFFI.) Look at him, people take him for a famous writer, and he's really nothing but a clown!

SALTER: Oh, leave me out of this!

THE WOMAN: How can I when you go on about your poor, ruined life. Do you imagine it will frighten me?

SALTER: You're already afraid.

THE WOMAN: I've never been afraid of you.

SALTER: Then it's time you were now!

THE WOMAN: Because of your revolver? Look—I'm going out with this gentleman. I'm Cia, and he's taking me for a walk as he did when I was a child. Then you can pull the gun out of your pocket and kill me, as though it were a game. Shall we try?

SALTER: Don't tempt me!

THE WOMAN: It's all right by me. (*To* BOFFI, *taking his arm*.) Come, Boffi, let's go. (SALTER *takes out the gun*.)

BOFFI (*immediately putting himself between them*): No! Put that gun down!

THE WOMAN: Look—I've been through the war. Let me have myself killed if I feel like it. Besides, he'd have to kill himself afterwards, and he hasn't got the courage.

SALTER: I have—you know very well I have!

THE WOMAN: What a nerve he's got! (*To* MOP.) Mop, isn't it true that he left your mother because she kept on complaining that he didn't behave as a famous writer ought to behave?

MOP: True enough. He had that nasty affectation of pretending not to believe in himself when visitors came to the house. 'Excuse me, ladies, but I find it impossible to be serious in the presence of my wife who—as you can see—watches over my reputation like a sitting hen!'

SALTER (*exasperated*): I couldn't be serious! I just couldn't! (*To* BOFFI.) It's terrifying how something like that—something quite stupid perhaps, you say for a joke, you see what I mean? How it can harden into an idea that sticks for ever—that's why she calls me an old clown!

THE WOMAN: Well, isn't that what you were—weren't you clowning in front of all those people when I first met you?

SALTER (*interrupting, wildly*): Because I was trying to hide the misery I felt inside me! My life was impossible!

THE WOMAN (*to* BOFFI): Did you see before how he chased away those poor young men who'd only had a drop too much to drink and wanted to have a little fun?! He was afraid their presence might compromise his precious reputation! He's become just like his wife! (*More furious than ever.*) You wanted me to make life possible for you, didn't you? With your daughter who . . . oh, God! (*She covers her face in her hands—disgust, exasperation, desperation.*)

MOP (*running to her, terrified*): No, Elma, no! Please!

THE WOMAN (*almost a scream, pushing her away*): Get away! I must say it!

MOP: Say what?

THE WOMAN: What you've done to me!

MOP: What have I done?

THE WOMAN (*almost beside herself*): You—all of you—I can't stand it any longer—this lunatic asylum—I'm drowning in it—my stomach's splitting open—drink, drink, drink—lunatics laughing. Hell let loose—mirrors, bottles, glasses—all whirling, crashing—they're screaming and dancing—twined together naked—all the vices under the sun mixed in together. And all because they can't find satisfaction any more! (*Grabbing* BOFFI *by one arm and pointing at* MOP.) Look, look at Mop, and tell me if you can see an atom of humanity in that face! (*Pointing at* SALTER.) And Salter over there—with a dead man's face—with all his vices crawling like worms in his eyes—and me dressed like this—and even you with a face like the devil! Look at this house—and not only this house—this whole city—writhing, screaming mad! (*Pointing at* MOP *again*.) She arrived—I knew nothing about her, it was evening and I was at the night-club, I came back—drunk: well, obviously—I knock down champagne bottles and then I drink them—it's called 'Champagne Bubbles'. (*Showing her dress.*) You see? It's my most famous dance—so obviously I'm drunk every evening—and that evening I came home to find her with her face covered in blood . . . a scratch from the forehead to her cheek! God knows what happened between them! (*She takes* MOP's *face and turns it so that* BOFFI *can see.*) Take a good look: she still has the scar!

SALTER: I didn't do it!

MOP: I did it myself . . . but you never believed me!

THE WOMAN: I was so drunk I didn't even see who took me up to bed that night.

MOP (*trembling, she almost throws herself on* THE WOMAN *to stop her going any further*): Elma, stop, I beg you!

THE WOMAN (*pushing her away*): No, I'm going to tell them everything! (*Indicating* SALTER.) He'd gone out . . .

MOP (*clinging to her*): What are you saying? Are you mad?

THE WOMAN (*pulling away from her and throwing her into the armchair, where* MOP *huddles with her face hidden*): Oh, yes, I'm mad all right. Only the mad can shout these things from the roof-tops in front of everybody! (*To* BOFFI, *pointing at* SALTER, *who is smiling*.) Look at Salter, he's laughing—just as he laughed that morning when he found out what had happened the night before.

SALTER: Only because you . . .

THE WOMAN: Because I was disgusted and you didn't think it mattered. Nothing matters to you. But what about Mop, look at her!

SALTER: She's suffering from remorse now!

MOP (*jumping up and shouting wildly*): No! Because it's not fair!

THE WOMAN (*to* BOFFI): They're really proud of what they do, you see? It's their right, they say. But accuse them and they scream that it's not fair! I must get away from here—away from all of them—all of them—even from myself—get away—away—away! I can't stand it any longer!

BOFFI: Then come away, I'm offering you the chance to pick up your own life again.

THE WOMAN: My life? What life?

SALTER (*with fierce mockery*): Your life as Lucia . . . with your husband . . . or had you forgotten that?

THE WOMAN (*to* SALTER, *with pride*): No, I hadn't forgotten! (*Changing tone, to* BOFFI.) This man you say . . . is he still looking for his wife after ten years?

SALTER: His Cia.

BOFFI: Yes, his Cia! In spite of all the opposition from people who wanted to think her dead after ten years . . .

THE WOMAN: But how can this husband still think she's alive, if she hasn't come back to him after all this time?

BOFFI: Because he believed that after all that happened to her . . . to you . . .

THE WOMAN: The woman he's searching for **is no more!**

BOFFI: That's not true. He was convinced you were alive but were too afraid to come back because after what happened to you . . . you feared you would never again be the same for him.

THE WOMAN: Does he really think she *could* be the same?

BOFFI: Why not, Signora . . . if you choose to be.

THE WOMAN: After ten years? After all the things that must have happened to her? The same person? It's impossible—and the fact that she's never gone back to him proves it.

BOFFI: But I'm saying that now . . . if you want to, Signora . . .

THE WOMAN: If I want? I want to escape from myself— that yes—to have no more memories of anything—anything at all—to empty myself of all the life that's in me. Look at this body. You say it's *hers*? That I am like her? I no longer feel anything—I no longer want anything—I don't even know myself! My heart beats, and I don't know it—I breathe, and I don't know it. I no longer know I'm alive. I'm just a body without a name—waiting for somebody to take it over! All right, then . . . if he can re-create me . . . if, out of his memories, he can give back a soul to the body of his Cia . . . let him take it. Let him make a happy life . . . a new life . . . a beautiful life! I no longer want my own!

BOFFI (*resolutely*): I'm going to telephone him!

SALTER: You'll call nobody from my house!

THE WOMAN (*starting to run towards the study*): Then I'll call him!

SALTER (*immediately, stopping her*): No, wait. I'll go. I'll call him from the study. Then we shall see . . . (*He goes quickly into the study.*)

THE WOMAN (*perplexed, stunned*): He's going to . . . But why is Salter going to . . . I thought he . . .

BOFFI: Signora . . . what do you want us to do?

MOP (*who has moved to the door to see what her father is doing—a scream of horror*): No! (*She starts to run into*

the study as the sound of a revolver shot is heard.) Father!
Father!

BOFFI (*running into the study*): Good God, what has he
done?

THE WOMAN (*also making for the study*): He's done what
he always said he would do.

*Their voices come from the study where they are now grouped
round* SALTER's *body. They examine him, later lift him
from the ground to lay him on the sofa.*

MOP: He shot himself in the heart.

BOFFI: No—he's not dead. His heart's still beating.

MOP: There's blood coming out of his mouth.

BOFFI: The bullet must have pierced his lung!

THE WOMAN: Lift him up! Lift his head a little!

MOP: No—gently. Let me do it. Father! Father!

BOFFI: We'd better move him. Put him on the sofa there.
Give me a hand!

MOP: Gently! Gently!

BOFFI: Come round this side—that's right . . .

MOP: It's Mop, Father—your Mop. Over here—that's
right . . . easy . . . mind his head . . . give me that cushion,
there.

THE WOMAN: We must get a doctor!

BOFFI: I'll go—I'll go . . . (SALTER *groans and tries to
speak.*)

MOP: What is it, Father? What are you trying to say? (*To*
THE WOMAN.) He's looking at you!

THE WOMAN: It's not serious—you'll see it's not serious—but we must get a doctor . . .

MOP (*to* BOFFI): Yes, a doctor: there's one living here in
the block! Fetch him quickly, please, quickly! (*The door-
bell rings.*)

BOFFI (*moving back to the living-room*): All right, I'll
go . . .

THE WOMAN (*following him*): His flat's on the floor
below. Doctor Schultz. I'll show you.

BOFFI *has opened the door and a huge, typically German house-porter enters. He is furious, and is just finishing dressing.*

PORTER: What's going on here? I heard a gun shot. Are we ever going to have peace in this place?

THE WOMAN: Herr Salter has wounded himself. He's over there.

PORTER: Wounded *himself*? How?

BOFFI: Shot himself through the lung. It's serious.

THE WOMAN: You must call Dr Schultz. Quickly!

PORTER: At this time of night? He'll be fast asleep.

THE WOMAN: Then wake him up. For God's sake!

PORTER: Not on your life! He'd have me sacked!

BOFFI: I'll call him.

PORTER (*holding him back*): You're not leaving this room—not while there's a wounded man here!

BOFFI (*wrenching his arm free*): You're mad!

PORTER: Not me, sir . . . it's these tenants here. They've turned this block into a mad-house. Anyway it's the rules of the place. Where's this man you say shot himself? Oh, I see him. Is it serious?

BOFFI: Of course it is, you fool. Why d'you think we need a doctor?

PORTER: Well, if it's that serious . . .

MOP (*enters from the other room*): I think we should take him to hospital—right away!

PORTER: Now you're talking. I'll call an ambulance.

MOP: Please! (She *returns to her father. The* PORTER *exits, mumbling to himself.*)

BOFFI: He wasn't very helpful.

THE WOMAN: That's how it is here. The Porter runs the place!

BOFFI: So, you're now free to come with me.

MOP (*calling from the study*): Elma, Elma, come quickly!

THE WOMAN: How can I come with you now?

BOFFI: But, Signora Lucia . . .

MOP (*appearing in the archway*): Elma!

THE WOMAN: She calls me Elma, you hear?
BOFFI: Then I'll fetch your husband.
MOP: Elma, you can't leave him now! You mustn't go!
BOFFI (*taking her arm*): After you've all been insulting her
    all evening? I'll bring him back here, Signora—and I'm
    certain that as soon as you see him, you'll . . .
MOP (*takes her other arm*): Elma, he's asking for you. He
    wants you.

BOFFI *gives up. He shrugs and goes out determinedly.*

THE WOMAN: All right, Mop. You go to him. I'm coming.
MOP (*takes a step, then turns*): Promise you won't leave?
THE WOMAN: I told you I'd come to him. In a minute.
    I need a moment to myself.

MOP *exits to the other room. Left to herself* THE WOMAN
*presses her fingertips against her face, then suddenly takes
them away and holds them against her temples, as though to
support her head, raised in desperation. She closes her eyes.
She murmurs.*

THE WOMAN: Just a body without a name! Without a
    name!

CURTAIN

ACT II

*A large, richly-furnished ground-floor room of the Pieri villa,
near Udine in the north of Italy. Four months have passed
and it is an afternoon in April. At the back is a loggia with
a marble balustrade and four slender columns supporting the*

glass roof. The sunny, green and peaceful countryside, which can be seen from the loggia, is delightful and, like the room itself, full of clear, light colours. Towards the end of the Act, violet coloured shadows settle over it. A staircase leads to the upper floors of the villa and on one wall hangs a large portrait in oils of Lucia Pieri as a young woman—as she was when she was newly married before the First World War.

AUNT LENA CUCCHI *is discovered talking to someone in the garden. She is about sixty, sturdily built, with an unfeminine face and a mass of grey curls. She has thick, dark eyebrows and tortoise-shell spectacles. She is dressed in black with a stiff, starched collar. Her manner is direct and efficient.*

LENA: Do come in. That is quite enough, for Heaven's sake! Well, really—look at that bunch! They're falling all over the place! No, no, don't waste time picking them up! (*She turns away.*) He'd strip the garden bare if he got half a chance!

UNCLE SALESIO NOBILI *enters through the glass doors, carrying a huge bunch of flowers he has just cut. He is a wizzened, dried-up old man who would still be energetic if it weren't for the fact he has a bad back and has difficulty moving his neck. He is wearing his Sunday best clothes and his hair and little moustache are well 'pomaded'. The moustache resembles a couple of dabs of soot under his large nose.* SALESIO *is always concerned with looking smart—his most important aim and perhaps the cross he has to bear! He wears a stiff high shirt collar which he assumes gives him an air of elegance.*

SALESIO: Here we are then—here we are! Now let me explain why . . .
LENA: I don't want to hear any explanations. Put those flowers down!
SALESIO: No, no, no, dear cousin, I wish to explain!
LENA: Give me the flowers. (*She starts to arrange them in various vases.*)

SALESIO: I didn't pick them for the visitors, you know—I only meant to . . .

LENA: I don't care who you picked them for—you picked far too many!

SALESIO: Let me explain . . .

LENA: Explain! Explain! You spend half your life explaining!

SALESIO: And a lot of good it does me! No one ever tries to understand.

LENA: If you must explain . . . then tell me why I feel so fit today—while you're under the weather.

SALESIO: That's not true. I'm feeling *very* well.

LENA: Very *bad*!

SALESIO: Why should I feel bad?

LENA: If you need explanations for that, it just goes to show that you've no idea of what you've done.

SALESIO: What have I done?

LENA: Never mind that now. God willing, it's all over! Today they'll be agreeing on this blessed affi . . . affi . . . affidated . . .

SALESIO (*laughing*): Affidated? Oh, ha ha! That's good— that's very good! Affidated indeed! It's an affidavit.

LENA: Well, affi . . . whatever it is, that'll be the end of it. If I had my way . . . I'd pension you off! With Cia here, there's no room for both of you.

SALESIO: That's a fine thing! That's all the thanks I get after robbing myself of everything for my niece's sake!

LENA: Nonsense. When you gave Cia the villa and grounds as a dowry, you weren't robbing yourself of anything! You were rich then—and it hardly meant a thing to you.

SALESIO: And now that I'm poor, I'm to be thrown out like an old coat!

LENA: That's what you deserve for not sharing Bruno's faith that poor Cia was alive.

SALESIO: And just how much faith did you have, eh?

LENA: I never had anything to do with declaring her legally dead.

SALESIO: Only because nobody asked you to.

LENA: I wouldn't have done it even if they had asked. Trying to rob poor Bruno of the villa and the estate!

SALESIO: But, for Heaven's sake, they were never his! You keep forgetting that there was no evidence she was alive. Bruno just wasn't one of the family any longer.

LENA: It's you who are forgetting how much Bruno put into the place! Rebuilding the villa and increasing the value of it all. And now you would deny him the right to . . .

SALESIO: He had no right!

LENA: Oh yes, I know what you're getting at! That nasty little scheme Ines and you concocted to try and get the State to be responsible for all the repairs! I refused to have anything to do with that dirty affair!

SALESIO: But Ines was my only other niece—and when she got married I was too poor to do anything for her!

LENA: So you admit it was all on her account! The idea of getting back what you'd given Cia! It turns my stomach to think about it! That's why I could never face marrying one of your family.

SALESIO (rebelling after having swallowed so much): And they—let me tell you—they could never face marrying you!

LENA: I'm perfectly happy to admit it.

SALESIO: And you know why, Lena? You're ugly. And you've got an ugly character, too. You just won't admit that I'm poor because I've given away so much.

LENA: On the contrary—I've accepted your motives, as a poor man, for trying to get your property back. But as far as your other niece is concerned. I'm sure that even you must have felt sickened at her crocodile tears when her sister was declared dead!

SALESIO: She was upset over the unpleasantness with Bruno. It's strange that Bruno understood my predicament—but not you!

LENA: . . . Because I used my gumption and didn't take sides! I can understand Bruno's behaviour—and in a way I can even understand your own motives in trying to recover your gift to your niece once you'd become so poor—I can understand—even though I find it despicable, all the same! But as for that niece of yours . . . that Ines, who has the nerve to face her sister today . . . if I had my way I'd make sure the villa would never become hers! Never! I'd see her dead first! (*She catches sight of* THE WOMAN *coming down the stairs.*) Ah, here she is—our dear Cia! (CIA's *appearance seems to stun the two of them for she has dressed herself to look like the large portrait hanging on the wall.*)

LENA: But . . . dear God—you've turned yourself into her . . . !

SALESIO: The very image of the portrait.

THE WOMAN: I was just coming down to check. The part, after all, has got to be played . . .

LENA: The part?

THE WOMAN: Well, aren't they all coming to see me playing it? And then, when one's been dead for ten years, you never know, do you? It's better to go back where one started . . . Except that I . . . (*She strikes her stomach as though it were independently in revolt against what she is doing.*) No! Tell me, who's coming, apart from my sister Ines?

LENA: Her husband.

THE WOMAN: Livio?

LENA: Silvio . . . Silvio!

THE WOMAN: I don't know why, but I keep thinking of him as Livio.

SALESIO: He's a lawyer, so be careful.

LENA: Why should she be careful?

SALESIO: Well, after all, it was he who was responsible for . . .

LENA: Oh, for Heaven's sake, he won't be thinking about that any more. He's polite . . .

SALESIO: Oh, a gentleman in every sense of the word . . .

THE WOMAN: I shall be delighted to meet him.

LENA: But you've already met him. Oh, of course he wasn't your brother-in-law then . . . just a friend of Bruno's.

THE WOMAN: Yes, of course. Bruno must have had so many friends. I hope I shan't be expected to know them all if he brings them here . . . now that it's open house for everybody . . . Who else is coming?

LENA: Your cousin Barbara, that is if Bruno thought to send for her.

SALESIO: She doesn't count.

LENA: What do you mean 'doesn't count'? She's the worst of the bunch!

THE WOMAN: And Boffi? Will Boffi be here too?

SALESIO: I don't know if he's in town.

THE WOMAN: Oh, he is, he is! I told Bruno to make sure that he was here. I want Boffi . . . he must be here! (*She looks at the portrait, then at herself.*) It's a perfect resemblance, isn't it?

SALESIO: You might have walked out of the frame!

LENA: True enough—but I must say I never thought that that portrait was really you.

THE WOMAN: No? And yet Bruno said that it was painted from a photograph.

SALESIO: Oh, indeed it was.

THE WOMAN: And that he'd given the painter all the details about me.

SALESIO: And now we can see for ourselves just how like you it is! Couldn't be more exact, for God's sake—what I've always said—there you are—you!

LENA: Yes, but it was—the eyes. May I . . . just a second . . . (*She takes* THE WOMAN's *face and looks into her eyes.*) That's it. Her eyes. Her eyes as I always knew them. These are her eyes . . . not those in the picture.

THE WOMAN: Cia's eyes?

LENA: Yes! Cia's eyes!

SALESIO: But aren't they the same as the ones in the portrait?

LENA: Of course not! These are her eyes—not those! Just
a hint of green . . .

SALESIO: Green, rubbish! They're blue!

THE WOMAN (*to* LENA): For you, Lena, green. (*To*
SALESIO.) For Uncle Salesio, blue. And for Bruno,
grey . . . under black eyelashes. You see? And then, of
course, the painter must have had his say, too. What
were Cia's eyes really like? Go and check for yourselves,
the portrait's as good a test as any.

SALESIO: I don't need to check. I was your father's best
friend, and you've got his eyes.

LENA: His eyes? Oh, no! Ines has got his eyes. They're not
like these at all! Believe me, Cia, you've got your
mother's eyes. We grew up together—two cousins with
the same name, poor Lena and me, it's hardly likely that
I shouldn't know. (SALESIO *laughs.*)

LENA: That's right, laugh!

THE WOMAN: Why are you laughing?

LENA: Because, since we were girls, boys used to tease us
when they saw us together . . .

SALESIO: They would call out, 'Pretty Lena and Ugly
Lena!'

THE WOMAN: Oh no, not ugly Lena!

LENA: That's exactly how I used to reply, 'I'm not ugly!'.
And that 'ugly' one . . . when the 'pretty' one died . . .
became like a mother to you . . .

THE WOMAN (*disturbed*): Don't Lena . . . please.

LENA (*as though to keep a promise she had made*): All
right dear, I won't. But I don't see why it should upset
you.

SALESIO: Can't you see it does?!

LENA: But she was so tiny . . . she can't possibly remember. (*Changing the subject.*) But you really are your
mother all over again. She was just like you when she
died.

SALESIO: Well, if you want to know, I see her completely
differently.

LENA: Arrgh!

THE WOMAN: There we are, Uncle, that's the play I'm going to act in. It'll be about how you see me, and how Lena sees me. It'll be about how you recognize somebody, missing believed killed, after an army's trampled all over her. (*She sits and invites them, with a gesture, to sit, too.*) But in the meantime I should like you both to explain to me exactly what is Bruno's position with regard to this villa and the estate.

SALESIO: You mean you don't know?

THE WOMAN (*dryly*): No. I don't know.

SALESIO: But Bruno must have told you . . .

THE WOMAN: He told me—it wasn't very clear—something about having his rights denied him. He was so over-wrought . . .

LENA: Oh, I know what you must have felt. When I tell you how it turned my stomach to hear . . .

THE WOMAN (*with the air of someone who suspects something which both saddens and disgusts her*): No, Lena, it's not what you think. It was something else that shook me. Bruno just shrugged his shoulders and said: 'Oh, don't worry anyway. It doesn't matter if you don't know anything about it. Indeed it's just as well for them to realize that I haven't told you anything.' But I want to be told. I want to be told everything!

SALESIO: But the situation could hardly be clearer now . . .

LENA: Now that you're back . . .

THE WOMAN: But the certificate of Cia's death hasn't been invalidated yet?

LENA: What does that matter? It will be invalidated with the affi . . . affidated they're making out now.

SALESIO: It would have been invalidated already if only you had . . . right from the start . . .

THE WOMAN (*with a contempt which she cuts off short*): From the start, I never wanted to have anything to do with all this . . .

LENA: Well, of course we know that. You should have been spared at least this bitterness about the death certificate.

THE WOMAN: If it was only bitterness!

LENA: But you see, there are financial interests involved.

THE WOMAN: Nobody told me anything about that!

LENA: Your interests, too.

THE WOMAN: I have no interests!

SALESIO: But of course you have interests . . .

THE WOMAN: No. Oh, no. I'm not having anything to do with interests. And if there's any question of that . . . I couldn't dress like this any longer. Like the portrait. That would be really horrible!

LENA: But of course it wouldn't! Why should you think that?

THE WOMAN: Because that's how it is. And you know something? The death certificate is right.

SALESIO (stunned): What do you mean—right?

THE WOMAN: Just what I said. Right. I told Boffi so in Germany, I even told Bruno. Ten years you waited for her to come back. And did she? No! Why didn't she come back all that while? It's not so difficult to see the reason, is it? She was dead. Dead. Or at any rate dead to every memory of a life that she didn't want any more—it's clear she couldn't have wanted it any more. Assuming she was alive at all.

LENA (moved): Of course, dear child, you're perfectly right. Don't think I don't understand you.

SALESIO: And I understand, too. Oh, yes, indeed. But you see, now that you've come back . . .

THE WOMAN: Quite ignorant of all these conflicting interests—not knowing that I should be forced to play a part that disgusts me. I came for Bruno's sake! I did it only for him! And I made it quite clear that nobody should expect to be recognized by me—no memories should be awakened. At first, I wouldn't even see you two, even though you were living here with him . . .

SALESIO: Didn't we keep away for more than a month?

THE WOMAN (rising, furious): He should have told me! He ought to have told me! I wouldn't have come!

LENA (*after a pause, timid*): Perhaps he didn't want to hurt you, because after all, it was your own sister . . .

SALESIO: After you'd disappeared, mind . . .

LENA: There you are, he's trying to excuse her again!

SALESIO: I'm not excusing anybody, I'm just explaining. Cia says exactly the same thing herself—after ten years . . .

THE WOMAN: . . . My sister very rightly asked for a death certificate so that the estate and the villa could go to her. Isn't that right?

LENA (*correcting her*): No, no, not to her, to Salesio. He had given them to you as a dowry . . .

THE WOMAN (*to* SALESIO, *with joy*): So it's all come back to you? It isn't Bruno's any longer?

LENA: Oh no, it's Bruno's all right . . .

THE WOMAN: But what about the death certificate? I thought that had solved everything, and freed me from . . . I thought it had freed him, too . . . (*Sitting*) Explain it to me better . . . How can it all still be Bruno's?

LENA: Because Bruno quite rightly opposed . . .

SALESIO: No, that's the whole point! Not rightly! No!

LENA: He was absolutely right . . .

SALESIO: No, he wasn't!

THE WOMAN: But don't you see, Lena, I should be perfectly happy if it had all come back to Uncle Salesio, so that he could give it to Ines.

LENA: No, no!

SALESIO: No, indeed! What's Ines got to do with it? Your return cleared up everything. It's just that before you came down, Lena and I were discussing the motives behind the quarrel—quite academically. You can imagine for yourself what it was like here after the war—just a heap of rubble.

LENA: And while it remained like that nobody thought of having you declared dead! They started to get greedy only after Bruno began putting things right.

SALESIO: If you're going to do all the talking . . .

LENA: Can you deny that it's true?

THE WOMAN: Let him talk, Lena, I want to know what he thinks, too.

SALESIO: You always did have enough common sense for everybody, Cia. And now you want to know the whole truth.

THE WOMAN: That's exactly what I do want.

SALESIO: Well, then, I have your permission to continue, Lena? Thank you. (*To* THE WOMAN.) This is the point. Who was responsible for repairing the damage after the war?

LENA: The government. Go on, tell him it was the government and make him happy. And so, you see, Cia, any claim Bruno might make for having rebuilt everything in the hope that you'd turn up at any moment was opposed by the others. 'That's all very fine,' they told him, 'but the repairs don't give you any rights at all because the government would have got round to doing them anyway, sooner or later!'

SALESIO: And that was how things stood when . . .

LENA: When the news of your return from the grave exploded like a bomb. (*Pause.* THE WOMAN *is rapt in gloomy concentration.*)

THE WOMAN: So if there hadn't been this return from the grave as you call it, Bruno would have lost the villa and the estate, everything?

SALESIO: Of course he would, absolutely everything!

LENA: And when the death certificate was obtained . . .

THE WOMAN: Did Boffi know all this when he came to Berlin?

LENA: Indeed he did. It would have been hard for him not to know. It was all such a dreadful scandal.

SALESIO: All this while, nobody's been talking about anything else here . . .

LENA: Reasons of the heart on one side and reasons of the pocket on the other, serious ones, too, because the estate's so big, and it's worth so much after all Bruno's done to it. And the opposition had a strong hand to play because poor Bruno's reasons of the heart, well, there were nasty-minded people who sneered at them as though he'd invented them just to protect his own interests.

THE WOMAN: Ah, so they said that, too, did they? His heart was just an excuse for looking after his pocket?

LENA: Only nasty-minded people!

SALESIO: They'd all become so bitter, you see . . . (*Pause*)

THE WOMAN (*darkly, more and more shaken by a suspicion which has assailed her*): I see . . . I see . . .

LENA (*to distract her*): But come now, that's all over. We'll stop talking about it altogether. Of course it must upset you now . . . seeing it all again . . .

THE WOMAN (*a burst of contempt*): Oh, no, for God's sake . . . that doesn't bother me! (*Change of tone.*) It's something else that upsets me . . . (*Then falling back into her black mood.*) Because in Berlin, too . . .

LENA (*timidly*): What?

THE WOMAN: No, nothing.

LENA: You see, this is all just a formality. You're officially dead, and so you must be officially brought back to life.

THE WOMAN (*without listening to her*): Boffi told me that he'd called Bruno just as soon as he thought he'd recognized me.

LENA: So he did—and you can imagine how Bruno came running.

THE WOMAN: . . . Because there was the problem of the death certificate and he stood to lose the case . . .

LENA: Good God, no! Whatever put that into your head?

THE WOMAN: I'm right, Lena. Believe me, I've hit on the truth!

LENA: You're wrong! He was the only one who never believed you were dead! He never gave up!

SALESIO: That's true.

LENA: He tore straight off to fetch you, trying to imagine all the reasons that you've described yourself to explain why you hadn't come back before.

THE WOMAN (*rising, very strained*): You know where I was when he found me? It was night-time, and I was going to hospital with a girl whose father had just tried to kill himself . . .

LENA: For you?

THE WOMAN: Yes . . .

LENA: Oh, how dreadful!

THE WOMAN: He didn't want to let me go—he still writes to me now. Then at the door, as I was following the stretcher-bearers, I saw him standing in front of me . . .

SALESIO: Bruno?

THE WOMAN: Yes, Bruno. Boffi had gone to fetch him at his hotel, and he didn't want me to go to the hospital. I told him he was raving—I told him to let me go—that I had no husband—that I'd never had one.

SALESIO: And Bruno? What did he do?

THE WOMAN: I went away with the man on the stretcher before he had a chance to say anything. When I came back two hours later, they were both still there. Obviously Boffi must have told him that I . . . (*To* LENA.) You see, Lena, trapped as I was . . . that lunatic had a gun in his pocket, and he'd already threatened me . . . to get away, to find some sort of escape . . . I had given way . . . I'd admitted something or other. Oh, I don't know—that I knew him—that I'd been alone in the villa . . . But then seeing them there again—knowing perfectly well that they'd been discussing these stupid admissions together—I denied everything—the whole story! I told them that I'd been forced before . . . I told them to get the Hell out . . . to go . . . to stop the idiotic farce which Boffi insisted on sticking to. Pretending he had recognized me.

SALESIO: But Bruno recognized you immediately, too!

THE WOMAN: No! That's a lie . . . he didn't!

SALESIO (*stupefied*): He didn't?

THE WOMAN: That's why I call it a farce. He didn't. I saw perfectly clearly that he didn't. When I saw him in front of me for the first time—he just didn't see the likeness that Boffi had told him he would. He was disappointed. I saw it! You know how it is . . . you spot a likeness and you tell somebody else about it. He looks, and it's just not the same as it was for you. (*Almost to herself.*) That's what worries me . . . why? Why? If he didn't recognize me . . . (*Then to the others.*) Oh, yes, some likeness there must have been. I admitted it—I could hardly do anything else. I admitted that I came from near Venice, too—but not from here—not here! I told them so much, I did so much, that in the end I managed to persuade them both that it really was just a likeness. Oh, a strong one, perhaps, a string of coinciden- ces, too, but no more than that. In fact I persuaded them that it wasn't me. What more could I have done? But then . . . I don't know why . . . I . . .

LENA: You repented?

THE WOMAN: No! But in the state I was then—(*Almost to herself.*) That shouldn't be an excuse for him now . . . he shouldn't be taking advantage of it. But if he has done . . .

LENA: Oh, no . . . why torment yourself like this? What are you trying to say?

THE WOMAN (*letting herself be overcome by misery*): Oh, Lena, I was so tired . . . and desperate in a way I'd never been before . . . Lost and finished . . . So sick with disgust at that life that I just couldn't go on any longer. And it was on that terrible night when my whole life seemed to be hanging over an abyss of pain . . .

LENA (*moved*): Oh, my poor child!

THE WOMAN: It was then that he began to talk about his Cia . . . what she was like . . . what she'd meant to him in that one year she'd been with him. He was so desolate, that listening to him, I began to cry and cry, not dreaming that he might see my tears . . . tears for my own misery . . . as a sign of repentance for having denied so much. And there was my body as a living proof that I was his Cia. I let him embrace it, pull it against his body so hard that I couldn't breathe. But I did it for no other reason . . . I . . . I came here with him only for that. I made him understand and promise that it was to be only that . . . that I should come as from the grave . . . for him only . . . only for him!

LENA: Oh, yes, I see . . . with your old life cut right off behind you . . . I could see it so clearly in your eyes as soon as you let us see you.

THE WOMAN: Did you recognize me, too . . . immediately?

LENA: No, my poor child, even I didn't recognize you immediately.

THE WOMAN: Even you?

SALESIO: Come to that, neither did I. But that's easy to understand . . . after all those years . . .

LENA: The years have got nothing to do with it—on the contrary . . . No, it was—I don't know, something about her, her bearing—even her voice a little . . .

THE WOMAN: Did you notice a difference in the voice?

LENA: Yes, I thought . . .

THE WOMAN: So did Boffi . . . he told me afterwards . . . it was the only difference he noticed! (*Pause*) It's odd that Bruno must have noticed it, too . . . but he didn't say anything. (*Rising, almost to herself.*) So many impressions are beginning to make sense now . . .

LENA: But you were away for so long, talking a foreign language. And then—the change in your heart above all. 'Lena,' you said to me, just like that, in a dead voice— and I could hear—in your voice—that everything you'd been before was dead.

THE WOMAN (*completely rapt in herself, she hasn't listened to what LENA has been saying*): I wonder . . .

SALESIO: It's time that you stopped wondering now!

THE WOMAN (*still to herself*): Of course, that's it . . . that's how he tricked me at the beginning . . . he told me there was every reason in the world for me not to see her . . .

LENA: You mean Ines?

THE WOMAN: Oh, Ines doesn't concern me . . . I'm talking about this double game that he's been playing with
me. At first I refused to come here because I knew . . .

LENA: You knew what Ines had done to you?

THE WOMAN: No, not that! I didn't know anything
about that at the time. But then he used precisely that to
get me to come here—he pretended that I wouldn't see
her—that what she'd done was the reason I could give
to everybody for not seeing her. And now he's doing
just the opposite—he's using what Ines has done—this
death certificate she's asked for—to force me into seeing
her!

LENA: Remember, though, he never wanted this quarrel
with your sister!

SALESIO: And after all you have been closed up here by
yourself for four months.

THE WOMAN: Perhaps even that was a part of his plan.

LENA (shocked): Part of his plan?

THE WOMAN: I'd swear it was!

SALESIO: What do you mean?

THE WOMAN: What do I mean? (She stops herself.) It's
flawless, the whole scheme—even the way he's looking so
strained and tense now!

SALESIO: No, no, no! You're being unfair, Cia! Believe
me you are!

LENA: Yes, I think you are, too.

THE WOMAN: You think that only because you don't
know everything!

SALESIO: Then let me tell you that you don't know
everything either, or rather, forgive me, you don't wish
to know; Bruno's got every reason in the world to feel
strained and tense. After all, you must remember the
curiosity which your reappearance gave rise to after ten
years, and all the . . . the fermentation of that curiosity in
the four months you've been closed up here—what
people are thinking and saying . . .

THE WOMAN: Ah, yes—of course, the wagging tongues
will be busy.

SALESIO: Naturally. What with the lawsuit—and your refusing to see your own sister . . . your husband's relatives have been saying . . .

THE WOMAN (*interrupting*): . . . Every spiteful thing they can think up. Especially about my life, up there, that must give them a wonderful cause to gossip. They must know everything about me by now. And Boffi . . .

SALESIO: Oh no, Boffi would never . . .

LENA (*interrupting*): No . . . no . . . no . . . he has always taken your part. Believe me. I know!

THE WOMAN: But he must have told them where he found me: what sort of life I was leading. Even if he didn't tell them in so many words, with his eyes, his gestures—and that horrid little twich of his—he doesn't need to hide anything! Goodness only knows what they must be thinking! Do they know I was a dancer?

LENA: Don't pay attention to them and their malicious slander.

THE WOMAN: But it's true. I was a dancer. And worse! Much worse! You can't imagine the things I've done. I used to make up my own dances to the music. Erotic movements which drove the men crazy. And the less I wore, the more they liked it.

LENA: Does . . . does **he** know?

THE WOMAN: Bruno? Of course he does! But what's worse—**they** know! They do, don't they, Uncle Salesio? What do they say about me?

SALESIO: They say so many things, but you shouldn't . . .

THE WOMAN (*interrupting*): Do they say he's decided to overlook all that because I can be useful to him now?

LENA: No . . . No!

THE WOMAN: I wasn't asking you.

LENA: Who do you suppose could have said such a thing? Or even thought it!

THE WOMAN: Tell me the truth, Uncle Salesio. Is that what they are saying?

SALESIO: Yes, it's true. They do say that.

THE WOMAN: You see?

LENA: Who says it?

SALESIO: Various people.

THE WOMAN: It's all so sordid! Who'd have thought that business interests would . . .

LENA (*interrupting*): It's not Bruno's fault!

THE WOMAN: All the same, if I thought . . . (*She stops as the sound of a car driving on gravel is heard outside.*)

SALESIO (*shaking himself*): Ah, here they are—this must be them now!

THE WOMAN (*suddenly coming to herself, with a tone of challenge*): All right then—let's have it out!

LENA: Have they come so early?

SALESIO (*looking into the garden*): No, it's Bruno.

LENA: I thought they said six o'clock.

SALESIO: There's Boffi, too, you know . . . Boffi, too.

LENA: You see? Bruno did bring him. (*Long pause.*)

THE WOMAN: What are they doing?

LENA: Bruno's reading a letter.

THE WOMAN: A letter?

SALESIO: The porter's just given it to him.

LENA: Whatever are they doing now? Boffi's going away with the letter.

THE WOMAN: No! Run and call him back, Uncle Salesio. I want him here!

SALESIO (*going into the garden*): Bruno! Boffi! Come here! Both of you! You, too, Boffi!

BRUNO *and* BOFFI *enter, followed by* UNCLE SALESIO. BRUNO *is very upset and is in the throes of a nervous crisis which has drained his face of all colour and made him restless and impatient in every glance and gesture.*

BRUNO: Whatever do you want Boffi for? Let him go, please.

BOFFI (*to* THE WOMAN): Good evening to you. Yes indeed, it's better if I go at once.

BRUNO (*anxiously*): Yes, straight away. And at all costs stop . . .

THE WOMAN: Stop what?

BOFFI: Another letter's come.

THE WOMAN: From Salter? Another?

BOFFI: He's taking advantage of the fact that he isn't dead after all. And he's getting his own back.

THE WOMAN: What does he say?

BRUNO (*to* BOFFI, *impatiently*): Go on, please Boffi— don't waste time!

THE WOMAN (*to* BOFFI): No, wait a moment! (*Then to* BRUNO.) Bruno, I want to know. Give me the letter.

BRUNO: Oh, for Heaven's sake, the letter's not important. If it were only a letter! (*Turning to* LENA *and* SALESIO.) Lena, please—and you, too, Uncle—would you mind leaving us?

LENA: Yes, of course, immediately.

SALESIO: Come along then, let's go. Yes, yes, yes. (*They both exit up the stairs.*)

THE WOMAN: Why? What's the matter?

BRUNO: It just would have to happen today . . . today of all days. This persecution's become outrageous.

THE WOMAN: What's he written this time?

BRUNO: Written! He's done a great deal more than write. He's coming here. He says that he's coming to prove you're a fraud.

THE WOMAN: A fraud? Is he bringing his daughter with him?

BOFFI: No. It's the same old line. You remember the threat he made . . .

THE WOMAN: What threat?

BOFFI: About some doctor friend of his in Vienna?

BRUNO: Well, he's gone to Vienna! He's written from Vienna! (*He shows her the letter without giving it to her.*) There you are, look!

THE WOMAN: But—what's he gone there for?

BOFFI: He's playing his last card—and he's staking everything on it!

THE WOMAN: But what does he say in this letter, for God's sake?

BRUNO: I'm telling you, darling. He says that he's coming here this evening with some imbecile woman—and the doctor who looks after her. And he says that he's got proof . . .

THE WOMAN (*watching him closely*): Proof? Proof of what?

BRUNO: That she . . . that it's she . . . and not you!

BOFFI: And he's bringing her here.

BRUNO: Now do you understand?

THE WOMAN (*unmoved, still staring at* BRUNO): Here? But how can he bring her?

BRUNO: He wrote to us both several times—to you and to me—perhaps we were wrong not to answer him . . .

THE WOMAN: But he never said anything to me about this!

BRUNO: Well, he did to me. As a matter of fact he asked me to go to Vienna to see the woman . . .

THE WOMAN (*surprised but still watchful*): Oh, yes?

BRUNO (*irritated at being watched so closely*): Yes, I tell you! He wanted me to talk to the doctor at the hospital there—this friend of his who's arriving with him now!

THE WOMAN (*still staring at him, as though she were interested in nothing more than his reactions*): Why did you never tell me anything about this?

BRUNO: I was hardly likely to tell you that I'd been asked to go to Vienna to see another woman . . .

BOFFI: You should, you know, Bruno . . . you really should . . . have answered him at least—even if only to tell him he was mad!

BRUNO: When I knew that he was only doing it to revenge himself on Cia?

THE WOMAN (*very distinctly*): I should have advised you to go.

BOFFI: There you are, you see?

BRUNO (*more and more irritated*): What should I have gone there to do? To look at a poor idiot, giggling and senseless, with a face to . . .

THE WOMAN: How do you know?

BOFFI: He sent me a picture of her.

THE WOMAN: Have you got this picture?

BOFFI: Yes . . . not with me though . . . But believe me, it's nothing to worry about . . . there's not the slightest possibility . . . In fact, I was just going to answer him . . . but when the injunction came . . . (*Indicating* BRUNO.)

THE WOMAN: What injunction?

BOFFI: The one he sent me . . .

THE WOMAN: I don't know anything about it . . . I'm learning everything for the first time now. And yet, I did have a right to know. Pictures . . . injunctions . . . what injunction is this?

BOFFI: Well, you see—when Salter got no answer to his letter he must have thought that it was in your husband's interests—having once recognized you—not to come out with another claimant. So he wrote to me. He sent me an injunction ordering me to show the photograph to other relatives—if there were any—to see if they could identify her. He even wanted them to go to Vienna!

BRUNO: It's become a mania with him!

BOFFI: Well, of course we just didn't know what to do. You see, the picture only came a few days ago. Should we show it to the relatives? Things were complicated enough as it was. Should we go to Vienna? Well, in fact, I was in favour of that idea. There, face to face, we could have cut it off short.

BRUNO: Just leave like that? It's easier said than done. But how? Secretly?

THE WOMAN: Why secretly?

BRUNO: Would you have liked them all to know about it? A hint's quite enough round here, and everybody knows everything! They do nothing but look at us and talk about us . . .

THE WOMAN: And so . . . you told me nothing, you didn't answer—you didn't make a single move.

BRUNO: I'm just telling you why.

THE WOMAN: An ostrich with your head in the sand . . .

BOFFI: It's true that if you'd gone there you might have stopped him . . .

BRUNO: Was I to know that they'd come here?

THE WOMAN: But I wonder how he managed to persuade the doctor?

BOFFI: He explains that in the letter. Apparently he's got money to throw away. And somehow he's just convinced this friend of his, the doctor. There are four of them making the journey ... Salter, the doctor, the woman and a nurse. He's obviously persuaded the doctor that it's in all our interests here not to discover the truth—and then, perhaps, that the sight of all these places might awaken in that poor wreck of a woman—I don't know ... but what proof can they possibly have ... ?

BRUNO: He's only out for revenge!

BOFFI: I was talking about the doctor! Of course, we know *his* motives! But what possible 'proof' could he have? (*A pause. They all three stand there for a moment, hesitant, hovering, motionless.* THE WOMAN *studies* BRUNO, *then suddenly asks him.*)

THE WOMAN: What do you want, Bruno? (*He does not reply.*)

THE WOMAN: You seem anxious. I'd even say afraid!

BRUNO: Nonsense. Why should I be afraid?

THE WOMAN: What are you hoping for?

BRUNO: I want, oh, darling, for God's sake, what can I possibly want now, with things as they are? You tell me! I was just sending Boffi to find out what train they might arrive on.

THE WOMAN: I see. And then?

BRUNO: Then do something at least to stop them coming in when the others are here.

THE WOMAN: Why? They've left Vienna—sooner or later they must arrive here. You look to me so ...

BRUNO: How do you expect me to look? Naturally I'm concerned ...

THE WOMAN: No, my darling, more. You look to me like someone who's expecting that at any minute the house will fall about his shoulders.

BRUNO: But, don't you understand, they're going to descend on us while the relatives are here, bringing some

sort of proof with them? Proof that they must consider
more or less valid, I imagine, if the doctor's come all this
way with a sick woman?

THE WOMAN: Ah, I see . . . it's the proof that you're
afraid of.

BOFFI: Of course it's not. Bruno's afraid that the others
might try to trade on . . .

THE WOMAN: On what? On the proof?

BOFFI: Well, on any doubt they might feel faced with the
proof that . . .

THE WOMAN: That she is really Cia . . . and I'm a fraud?

BRUNO: Not that they really believe that! But it would
suit their ends!

THE WOMAN (*ironically*): I see. You're saying that they
might wish to play on this doubt in their own interests?

BOFFI: Exactly. Doesn't that seem likely to you?

THE WOMAN: But if you stopped that happening today,
you couldn't stop it tomorrow. That's a game they can
always play, even if they do recognize me today. I have
no proof.

BOFFI: But you don't need any.

THE WOMAN: I don't? Dearest Boffi, nothing could be
easier than to doubt me. Listen, I could show you all the
reasons I have to doubt myself . . . I . . . to doubt myself!
Seeing Bruno like this . . . (*With a violent movement of
contempt.*) Just think that whichever way things fall out
now, he can't lose.

BRUNO: I? What do you mean?

THE WOMAN: I mean you can't lose what's worrying
you most at the moment.

BRUNO: What's worrying me at the moment is the scandal that's going to be created! There's already been
enough gossip about our living here without seeing anybody for four months.

THE WOMAN: Are you complaining about that?

BRUNO: No! But now you can see for yourself the
effect . . .

BOFFI: Bruno's right.

THE WOMAN: Well, if the worst comes to the worst, my darling, there's no need for you to worry. You will just have been tricked.

BRUNO: What do you mean—tricked?

THE WOMAN: Tricked into thinking that I was Cia. Like Boffi in Berlin . . . Like Lena and Uncle Salesio here. You're in good company, aren't you? And you wouldn't lose a thing over it because it'll be my imposture which will have tricked you! (*She laughs.*)

BRUNO: Oh, rubbish! What trick are you talking about? That you are Cia?

THE WOMAN: That's right . . . Cia. Oh, we've settled that for sure. You don't have to worry about that. Look at the portrait! What more could you ask for? (*She laughs.*) You'll bear me witness, Boffi, that I did everything I could to save him from being taken in by a possible—suspected imposture. Never mind, though—here I am! Ready to answer. But only for myself, mind! I'm not answering for you any more. Because I've been tricked, too,—did you know that?

BRUNO: You? About what?

THE WOMAN: About you—if only you knew how much! (*Turning to* BOFFI.) Go away then, Boffi—but don't go looking for easy ways out any longer—it's a waste of time. Indeed, I'd like you to try and see that they arrive while the others are here.

BRUNO: What are you going to do?

THE WOMAN: You'll see.

BRUNO: The family should be here at any minute now . . .

THE WOMAN: I've told you that I'm quite ready. I just want a few words with you first. Perhaps you won't be able to understand me, but that doesn't matter. Oh, and don't worry that the game's going to be all in their hands—it isn't. I'm going to do all the playing there is to do myself. I feel well in the spirit of it already! And it's going to be a hard-fought game for everybody—even for me. (*To* BOFFI.) Go on, Boffi—go now!

BOFFI: So you really want me to bring them here?

THE WOMAN: Yes, bring them here.

BOFFI: All right. I'll be off then. (*After* BOFFI *has gone through the door into the garden, she continues in a burst of exasperation.*)

THE WOMAN: It's a waste of time—hard facts must always win in the end. There's no getting away from this heavy earth of ours. Your soul may fly up for a moment—escape—soar beyond even the most appalling things that fate may have made you suffer—go on, little soul, fly—create a new life for yourself! But when you're all full of that life, down you come again—there's no escaping it—down until you smash into the hard facts that begrime your sweet new life for you—down into the profit and loss, and the mean little family squabbles . . . You know very well that I know nothing of all that. But it doesn't matter. I just want to say this to you. I've been here with you for four months. (*She grips* BRUNO *by the arm and pulls him round to face her.*) Look at me! Look in my eyes! Right into them. They haven't been seeing for me any longer—not even to see myself with! They've been like this—see—fixed in yours—all the time—so that the image of myself as you saw me might be born in them from your eyes—and with it the images of all things and of life itself as you saw it! I came here and I gave myself to you completely—I told you: 'I'm here and I'm yours. Now make me—make me yourself just as you want me, as you desire me. You've been waiting for me for ten years? Pretend they don't exist! No—there's no memory of hers any longer in me. Give me your memories! And now they'll come alive again in me, alive with all your life, with your love, with the very first joys that she gave you!' How many times have I asked you: 'Like this?' Is it like this?' And I was blest in the joy that was being re-born in you from my body—and my body shared the joy!

BRUNO (*almost drunkenly*): Oh, Cia—Cia!

THE WOMAN (*stopping him as he tries to embrace her. She seems almost drunk too, but with pride at having been able*

to create herself as she has): That's right—Cia! I . . . I am
Cia! Only me! Me! Me! Not her! Not the portrait. She
was! Don't you see that existence by itself is nothing?
Existence means creating oneself. And I have created
myself as her. And you have understood nothing!

BRUNO: Oh, yes, yes—I have understood!

THE WOMAN: Understood what? Haven't I felt—haven't
I felt your hands searching my body here . . . (*She indicates vaguely a point on her body somewhere above her
hip*.) . . . For . . . I don't know—some mark you knew
you should find there. And because of a mark that isn't
there—or for some other reason—I'm not Cia after all,
am I? I can't be Cia, can I? Or maybe the mark's
disappeared? I just didn't want it any more, and so I had
it removed. Yes, that's it! Because I knew—I'd realized
that you were searching me for it—and you were, weren't
you?

BRUNO: Yes!

THE WOMAN: You see? But now you're terrified that
Ines, with all the intimacy of a sister, or even Lena, might
want to find this mark on me again—as a nice, legal
proof, signed and sealed. And you're terrified they won't
believe what I've told you. 'Oh. Disappeared. That's
serious! How can a mark like that disappear?' They'll
want to call in doctors. All the more so as this poor
imbecile creature who's coming now might perhaps really
have the mark herself. If she had it and I didn't . . . that
really would be the end! Poor, poor Bruno! So worried
about all these documents and proofs that might be
brought forward! But you mustn't worry. I am Cia—a
new Cia! You want so much. And I wanted nothing when
I came here—absolutely nothing. I gave you back alive
the woman who I thought you'd waited for with love for
ten years, so that I could live a pure life myself, too, after
so much squalor and shame. And to show you just how
true that is, I'm ready to shout in all their faces, in spite
of all proof, and even against you—yes, you, if you're
forced not to recognize me in order to save your own

interests—I'll shout in their faces that I am Cia—I
alone—because she up there on the wall—can no longer
have that life, except in me! (*Once again the sound of a
car on the gravel outside.*)

BRUNO (*strained and shocked*): It's them! The family!
They're here!

THE WOMAN: Leave everything to me! You just go and
receive them. I can't show myself any longer dressed up
like this! I'll be down straight away. (*She goes quickly
towards the stairs and begins to climb them.*)

BRUNO (*almost a plea*): Cia . . .

THE WOMAN (*stopping and turning; she is very calm and
speaks with a voice that indicates that what she is saying
is now unarguable*): Yes. Of course. Cia.

CURTAIN

ACT III

*About twenty minutes have elapsed and it is now almost
evening. The room is flooded with a violet aftermath of sunset
which streams in from the open loggia. The landscape is more
peaceful than ever. The tiny lights of another village twinkle
in the distance.*

BRUNO *and* UNCLE SALESIO, CIA's *sister* INES *and
her husband,* MASPERI, *are waiting impatiently. Although*
INES *is younger than* CIA, *she looks older. She is elegantly
dressed and has everything that a woman of her sort should
have. She asked for the death certificate because it was right,
not because she is greedy and certainly not in order to harm
her sister, for whom she has sincerely grieved ever since it
was believed that she had died. But* UNCLE SALESIO *didn't
part with the villa and the estate to have them enjoyed by an*

outsider, and as CIA *was presumed dead, it was only right that the property should come back to the family.*

BARBARA *is an unmarried woman in her forties. She has shiny black hair tinged with grey. She is full of complexes, stemming from a tortured sense of having been born ugly.*

MASPERI *has an odd face: his upper lip looks as though it has been thrust onto his face and pasted under his nose. He has protruding teeth and a pink complexion which looks almost artificial. He wears spectacles which he fidgets with and frequently adjusts on the bridge of his nose. He is a man of the world and knows just how things should be done. He likes to be polite but now he can hardly restrain his annoyance at the ill-mannered reception he and his wife are being given. After all, they have already waited four months for a confrontation which should have taken place immediately.*

At last, LENA *comes down the stairs.*

BRUNO: What's she doing, for Heaven's sake? Did she say she was coming down?

LENA: Yes, she said, 'I'm coming,' but . . .

BRUNO: But what?

LENA: She was standing there surrounded by all her clothes—she'd opened all the trunks.

BRUNO (*dazed*): The trunks?

LENA: Perhaps to look for something . . . Or to put something back . . . I don't know . . . (*Pause*)

INES: She doesn't by any chance intend to—go away?

BRUNO: No, for Heaven's sake, why should she? I suppose you didn't ask her what she was doing, Lena? (*To the others.*) She did say something about wanting to change . . .

LENA: In fact, she has changed. And she looked so nice as she was!

BRUNO: Why isn't she here then?

LENA: She's terribly nervy. She almost pushed me out of the room. 'Go on down,' she said, 'Go down and say that I'm coming.'

SALESIO: Then she will come! (*A pause.* BARBARA *goes over to the loggia.*)

BARBARA: What a lovely view you get from here. The countryside is enchanting . . . and those lights . . .

MASPERI (*who has joined her*): Yes, it's a beautiful evening. (*Pause*)

BRUNO (*whispering to* LENA): How is she?

LENA: I'd swear she'd been crying.

SALESIO: She is indeed very upset. And after all that's most understandable—the idea of seeing . . .

MASPERI: Oh no, no, no! I'm sorry, Uncle Salesio, but it's nothing to do with seeing anybody. Unless, by any chance she's got a grudge against her sister.

LENA: No, no, not against her sister! What makes you think her sister's got anything to do with it? I hope you haven't been listening to Salesio's explanations?

BRUNO (*stressing each word*): No, the grudge she bears is against me.

MASPERI: Oh well . . . if it's something between the two of you . . .

BARBARA: That's all very well, but we've been kept here waiting for a quarter of an hour. (*Pause*)

INES: She shouldn't bear grudges now . . .

LENA (*to* INES): But who's saying anything about grudges? She even told me that what you did was right, Ines. What more could you ask for? She said she'd be happy if everything here were to be given back to Uncle Salesio so that he would then be free to give it to you.

INES: Why should she want me to have it?

LENA: Well, it all goes to show how she really feels about things.

SALESIO: After ten years, she said, it was only right that you . . .

INES: I didn't do it for myself. You know I didn't, Uncle. It was for you. And then . . . yes, I admit it—because I have a daughter.

MASPERI: She must have understood that Ines and I didn't wish to do anything against her.

BRUNO (*very clearly*): What she won't understand, Masperi, is what you have all done against me.

MASPERI (*spreading out his hands*): Oh, please, I devoutly hope we haven't come all the way here to start discussing that again!

BRUNO: No, no, it's not that, that I . . .

MASPERI (*trying to continue*): We are all waiting here . . .

BRUNO (*cutting him off*): It's that I want to understand what she really feels . . . for myself as well as for you. I want to be able to see things straight myself! (*With an outburst of anger.*) I tell you I'd rather be anywhere else than here at the moment . . . Lena, Salesio—she's talked to you—what is it that she's got against me? Has she started suspecting that I . . . ?

LENA: I think . . . she has.

SALESIO: She said that if she'd known she was going to find herself in the middle of a squabble about financial interests . . .

MASPERI: What squabble? As soon as she came back all squabbling was bound to be cut off short!

SALESIO: Exactly, Masperi. Just what we told her!

INES: Oh, I would have rushed here immediately . . . if Bruno . . .

MASPERI: Precisely. If Bruno hadn't told us all . . .

INES: That she didn't want to see anybody. And least of all me! I could have shown her that I never, but never, oh, the idea! God alone knows how much I cried for her . . . (*Moved, she covers her eyes with a handkerchief.*)

MASPERI: Oh, don't start that again, Ines. Besides it seems pretty clear that she's accepted your side of it—so you're all right. Here and now it seems that other factors are involved—haven't you gathered that?

BRUNO: I didn't say that she didn't *want* to see anybody, I said that she *couldn't*!

LENA: And that's absolutely true—she really couldn't! She couldn't! She couldn't even bring herself to see Salesio and me at the beginning. After all, we must remember that the poor girl has been through a terrible experience!

SALESIO: All the horror of the past—and then coming back here. She could only bring herself to do it because she loved Bruno so much. She didn't want to come . . .

LENA: She was forced to! (*As* BRUNO *looks at her angrily, she adds.*) That's what she said—forced! (*Pause*)

MASPERI: And this . . . suspicion of hers that you mentioned . . . ?

BRUNO (*unable to evade the question any longer*): All right, then . . . she suspects that I did just that . . . that I forced her, as you put it, to come here—because I needed her in my quarrel with you. It's true that she didn't want to come. And I think that she began to suspect, because I promised her there in Berlin that she wouldn't have to see anybody. I told her there was a perfect excuse for her not to see you—the family quarrel. And she came to think of it as no more than an excuse. I was sure that after a while, when she'd got over the first moment, when she'd calmed down a little and with the passing of time, she'd have been able to conquer this fear of you all.

INES: But I could have made her conquer it straight away simply by assuring her . . .

BRUNO: In a sense, it wasn't so much you that frightened her as herself—at least, that's how it seemed to me . . . (*With anger.*) There you are, Lena! That's all the force I used, if you can call it force! I put no pressure on her whatsoever! (*Getting more irritated.*) Then there had to be some way out of this situation, hadn't there? I had to try and convince her that we couldn't go on for ever like this—that the excuse would have to stop . . . (*turning to* LENA *and* SALESIO.) Particularly as she'd made it so plain to Lena and Salesio that (*turning towards* INES,) she had nothing against you, Ines—I mean she put an end to the excuse herself. (*Sweating and agitated.*) I just don't know! (*Little pause, then a fresh outburst.*) And don't think I enjoy having to give the impression of justifying myself before you . . . (*Pacing the room.*) And now she suspects me. As if I wasn't the only one here who consistently refused to believe she was dead! I was so sure that I didn't hesitate to spend all that I did spend to re-build everything here. And why? I'd have been an idiot to do it just so that you could come along and take it from me, wouldn't I? All right—I admit that I took a pretty firm line with you about it, I may even have been spiteful. God knows it's natural enough. I've had to fight—I've had to defend my property as well as my feelings. That's not a crime . . . (*Angrily looking towards the staircase.*) What's she doing, for Heaven's sake?

INES: Exactly. Because if she doesn't intend to come down there seems to be no point in our going on waiting for her.

LENA: Try and be patient. She's obviously trying to calm her nerves first.

BRUNO: But she must realize that at any minute now . . . (*He stops, then goes on immediately to* LENA.) Lena, will you please go back up there and tell her from me to remember where Boffi has gone and why. She must be here when . . . And anyway we've been waiting for long enough already. There are limits.

LENA: All right. I'll go. (*She goes towards the staircase.*)

INES: To see how she is, too.

LENA: Yes, of course. (*She exits up the stairs.*)

INES: Because if she really doesn't feel up to it this evening we can just go! (*Pause*)

MASPERI: I'm only sorry that something which was all cleared up for us as soon as we heard she was coming back should be causing trouble now between you two . . .

BRUNO: Unfortunately, there's something else which . . . You see, not everything has been cleared up between all of you and me. There's something else . . .

MASPERI: Something else? What?

BRUNO (*with a gesture towards the floor above*): Cia knows very well what! And she shouldn't leave me like this now! (*Pacing again.*) You'll have to excuse me—I really am a bit shaken ... Oh, God, if I'd even dreamt that something like this ... It's all very well to ignore facts. How can you ignore them when they happen? (LENA *comes back down the stairs.*)

INES: Here's Lena ...

BRUNO: Well, what did she say?

LENA: I hardly know ... she said that what you said about Boffi was the very reason why she wasn't coming down yet ...

BRUNO: What I said?

LENA: Yes.

BRUNO: So she intends to wait until ...

LENA: Until Boffi comes back.

BRUNO: She said that? She really wants to drive me quite mad!

LENA (*shrugging her shoulders*): What can I do about it? I'm just telling you what she said.

BRUNO: I'll go and see her myself. (*He runs up the stairs.*)

INES (*rising and going to* LENA): What exactly is going on, Lena? What's happened?

SALESIO: Must be something behind all this ... something new!

LENA: It looks like it.

MASPERI: In fact Bruno himself hinted that ...

INES: Yes, but what? He said that perhaps everything's not cleared up yet ...

MASPERI: So he did! Between us and him. But I can't think what he was talking about.

LENA: I think it must have something to do with that letter ...

INES: Letter?

SALESIO: That's right. I think so, too. You can be sure ...

INES: But what letter?

LENA: A letter they got a little while ago ... apparently it came from abroad.

SALESIO: They were talking about it together for a long
   time . . .
LENA: That's right . . . About somebody who . . . Oh, I
   don't know . . . in Austria or somewhere . . .
SALESIO: Threw 'em into a fine old how d'you do.
LENA: There was Boffi, too . . . then they sent him away
   immediately . . . I don't know where . . . to stop something . . .

*Through the loggia comes the dazzling gleam of car head-
lights. We can hear a car horn and, once again, the sound of
tyres on the gravel.*

SALESIO: Ah! There we are! That must be Boffi now!
LENA: Good, good! Now she'll come down. She was just
   waiting for him . . . (*Looking through the French win-
   dows.*) Yes, here he is . . . (*With a gesture and an express-
   ion of surprise.*) But . . . he's not alone!
SALESIO (*also looking out*): There're several people . . .
MASPERI (*also looking*): Whoever are they?
INES: Who's that strange woman? What is going on?
SALESIO: They're getting her out of the car . . .
MASPERI: They're helping her out . . .
INES: Oh, God, what is it? What's happening?
SALESIO: They look like Germans.
LENA: Oh yes, they're foreigners all right . . .
MASPERI: Look at that . . . Look at that woman! She's . . .
INES (*going back*): Oh, how horrible!

*The MADWOMAN enters supported by the NURSE and the
DOCTOR, and followed by BOFFI and SALTER. The
MADWOMAN is fat, flaccid, with a wax-like face, hair in
disorder, motionless, empty eyes. There is a perpetual idiot-
smile on her mouth—a wide, empty smile which never ceases
even when she is making odd noises or babbling one or two
words, clearly without any idea of their sense. The DOCTOR
and the NURSE are typically German in appearance and*

manner. Even SALTER *seems more German-looking than before.*

SALTER (*approaching*): Come along, come along, my dear. This way, now . . . In here, that's right . . . Come along . . .

MADWOMAN: Le—na . . . Le—na . . . (*These two syllables, which are no longer a name to her but rather a sound which has long since become automatic, are uttered by her large, breathy mouth almost in cadence.*)

LENA (*shattered*): Oh God—but what . . .? Is she calling me?

INES: Who is she? For God's sake, what's happening?

BOFFI (*entering, distraught*): Where's Bruno? Where's Lucia?

MADWOMAN: Le—na . . .

LENA (*looking from face to face, bewildered*): She's speaking to me!

SALTER: Do you belong to the family? Is your name Lena?

LENA: Yes . . . I'm the aunt . . .

SALTER (*to the* DOCTOR): There now, Herr Doktor. D'you hear that? There is somebody in the family called Lena! That's another proof! Oh, it's absolutely certain now! We didn't know that!

MASPERI (*coming forward*): What is absolutely certain?

BOFFI: Don't pay any attention Masperi! She makes that sound all the time . . . she's been doing it all the way here.

MADWOMAN: Le—na . . .

MASPERI: But she really is saying Lena though.

BOFFI: Yes, but she's not saying it to anybody. And she laughs all the time like that . . . (*Then referring to* BRUNO *and* THE WOMAN.) For Heaven's sake, where are they? Where are Bruno and Cia?

INES: Oh God, has everybody gone mad?

MASPERI: What is all this about? What have they brought this woman here for? Who are these people?

BOFFI (*still speaking about* BRUNO *and* THE WOMAN): How can they possibly stay upstairs now? Would somebody please call them?

SALTER (*to* BOFFI, *indicating the others*): Are these ladies and gentlemen also relatives?

BOFFI: Yes ... (*Introducing* INES) ... This is the sister, Signora Ines Masperi.

SALTER: Her sister? So there *is* a sister! Her sister? Right then, we'll soon know ...

INES: Who is this gentleman?

BOFFI: His name is Carl Salter. He's a writer.

SALTER (*to* INES): Will you please look at her, Signora Masperi. Look ... There she is.

INES: Me? (*To* BOFFI.) Boffi, what is he talking about? Look at who?

BOFFI: He will insist on believing ...

SALTER (*to* INES): Don't tell me that she doesn't remind you of somebody?

INES: No ... who? Oh, God! Who should she remind me of?

BOFFI (*ironically*): Your sister!

MASPERI: What?

INES: Cia?

LENA: Where? What is he talking about?

SALTER: Yes! This woman! This woman!

SALESIO: Then he must be off his head, too!

SALTER: I've brought her all the way here ...

MADWOMAN: Le—na ...

SALTER (*at the sound of her voice, gesturing towards her*): There! Isn't that proof? You must accept that as proof! She's saying Lena! The doctor says that for years now she's kept calling for Lena!

LENA: Oh, no! It's impossible!

SALTER: Don't you recognize her? Look in her eyes! How can you fail to recognize her?

LENA: What ... who can you expect me to recognize?

SALTER: My friend here, the doctor who's been studying her case for years, he's got documents, proof ...

MASPERI: What proof? Let him show it then!

INES: Oh, but it's impossible!

MASPERI: Please, Ines, let him talk. We've been so taken by surprise that . . . What proof?

LENA: But our Cia's upstairs!

SALTER: I know the lady upstairs. Very well.

SALESIO: This really is the most extraordinary thing . . .

MASPERI: Please, Uncle Salesio, let him say what he has to say! (*To* SALTER.) So you know . . .?

SALTER: The lady upstairs . . . only too well!

LENA: Do you think you know her better than I do? I who was a second mother to her?

SALTER (*gesturing towards the* MADWOMAN): No, to her! To this poor woman here.

LENA: Rubbish!

MASPERI: If you think that you really have proof . . .

SALESIO: But what are you talking about proof? Masperi, you don't seriously think . . .?

MASPERI: No, but I'm just saying that if they think they have this proof, the simplest thing is to . . .

BOFFI (*ironically*): Here we go!

SALESIO: This proof would only make us laugh, or weep with pity more likely!

MASPERI: . . . The simplest thing is to go to the proper authorities . . .

BOFFI: Even when you know why all this is being done?

MASPERI: I have no idea why it's being done!

BOFFI: But I have . . . so have Bruno and Lucia! Where are they?

SALTER: Here's the motive you want . . . revenge!

BOFFI (*to* MASPERI): There you are!

SALTER: But I should add . . . punishment!

MASPERI: I don't know this gentleman . . . I can't possibly . . .

SALESIO: Oh ho! Anyway the gentleman's motives have no great importance. Out with them then! These documents and proofs if you've got any! Because we don't want anybody round here getting any funny ideas into their heads because of this . . . revenge . . . or punishment or whatever it is.

BOFFI (*to* MASPERI): I knew it, you know.

MASPERI: What d'you mean you knew it? Who could possibly have known a thing like this?

BOFFI: I mean I knew that you would start getting ideas.

SALESIO: But nobody is to start getting ideas!

INES (*contemptuous*): Of course not! (*To* SALTER.) Now look, all of us . . . I . . . her sister . . . her aunt here, her uncle, and Boffi, too . . . we are all of us looking at this poor creature you've brought here, and not one of us recognizes her.

SALTER: Perhaps because you have already recognized the lady upstairs?

INES: No! In my case, no!

SALTER: What? You mean you haven't recognized her?

INES: I haven't seen her since she arrived. I came here to see her today.

SALTER: You've had no desire to see her until today?

INES: No, it wasn't I . . . It was she who . . .

SALTER: Ah! So it was she. I see. Because she couldn't do it . . . not with a sister. With a sister—blood must tell— Her cheek against yours—that touch would be unbearable even for her. She was terrified you'd know something was wrong. But try—try now, and you'll feel there . . . (*Indicating the* MADWOMAN.) . . . that this woman's your sister.

INES (*horrified*): Oh no . . . for God's sake . . . stop!

SALTER: If you can only let your pity get the better of your horror—look! It *is* Cia! It's ten years remember! All the havoc, the war, the hunger she's lived through—I know the woman upstairs who's pretending to be her—if she seemed to resemble the image in your minds, then look—look well here—if you look carefully at this woman, if you search for the reality, underneath all the distortions and changes, she's got—she has got that face . . .

INES: Oh, no!

LENA: But where can you see it?

SALESIO: The man's talking rubbish!

SALTER: Look at the eyes . . . if they weren't so dead . . .

BOFFI: They're completely different . . . an altogether different shape . . . perhaps just the colour a little.

SALTER: She's been mad for nine years. She was found with an old uniform coat of a Hussar over her. It was torn to pieces, but there was still a flash on it!

INES: What flash?

SALESIO: Where was she found?

SALTER: At Lintz.

MASPERI: What's all this about flashes and coats?

SALTER: The flash was of the regiment to which that Hussar belonged. And that regiment had been here—right here!

MASPERI: Here during the invasion, you mean?

BOFFI: What does that prove? She might have begged it in Lintz off a Hussar who'd been here during the invasion.

MADWOMAN: Le—na . . .

SALTER: And she calls for Lena! You hear? Why? Why should she have only that name fixed in her mind? (*To* LENA.) And you, who say you were a second mother to her . . .?

LENA (*with sudden resolve, overcoming her own horror and surrounded by the horror of the others*): Wait! Let me look—let me speak to her. (*Pause*) Cia! Cia! Cia!

The MADWOMAN *remains impassive with her silent, empty laugh. They all watch her. Meanwhile,* THE WOMAN *has come down the stairs, followed by* BRUNO. *Nobody is aware of them. They become aware of her as she moves in front of them towards the* MADWOMAN *as soon as* LENA, *having abandoned her attempt, breaks from the* MADWOMAN. *It is an odd thing, but after what has happened and simply because the* MADWOMAN *is there, even though nobody has been able to recognize her, everybody*

. . . even those like LENA, SALESIO *and* BOFFI *himself who have hitherto believed implicitly in* THE WOMAN— *now looks at her with perplexity and doubt.*

THE WOMAN (*to* BRUNO, *in the silence which has fallen as they all look at her*): Well, Bruno, why don't you try and call her, too?

SALTER: Ah, here she is!

THE WOMAN (*quickly, proud*): Here I am!

INES (*perplexed, but feeling she must overcome it*): Cia . . .

THE WOMAN: Wait a moment. Let's have some light. You can't see anything here. (SALESIO *goes to the door and switches on the light.*)

INES (*looking at her in the light, repeats after another moment of hesitation*): Cia . . .

SALTER (*faced with* THE WOMAN's *arrogant certainty and the double 'Cia' of* INES, *his reaction is exactly the opposite of the others'—he begins to doubt himself. He turns to* INES): D'you really believe . . . ?

THE WOMAN (*to* SALTER, *indicating* BRUNO): Well, Salter, you see . . . I kept him upstairs, I stayed upstairs myself, deliberately to give you time to make your effect. I recognize your ruthlessness very clearly. Only you would be capable of doing something so abominable . . . bringing her here . . . Poor creature—I want to look at her. (*She goes up to the* MADWOMAN *and with a delicacy which is all compassion, she puts her finger under the* MADWOMAN's *chin, so as to look closer into the laughing face.*)

MADWOMAN (*as* THE WOMAN *studies her, chants her double note without altering her empty, soundless laugh*): Le—na . . .

THE WOMAN: Lena . . .? (*Overcoming a shudder, the* MADWOMAN *turns towards* LENA.)

SALTER (*quickly*): There you are, you see! She turned to look at her.

LENA: It's not me she's calling.

BOFFI: It's just a sort of chant she sings all the time.

SALTER: As far as I'm concerned, it's sufficient that she turned her head.

THE WOMAN: And that proves it, doesn't it? I can't be Cia.

SALTER: Even you suggested that he should try and call her too!

THE WOMAN: I knew that you wouldn't believe me. But then I discovered all the rest of you just now, while Lena was bending over her like this, calling 'Cia! Cia!'

LENA (*guilty, trying to excuse herself*): It was only because . . . Don't you see?

SALESIO (*at the same time, indicating* SALTER): This gentleman insisted so much . . .

BOFFI (*at the same time*): She kept on calling 'Lena . . . Lena!'

THE WOMAN (*topping them all*): But of course. There's nothing wrong with it. It's quite natural. (*To* LENA.) I can see how you look at me now, Lena.

LENA (*bewildered*): How I look at you . . . ?

THE WOMAN (*to* SALESIO): And you, too, Uncle Salesio.

SALESIO: Me? Oh, no, no, no . . .

THE WOMAN: Even you, Boffi . . .

BOFFI: No, that's not true at all. Nobody has recognized her.

SALESIO: We were all so . . . (*He doesn't know how to go on . . . surprised? Overwhelmed? And anyway, they don't give him time.*)

BOFFI: Even your sister saw immediately that . . .

THE WOMAN: Yes, Ines called me Cia, didn't she? Twice.

BOFFI (*to* SALTER): You heard, Salter? (*Then to* MASPERI, *deliberately.*) And you, Masperi, did you hear?

INES (*contemptuous*): I told you before that nobody here had any desire to take advantage of this situation.

BOFFI: I was making it clear because even Bruno might take advantage of this!

THE WOMAN (*in a burst*): Oh, no, he won't! He won't take advantage of anything. Besides, look at him . . . he's more bewildered than anyone else.

BRUNO (*shaking himself out of it*): Bewildered? No, dumbfounded at this man's impertinence . . . if anyone is taking advantage of things it's he!

THE WOMAN: Don't worry. He won't be able to take any advantage either—neither of me, nor of this poor woman.

SALTER: I considered it my duty . . .

THE WOMAN: To bring her here . . .

SALTER: Yes, to punish you!

THE WOMAN (*going up to him*): Punish me?

SALTER: Precisely. I nearly died because of you, and while I was lying between life and death, you calmly came down here to start cheating other people!

THE WOMAN: I have cheated nobody!

SALTER: You've cheated and cheated!

BRUNO (*with a menacing move towards* SALTER): Don't you dare!

THE WOMAN (*stopping him immediately*): No, no, Bruno, keep calm.

BOFFI: He's being deliberately provocative!

THE WOMAN: I can manage him by myself. (*Turning to* SALTER.) I take it you're talking about my famous imposture, eh? And have you proved it? How? Like this? By this ghastly thing you've done? Well, I assure you I'm delighted you've succeeded—doubt has been sewn.

LENA: No, no, it hasn't!

BOFFI (*at the same time*): When?

SALESIO (*at the same time*): Doubt? In whom? It's not true!

THE WOMAN (*almost yelling*): I say I'm delighted! (*With a change of tone.*) You all deny it . . . and yet I caught you just now . . .

SALESIO: But we didn't recognize her!

THE WOMAN: That doesn't matter!

BOFFI: You don't need to worry, Cia. I'll bet that he doesn't even believe it himself.

THE WOMAN: And that doesn't matter either. Let's examine this imposture of mine. It must be an odd sort of imposture, mustn't it, if I drew your attention myself

to the odd way you were all looking at me when I came
down just now. And you, Boffi, when you began to
doubt . . .

BOFFI: I swear that I never doubted for a moment . . .

THE WOMAN: Oh, yes you did. And to console yourself
for that doubt you went out of your way to notice . . .
and to point out to me . . . how Ines called me Cia
twice . . .

BOFFI: I noticed it because it was the truth. Besides what
possible doubt could I have because of this poor
wretched woman?

THE WOMAN: No, no . . . not because of her . . . because
of me . . . even though you couldn't recognize her. It was
a very natural doubt . . . as soon as I appeared unexpectedly . . . you were all so confused . . . (*She indicates*
SALTER.) And Salter had just the opposite doubt, when
he heard someone who hadn't seen me until then call me
Cia. Oh, it's all very natural . . . (*To* LENA *who is crying
quietly*.) It's no good crying, Lena. There's no certainty
on earth so firm that it can't be shaken as soon as even
the smallest doubt arises . . . and then you can never
again believe quite as you did before!

SALTER: So you admit yourself that you might not be
Cia?

THE WOMAN: I admit a good deal more than that! I
admit that this woman might be Cia! (*She points to the*
MADWOMAN.) If that is what they want to believe!

SALTER (*quickly, gesturing first towards* THE WOMAN
and then at the MADWOMAN): Yes, because she looks
like Cia while you don't.

THE WOMAN: Ah, no—that's not true! Not because I
look like her! I was the very first to say that my likeness
is no proof at all—the likeness that made you think you
recognized me. You know, that could well be a proof that
it's not me!

MASPERI (*struck by this, spontaneously*): That's true . . . I
hadn't . . .

THE WOMAN (*turning to him quickly*): It is true, isn't it
Signor Masperi? It proves that it can't be me. (*Back to*

SALTER.) You see, Salter? It's only just occurred to some people . . .

BRUNO: It seems to me that you're doing everything to . . .

THE WOMAN: But you recognized the strength of that argument, too!

BRUNO: I did?

THE WOMAN: Yes, you, Bruno!

BRUNO: When? What are you talking about?

THE WOMAN: When I pointed out to you there in Berlin. And you were shaken by it, too, Boffi. Understandable come to that. It's only when you believe in someone or perhaps when it suits you to believe in someone that you don't think of something as obvious as that, or maybe you don't want to think of it. Cia may well be this woman—precisely because she no longer looks anything like her.

BRUNO: You're taking a perverse pleasure in . . .

THE WOMAN: I told you I was going to explain my imposture to Salter.

BRUNO: Well, this is a fine way to do it—making everybody doubt you.

THE WOMAN: Exactly! That's just what I am doing. I want everybody to doubt me . . . just as he does . . . so that I can at least have the satisfaction of being alone in believing in myself! (*With a gesture towards the* MAD-WOMAN.) You haven't recognized her. Because she's unrecognizable? Because they haven't brought you enough proof? No. For none of these reasons! It's only because you don't yet feel that you can believe. It's as simple as that. Hundreds of poor devils have come back as she's done after several years—unrecognizable—without any memory—and sisters and wives and mothers—even mothers—have argued over them. 'He's mine!' 'No, he's mine!' They wanted to believe! And nothing can prove you wrong if you want to believe! You say it's not he? But for that mother it is! She believes in the face of all proof. She believes without any proof! Didn't you believe in me without proof?

BOFFI: There wasn't any need of proof—you are you.

THE WOMAN: That's not true! (*Turning quickly to* BRUNO *who is about to protest*.) Don't worry, Bruno, my darling, I'm not damaging your interests if I try to prove that Cia might really and truly be this woman. On the contrary. After all there has been so much suspicion. Uncle Salesio told me so. (*She indicates* SALESIO.) Suspicion when I stayed shut up here for four months without seeing anybody . . . .

BRUNO: But everybody understood why!

THE WOMAN (*smiling at* LENA): Except for the nasty-minded people, eh, Lena? (*Then to* BRUNO.) The trouble is that you imply it yourself . . . (*To* MASPERI.) And you're already thinking, too, aren't you, Signor Masperi? It's in your face.

MASPERI (*surprised*): No, no, I . . .

THE WOMAN: You can't deny it. It's written all over you—you're mulling over what I've been saying just now. On you go then. It's not going to be so very difficult to suspect—well, let's see now—that a person who wanted to ride on a likeness that other people found it useful to notice.

BRUNO (*spitting it out*): Useful to me . . . is that what you mean?

THE WOMAN: So somebody's already suspected it, have they?

BRUNO: You raised the suspicion.

THE WOMAN: Exactly! (*She crosses to* MASPERI.) Well then, is it so very difficult to suspect that I've been here, taking my time comfortably . . . (*She enigmatically smiles at* SALESIO.) . . . Four months—to get myself ready to turn myself into Cia—first of all saying that I couldn't bear to see anyone—and luckily, you see, there was a very good excuse . . . Very convenient for Bruno, too. (*She indicates* BRUNO.)

BRUNO (*quickly, to the relatives*): There you are—didn't I tell you that's what she'd say?

THE WOMAN: You may have told them so—but now it's me they're listening to! (*To* SALTER.) You see, Salter, there was a clash of interests between them! It's easy to pretend at the beginning that one just doesn't want to remember anything . . . You can even pretend that you really have forgotten everything . . . and then in the meantime, eh? . . . Slowly, slowly build up the memories . . . Bruno needed time, didn't he, to re-build the ruined villa and put the estate to rights. Well, I needed time, too, to build myself again, stone by stone, just like the villa—and to transplant all the poignant little memories of poor Cia into my soil—time to nurse them and let them blossom into life again . . . (*She crosses slowly to* INES *with her arms outstretched.*) Until one day, I should reach the point when I could even receive my sister . . . (*She takes her hands.*) . . . and talk with her about—oh, when we were little girls together, and about the jokes that we had, even though we were both orphans, brought up by an aunt. (*To the others.*) Do you know, I even went to the trouble to make myself a dress exactly like the one in the picture, so that when I came down I'd look as though I'd walked straight out of the portrait. Isn't that true, Lena? But then I changed my mind because I thought it was going a bit far! (*The others seem embarrassed.*)

THE WOMAN: You're really beginning to suspect, aren't you? If the suspicion's not already fully grown . . .

MASPERI (*almost horrified*): No, no . . . that never . . .

INES: Who could even think, even dream of such a thing?

THE WOMAN (*pointing to* BRUNO): Bruno could. He did . . . think . . . of such a thing.

BRUNO: I did?

THE WOMAN: You. And now you're terrified that this suspicion—which is quite feasible, after all—might turn out to be the truth.

BRUNO: Oh, rubbish. Could any of you ever believe it?

THE WOMAN: They do—they do! Because it really is true—it's the truth as the facts show it to be. It really is the imposture Salter believes it to be. (*She indicates* SALTER.)

BOFFI: But what are you saying?

SALESIO: How could it be possible?

BRUNO: This is just your revenge—and it's even fiercer than his!

THE WOMAN: Not my revenge—no! It's the revenge of the facts, my darling—the facts! By asking them to come here, you wanted us to reach this point, didn't you? But their recognition doesn't mean anything! It was you who should have recognized me—alone and disinterestedly—I didn't come here to defend a dowry! That would have been the imposture that he talks about! So look—if it's going to help you—so that it shan't seem like revenge against you—why don't you believe it? Face the facts as they are and believe it!

BRUNO: Believe what?

THE WOMAN: Believe that I really have been cheating. What more can I say?

BRUNO (exasperated, facing her): You're doing this to test me—it's all to test me!

THE WOMAN: No, I swear it isn't.

BRUNO: It is—it must be!

THE WOMAN: And what if this is just a new move of yours, too?

BRUNO: What move?

THE WOMAN: To let them think that I'm really only doing it to test you.

BRUNO: No!

THE WOMAN: No? All right then—accept the fact that I've tricked you. In fact there's nothing to stop you all accepting it—go on, all of you—accept in full what Salter says! (She indicates SALTER.) Accept that he is right about everything—even about this poor creature—that it may well be her—really Cia. Look at her! (She goes up to the MADWOMAN and with the same gesture of delicacy and compassion as before she puts her finger under her chin.)

MADWOMAN (as soon as she feels the touch): Le—na . . .

THE WOMAN (to LENA): Lena—you hear? She's really calling you. Why won't you believe it?

MADWOMAN: Le—na . . .

THE WOMAN: There you are . . . it's you she wants—really you—I didn't even want to see you. But she called for Lena as soon as she came—she's always called for Lena, Lena—and you just won't believe in her? Because she didn't answer you? But how could she? Look at her. (*She studies the* MADWOMAN *with infinite sadness.*) If she can call for Lena like that—with that laugh all the time—no human voice will ever be able to reach her again! (*To the* MADWOMAN.) Where are you calling from? From what distant, happy moment in your life where you've remained fixed—shut off in the blessing of that laugh—you're safe—immune . . . (*To* LENA, *who, almost repenting her instant dismissal of the* MADWOMAN *and pulled by the emotional magnetism of the scene has moved near her.*) Ah . . . so you've come to her again?

LENA (*frightened, almost in a whisper*): Oh, no, no . . . I just . . .

THE WOMAN (*gently*): Stay here. Perhaps Ines, too. I've got something to say to Salter. (*She indicates* SALTER *and takes him aside, then continues, staring hard at him.*) Apart from being an unpleasant man—you must be a very bad writer, too.

SALTER: Quite possibly.

THE WOMAN: It's all just a fake, isn't it?

SALTER: What . . . ?

THE WOMAN: Your 'literary works'. You can't have ever put anything that's really yours into it . . . no heart or blood—no trembling of the nerves, of the senses . . .

SALTER: In fact, nothing?

THE WOMAN: Nothing. I don't think you've ever suffered real anguish or despair! The despair which makes you want to take revenge on life—the life others have forced you to lead—by creating another more beautiful life—the one that might have been . . . the one you would like to have lived! And because you're like that yourself—because you knew me for three months as I was with you—you think I'm the same sort of fake that you are?

SALTER: I suppose you put your heart and blood and nerves and all the rest of it into it?

THE WOMAN: Why else should I have done it?

SALTER: To get rid of me.

THE WOMAN: I could have got rid of you without tricking somebody else.

SALTER: But I thought you'd just been confessing that you were in fact tricking?

THE WOMAN: All right, then—so you think that I really have tricked them?

SALTER: And now you may well have had your own good reasons to confess, with the inducement of . . .

THE WOMAN: Of what?

SALTER: Some chance of making something out of it . . .

THE WOMAN: That too, eh? It's very clear that your writing really is just a game you play to make money. Would you like to see somebody playing free, gratis and for nothing? It's all a question of what a person can become as a result of disaster. Look—you might become like that poor wretch—(*She points at the* MAD-WOMAN.) Having fallen into the hands of a savage enemy who rips you to pieces—beautiful as you were—and young—taken by surprise alone here in the villa, your body marauded, and your soul made havoc of, until you're hunted into madness, and reduced to what she is now, and all return is impossible. Or again, you might still crash, but with a difference, undergo all the shame and torment just the same, and be hunted just the same into madness—but with a difference—you might find in the very madness itself a sort of inspiration to revenge yourself on your own fate—and in the horror of what's been done to you, the feeling of being so completely filthied that you really do feel disgust and horror at the idea of going back to your old life . . .

SALTER (*calling her fiercely back to her terms of reference*): Remember, you said this was only a game!

THE WOMAN: Wait a moment! Let's say, for example, the old life here—in this villa—where—Oh, God! Like a flower, and quite innocent, only eighteen . . . and close, close to a sister you love . . . (*She is referring to* INES, *without, however turning to look at her, as though she were not there and she could only see her in the past when she got married at the villa given her in dowry by her Uncle. Very slowly as she goes on speaking she moves backwards towards* INES, *so that the last lines of the speech are said with her head leaning on* INES's *breast*.) . . . hugging her so tightly, never wanting to leave her. Not because I didn't love him . . . but because—knowing nothing that first night—what she said to me—oh, as ignorant as I was and she crying her heart out . . . 'You know what they say? Now he'll have to look at you . . .'

INES (*violently, excited, embracing her*): Cia! Cia!

THE WOMAN (*stopping her convulsively*): No! Wait! Wait a moment!

BRUNO (*with triumphant joy*): I never told you that!

THE WOMAN (*after looking at him, says coldly*): I could easily drive you mad, couldn't I, Bruno? No, nobody told me that. (*And she adds quickly as* BRUNO *turns almost involuntarily to look at* LENA.) Not even Lena. How could she? Something as intimate as that . . . it wasn't by accident I brought it up just now—no one could have told me that except the person who said it at the time. (*To* INES.) Could they, Ines?

INES: No, of course not!

THE WOMAN (*turning quickly to* BRUNO): You didn't search for your Cia well enough, you know! You rebuilt the villa immediately. But you didn't look—you never looked well enough among the rubble and the bricks to see if there was something of her still there, something of her soul left behind, some memory still really alive—but alive for her! Not for you! Fortunately I found it!

BRUNO: What do you mean?

THE WOMAN (*not answering him, turning to* SALTER): Are you following me, Salter? And so, too filthy ever to get clean again, off she went with the very stupidest of those officers—just exactly as I told you in Germany— off to Vienna first of all, for years there in all the chaos of a lost war. Then Berlin—that other lunatic asylum . . . and she learned to dance, and suddenly the madness grew bright, and there was applause, and there didn't seem to be any reason ever to strip off those coloured veils of madness—you could wear them to go down into the square, and walk through the streets with them—and in the all-night bars at three, four, five in the morning, with all the clowns in white tie and tails around you. Until one evening when you least expect it, (*she goes towards* BOFFI) someone passes close to you, slipping by like a devil, and calls you 'Lucia, Lucia, your husband's just round the corner. If you like I'll call him for you!' (*Moving away, with her face in her hands.*) God help me, I thought he was searching for somebody who couldn't exist any longer—somebody he realized he could find alive only in me, to re-make her, not as she wanted, because she no longer wanted anything for herself, but as he desired her! (*She makes a violent movement as though to liberate herself from a wild illusion, and goes towards* SALTER.) Stop! That's enough of that! (*To* SALTER.) So you came here to punish me for my imposture, did you? How right you were! D'you know how far this imposture of mine was going? To a point where I should have myself recognized by my sister and my brother-in-law . . . who I'm now seeing for the first time in my life!

INES (*shattered*): Cia, whatever are you saying?

THE WOMAN: Just as I'd never been here before until Bruno brought me!

BRUNO (*trembling—loud*): You know perfectly well that's not true!

THE WOMAN: It is! It is true!

BRUNO: You're trying to make us believe that it is. You're just saying it because . . .

THE WOMAN: Because I wanted you to go on believing that I was Cia! But now Cia's going! She's going back to dance again!

BRUNO: What?

THE WOMAN: I'm going away with him! With Salter! (*She indicates* SALTER.) I'm going back to dance in Berlin!

BRUNO: You're not moving from this house!

THE WOMAN: I told you you didn't search well enough for Cia! D'you know, my darling, that up there in the attic, without even realizing it, you let them throw away a little sandalwood cabinet. It's all broken, but there are still one or two little silver insects stuck onto the doors. Lena reminded me about that cabinet which Cia had kept because it belonged to her mother. D'you know what I found in a little drawer of that cabinet? A notebook of Cia's with the very words that Ines spoke to her on the day of her marriage: 'You know what they say? Now he'll have to look at you.' It's my notebook and I'm taking it everywhere with me. Particularly because, it's very odd, you know, but even the handwriting looks like mine! (*She laughs, starts off, then stops to add.*) Oh, by the way, there's something else. Don't forget to look on this poor woman's hip to see if there's . . .

SALTER: A birthmark—yes, there is.

THE WOMAN: Red? Slightly swollen? Is there really?

SALTER: Yes, it's slightly swollen, but not red—black. And it's not exactly on her hip . . .

THE WOMAN: In the notebook it says: 'Red and slightly swollen . . . on the hip . . . like a ladybird.' (*To* BRUNO.) There you are, you see? it may have darkened in colour. It may have shifted slightly. But she's got the birthmark. Another proof that it's she! Believe in her . . . all of you . . . believe in her! All right, Salter, let's go! (*To* BOFFI.) You'll send my things on, won't you, Boffi? (*To* SAL-TER.) You've got the car outside? I'll come just as I am. (*She runs to the door.*)

SALTER: Yes, just as you are! All right! Let's go! (*And they both almost rush out to the car in the garden.*)

BOFFI: No, no, wait a moment.

BRUNO: Wait . . . Cia . . . wait!

MASPERI: Perhaps it would be best to let her go.

BRUNO (*like all the rest of them, stunned and bewildered*):
Let her go? Just like that? I can't just let her go back . . .
Cia . . . Cia . . . (*And he goes off into the garden, too,
followed by the others. We can hear confused and agitated
voices off. Only the MADWOMAN and LENA remain on
stage. LENA, however, stays at some distance from her,
uncertain and bewildered.*)

MADWOMAN: Le—na . . .

LENA (*almost voicelessly, not quite able to bring herself to
believe*): Cia . . . Cia . . . Oh, no . . . Please God, not this,
not Cia . . .

LENA *buries her face in her hands as the*

CURTAIN FALLS

THINK IT OVER, GIACOMINO!

Pensaci, Giacomino!

1916

Translated by
Victor and Robert Rietti

CHARACTERS

AGOSTINO TOTI, a Professor of Natural History
GIACOMINO DELISI
ROSARIA DELISI, Giacomino's sister
CINQUEMANI, an old janitor of the school
MARIANNA, his wife
LILLINA, their daughter, and the wife of Professor Toti
SIGNOR DIANA, headmaster of the school
DON LANDOLINA
ROSA, a maid in Toti's house
FILOMENA, an old servant of Signorina Delisi

The action takes place in a provincial town in Italy.

ACT ONE

The hall of a provincial high school in Italy. Facing the audience, at equal distance from each other are three doors with the inscriptions: Class One—Class Two—Class Three. Down stage right, the Science and Natural History Laboratory. Facing it, down stage left, the headmaster's study. The school bell hangs on the back wall.

The only articles of furniture are a table and chair for the Janitor.

CINQUEMANI *is discovered, wearing his janitor's uniform, a cap with the school badge, an old grey woollen scarf round his shoulders, and a pair of woollen mittens. He paces up and down the hall with an air of 'great importance.' The voices of rather unruly students come from the laboratory where the lesson is about to end.* CINQUEMANI *raises his hands as if to say:* 'Heavens, what a noise!' *The headmaster suddenly bursts out of his study.*

DIANA: I must put a stop to this scandal once and for all. (*He crosses to the laboratory—opens the door, and the noise ceases abruptly.*) Professor Toti, is this the way you keep discipline in your class? You—boy—what are you doing over there by the window? And you? Yes you. Why aren't you at your desk? Leave the room, both of you. Pack up your books and go home! Professor Toti, take the names of those two students! I'll teach you how to behave properly in my school. You are suspended for three days. I'll inform your parents at once. Go! Professor Toti, please come here for a moment. (*The sound of a scuffle and of someone running is heard in the class-room.*) Hold that boy! Hold him—don't let him get out of the window. (*To the janitor.*) Cinquemani, quick—a student has jumped out of the window. Run and catch him! (CINQUEMANI *exits in haste.*)

TOTI *comes into the hall. He is an old man in his seventies. He wears a pair of canvas slippers, a black velvet cap and a green scarf with tassels round his neck.*

TOTI: I assure you, Signor Diana, that young man doesn't belong to my class.
DIANA: Then who was he? How did he happen to be there? (*The sound of boys giggling.*) Silence! (*Furiously, to* TOTI.) Explain, Professor. (TOTI, *embarrassed, hesitates to answer.*) Well? I am waiting.
TOTI (*quietly and good naturedly*): What can I say Signor Diana? I—don't know! I had my back to the class, writing on the blackboard—look, you can see it from here—I was drawing the species and sub-species of monkeys... (*There is a burst of laughter from the class.* TOTI *turns to them, with an almost comical display of anger.*) Silence when I'm talking to the headmaster—you bad boys!
DIANA (*impatiently*): Come, come! How did that boy get into your classroom?
TOTI (*shrugging his shoulders*): Through the window, I suppose, as he went out that way. (*There is another burst of laughter from the class.*)
DIANA: Silence, I say! Or I'll have the whole class suspended for two weeks! (*To* TOTI.) You allow strange boys to enter your classroom 'through the window' while the lesson is in progress?
TOTI: No, not exactly, Signor Diana. You see, it's partly the janitor's fault. He often falls asleep by the school gate and he doesn't notice if strange boys climb over the wall and get into the yard. Once they're there ... as you know the window of my room is practically on ground level ... they've only to lift one leg—and they're in.

DIANA: And you allow that to happen?

TOTI: Santa pazienza! Let's be reasonable. How can I be writing on the blackboard—and at the same time see what happens behind me? I don't have eyes at the back of my head, now do I?

DIANA: Oh!

TOTI: But you know, Signor Diana! it may be that that boy is a great lover of animals . . . (*He smiles good-naturedly and adds almost in parenthesis, as if to show that he can make such feeble excuses even in Greek.*) . . . a 'Zoophyte', in fact: that's it, a Zoophyte! He was so attentive and so very quiet that I didn't even notice him.

DIANA (*impatiently*): I see! Well . . . we'll speak of this later. Meanwhile . . .

CINQUEMANI (*enters panting*): No sign of him, Signor Diana. He must have run like the devil!

DIANA: Ring the school bell, Cinquemani.

TOTI: I give you my word of honour, Signor Diana . . .

DIANA: That will do, Professor. I told you we'll discuss it later—after you've dismissed the students. (CINQUE-MANI *rings the school bell. Professor* TOTI *talks to his class from the door.*)

TOTI: Now boys, you'd better get out of here through the other door. Make no noise or the headmaster will start thundering again. When you're home, have a good dinner and then get on with your homework . . . but don't work too hard, boys! Sh . . . sh . . . Quietly, please.

The headmaster has returned from his study during the above, and now approaches TOTI. *While the scene continues,* CINQUEMANI *takes off his cap, his woollen mittens and his scarf and from a drawer in his table, takes out a blue tunic and a large red handkerchief. He puts on the tunic and with the handkerchief, he fashions a kind of head-wear to keep the dust off his hair.* MARIANNA *and* LILINA *enter later with brooms, dustpans etc. to start cleaning up and express impatience at finding the headmaster and* TOTI *still there.*

DIANA: Now: tell me, Professor Toti . . . Do you imagine it is possible to continue in this manner? That I should be compelled to leave my work, in order to enforce discipline in your class?

TOTI: Really, Signor Diana!

DIANA: Let me finish! It seems that my presence is necessary to prevent a revolution breaking out in my school through your inability to control the behaviour of your pupils. Take this morning for example. Why the noise and laughter could even be heard in the gymnasium.

TOTI: They were happy, the dear boys. You know, Signor Diana, I like sometimes to crack a joke with them to keep their interest alive: I was describing the funny ways of monkeys . . .

CINQUEMANI (*shaking his head 'knowingly' and sighing*): There are monkeys—and monkeys!

TOTI: You, dear Cinquemani, keep quiet please, while I'm talking to the headmaster. They're only boys after all Signor Diana. They heard me talk of the pre-hensile tail of monkeys: of the fact that they use their tail and their feet in the same way they use their hands . . . which is as good as saying that monkeys have five hands. That reminded them that here in school we have a janitor (*looking at* CINQUEMANI) whom we call Cinquemani or 'Five Hands'—and boys as they are—that made them laugh. (CINQUEMANI *looks none too pleased at this*.)

DIANA: Stop making excuses for them. It only annoys me.

CINQUEMANI: That's right! It annoys me too!

DIANA: Cinquemani!

CINQUEMANI: Forgive my saying so, Signor Diana, but the noise they make in his class makes my head buzz!

DIANA: That will do, Cinquemani! Remember your place!

TOTI: That's right, Cinquemani, remember your place! Signor Diana, I admit that my pupils have been a little noisy this morning, but boys will always be boys, and after all, no harm has been done.

DIANA: No harm? And what about discipline? The dignity of my school?

TOTI (*resolutely*): Signor Diana, let's be serious for a moment. . . . .

DIANA: Serious? Did you imagine I was joking?

TOTI: Of course not: but I must tell you frankly that the cause of this 'lack of discipline' as you call it . . .

DIANA: Yes! . . .

TOTI: . . . is the timetable. The time for my class is badly chosen! It's the last hour of the day. The boys come to me already tired and anxious to get home. How can you expect them to be attentive and quiet? (*Suddenly*) Have you a penknife?

DIANA (*taken by surprise*): What on earth do you want a penknife for?

TOTI: If you will make a tiny cut in your finger, or if you prefer it, in mine,—it will soon become clear to you, Signor Diana, that at our age the blood is like water. But, Santo Dio, these boys have quicksilver in their veins. I get angry with them sometimes, I assure you . . . Yet I can swear to you that when I see them putting on that air of innocent saints, while I know they are planning some mischief . . . (*He laughs.*)

DIANA: It's little wonder you cannot command respect if you let them see you are amused.

TOTI: No, no! I can be very severe with them, and they know it. I have only to look at them! Believe me, Signor Diana, they don't lack respect for *me*; it's the 'Professor' they laugh at!

DIANA: Nonsense! (*Peremptorily*) Tell me! How many years have you been teaching?

TOTI (*warily*): I've never really worked it out.

DIANA: Answer me please.

TOTI: Well . . . Thirty-four years.

DIANA: And you have no family, have you?

TOTI: No. No family of my own. I only have a wife— when I go out for a walk in the sun.

DIANA: What do you mean?

TOTI: My shadow, Signor Diana: it walks, by my side. In my home there's no sun—therefore, no wife.

MARIANNA *appears in the corridor.* CINQUEMANI *nods to her to keep out of the way. Every now and then, she pokes her head round the door to listen to the conversation.*

DIANA: Pardon my asking, but how old are you?

TOTI (*smiling*): How old do you think?

DIANA: Sixty-six—sixty-seven?

TOTI (*pleased at this 'underestimate'*): If you say so.

DIANA: Well—shall we say seventy?

TOTI (*shrugs his shoulders*): If you insist.

DIANA: Very well. Seventy years old: no family, and you've spent thirty-four years teaching. It surely can't be very pleasant for you to continue teaching at your age?

TOTI: Pleasant? The very thought of it weighs on my shoulders like thirty-four mountains!

DIANA: Then why don't you retire? You could live on your pension. By now you're entitled almost to the maximum, and . . .

TOTI: Retire? You're joking! After more than a third of a century I've carried this cross on my back, the Government would pay me my miserable four-penny-worth of a pension for a few years—and then what? Does their responsibility to me end with that?

DIANA: But what more can you want? To retire: no work and plenty of rest . . .

TOTI: Rest? Be idle you mean! With nothing to do all day but feel old, miserable and alone. Take it from me, the Government . . .

DIANA: Come now, the Government is hardly to blame if you haven't a family!

TOTI: Isn't it? So the Government is not responsible for my having been forced to live most of my life in a sixth-floor garret? The Government is not responsible for my having had to do my own cooking, darn my own socks, scrub the floors. The joy of a family has never been mine. Indeed how could I have kept one with the miserable pittance the Government has been paying me? Why it couldn't feed me, a wife and eight or ten children . . .

DIANA: Ten children?!

TOTI: Naturally. You understand . . . when I was young! No, it would have been madness! I thank God I never married before: but *now* it's different. Now I mean to get married.

DIANA: Oh, surely not!

TOTI: Yes, Signor Diana. The Government is not going to get away with it so lightly! I reckon that I may live another five or six years, and I intend to take a wife—to compel the Government to pay my pension, not only to me while I am alive, but to my wife when I am gone.

DIANA: That's preposterous! You want to get married . . . at your age?

TOTI: Bother my age! What has my age got to do with it?

DIANA (*laughing*): But . . . but my dear Professor Toti, a wife . . . will expect more than a pension from . . . a husband. Why, people will laugh at you!

TOTI (*slowly*): I know what that look in your eye means, Signor Diana.

DIANA: But . . .

TOTI: It means that you are exactly like all the others; they see the Professor and they miss the man! They hear of my getting married and they laugh, thinking that at my age a wife will . . . well, you know what I mean. (*He makes the sign of a cuckold's horns over his head.*) Or they lose patience with me—as you did just now—believing that my pupils play pranks on *me* when they are only poking fun at 'The Professor.' The Professor and the man are different beings. Outside, the boys respect me, they raise their hats to me. In here, they too follow their profession; that of a student, and they naturally have to play tricks on whomever is their teacher, even if it be this squeezed-out old lemon. But I don't mind their good-natured laughter, just as I'm not affected by the mockery of evil-minded grown-ups. (DIANA *coughs, a little ill-at-ease.*) Yes, Signor Diana, I shall take a wife. She can be poor but she must be pretty and full of fun.

DIANA: Oh come now, Professor!

TOTI: Yes siree! Very pretty and fun-loving! I've had enough solitude and sadness in my life. I don't want any more! So I shall take a wife and the marriage will be legalized by both the Church and the State so that the Government can't get out of paying her my pension. But she'll be my wife and I her husband for this and *no other* reason, do you understand?

DIANA: But surely, my dear Professor . . .

TOTI: Oh I know, I know only too well the limitations imposed on me by my years.

DIANA: Quite!

TOTI: But for a while I will enjoy the comfort of a little gratitude for the good I will have done at the Government's expense—and 'après moi—le deluge!'

DIANA: I beg your pardon?

TOTI: Amen!

DIANA (*laughs*): You are quite a character my dear Professor. I admire your sense of humour: believe me—you'll need it!

TOTI: Ah, you already begin to see me with horns on my head, eh? (*He again makes the sign of 'the cuckold' over his head.*) The old cuckold!

DIANA (*remonstrating*): What are you saying, my dear Professor!

TOTI: But I assure you Signor Diana that I don't worry much on that score! I thought of that too and I know what to expect! Do you see: I know I cannot be, nor do I wish to be a husband in the true sense of the word. My marriage will purely be a gesture of charity . . . Therefore, that 'badge of ridicule' will not be placed on me; it will decorate only the head of the husband.—But as this is a part I will play in name only, if all the fools of the country want to laugh their head off, it won't matter a scrap to me!

DIANA (*ironically*): Well; yes Professor, looking at it *your* way, I see your point. Let us hope this marriage will take place soon.

TOTI: As soon as I have found the right girl. And, to tell the truth, I already have someone in mind.

DIANA: Good. I hope you will ask me to the wedding?

TOTI: But of course. You'll be the first to be invited.

DIANA: Thank you. (*He turns to* CINQUEMANI.) Cinquemani, fetch my hat and cane, please. (CINQUEMANI *nods and goes into the headmaster's study. He returns shortly with a hat and cane in one hand and a clothes brush in the other.*)

TOTI: You are no longer angry with me, I hope, Signor Diana?

DIANA: To be frank with you: as a man, no ... but in my capacity as Headmaster ...

TOTI: Of course, as a headmaster you admonish me: but as a man—you won't refuse to shake my hand.

DIANA (*laughs and extends his hand*): There!

TOTI (*smiling*): Looking at it *my* way! (*He moves towards the laboratory. At that moment* LILLINA *and* MARIANNA *appear. He glances at* LILLINA *and slowly returns to the headmaster.*)

TOTI: And you know, the girl I choose will be *very* young—and that will compel the Government to go on paying her my pension for at least fifty years after I die. They won't get away with it, I assure you!

DIANA (*smiling*): Goodbye, Professor. Take care of yourself.

TOTI: I will, I will—don't worry about that. (*He exits into the laboratory.* CINQUEMANI *starts to brush the headmaster's jacket.*)

CINQUEMANI: Ah, what a character! He's quite capable of doing it, you know? He's never cared a fig for what people say about him. You may be sure, if he says he'll take a wife—he'll take a wife!

DIANA: Well, we shall see. (*He takes his cane and hat.*) Good-day.

CINQUEMANI: Good-day, Signor Diana. (*As soon as the headmaster has gone, he turns to his wife and daughter who have been standing there, waiting.*) Come on—get on with your work!

MARIANNA: Listen to him! As if it was our fault we couldn't get on with it before! I'd have finished down here ages ago if it hadn't been for them making me waste my time with all that disgusting talk!

CINQUEMANI: Ssh! (*Pointing to the laboratory.*) The professor's in there.

MARIANNA: Let him hear me: it'll do him good! Why he nearly turned my hair red with shame! (*She goes into Class Three with her broom and things.*)

CINQUEMANI (*shouting after her*): Shut up! Get on with your work and don't waste any more time. (*He turns to LILLINA.*) And you go and clean Class Four.

LILLINA: Why? I usually do the lab.

CINQUEMANI: Do as you're told! Upstairs in the house your mother's mistress: but down here I give the orders, d'you understand?

MARIANNA (*re-entering from Class Three*): Listen to him! 'He gives the orders now!' ... 'You go into Three! You go into Four! You go into Five!' He thinks that because he wears that blue 'nightshirt' he can boss everyone around while he does nothing himself!

CINQUEMANI: Nothing?

MARIANNA: Yes, nothing! (LILLINA *laughs.*)

CINQUEMANI: So—you'd stand there laughing at me, would you? I'll teach you and your mother to show some respect for me. (*To MARIANNA as she returns to the class-room*) Shut that door while you sweep the floor ... and open the window, or the dust'll blow out into the corridor and I'll have to sweep it up again! (*To LILLINA.*) I told you to do Class Four.

LILLINA: I don't want to. It's so stuffy: I always feel I'm going to suffocate in there. (*Wheedling*) You do it for me, please papa. I'll do the lab.

CINQUEMANI: But can't you see ... Professor Toti's still there.

LILLINA: Well tell him to go. We can't wait all day for him.

CINQUEMANI: That's true. (*He calls to Professor* TOTI *from the doorway of the laboratory.*) Are you still here Professor? For heaven's sake go home and let us clean up the lab. We've wasted enough time as it is.

TOTI (*off stage*): Come here Cinquemani. I want a word with you.

CINQUEMANI: He wants to talk to me? (*He glances enquiringly at* LILLINA *and goes into the room.* LILLINA, *annoyed at being delayed from carrying on with her work in the laboratory sighs angrily, looks at her wrist watch and stamps her foot. She sighs again and suddenly puts her hand over her eyes as though she were very worried.* MARIANNA *comes out of Class Three with her cleaning things. Her face is dirty.*)

MARIANNA: Thank God—that's done. (*Agressively*) What are you doing here?

LILLINA: I'm waiting for the Professor to come out of the lab.

MARIANNA: Is he still there? And where's your father?

LILLINA: He's in there too, talking to the Professor.

MARIANNA: What's he got to talk about?

LILLINA: How should I know? Father asked *him* to come out, and he asked *Father* to go in. He said he had something to say to him.

MARIANNA: Is that so?! And of course you waste your time out here, listening at the keyhole.

LILLINA: I couldn't care less what they say. I'm only waiting for them to finish.

MARIANNA: That's fine! You wait; Your father talks— and I do all the work.

LILLINA: How you love to grumble about nothing! You never do more than two classrooms any day: well, finish your two and go upstairs. I'll see to the rest.

MARIANNA: I like that! Me clean two classrooms and then get on with all my own work upstairs while you hang around here for hours—like you do every day— doing nothing!

LILLINA: Doing nothing!

MARIANNA: Yes—nothing! When I call you from upstairs, you don't answer; and you always have an excuse
handy to stay behind when I've already finished down
here. (*Mimicking her.*) 'I'll just fill the inkpots in the
desks, Mother!' or 'There's no chalk by the blackboard—
I must go and find some!' You waste three solid hours
every day that way. What on earth do you do with
yourself?

LILLINA: Well you know what Father is! With the excuse
that he's been shut in here all day, the moment you go
upstairs, he hops out to 'get some fresh air' . . . out of a
bottle . . . leaving me to do three classrooms, the headmaster's study, the laboratory and the whole corridor—
on my own! And then you grumble at me! That's all the
thanks I get!

MARIANNA: Oh, it's no use talking to you. Get on with
your work. If the headmaster comes back he'll complain
that the place hasn't been cleaned. Oh why did I ever
have such a daughter! (*She goes off to the left.*)

LILLINA (*getting more and more impatient, looks at her
watch*): What the Devil are they doing there? (*She peeps
through the key-hole of* TOTI's *door. The door opens
suddenly and* CINQUEMANI *comes out. There is a look
of wonder mixed with joy on his face; as though he'd been
pleasently stunned by his talk with* TOTI. *He is so ab-
sorbed in thought that he hardly notices his daughter.*)

LILLINA: Well? Isn't the professor coming out?

CINQUEMANI: Eh? Oh no . . . he's waiting for you. Go
to him, dear. (*He chucks her under the chin and smiles
sweetly at her. She hesitates.*) Go—go in there . . . Lil—
li—na.

LILLINA: But . . . but what does he want with me?

CINQUEMANI: He'll tell you himself. He'll tell you, my
little Lilly. (*He chucks her under the chin again.*)

LILLINA (*puzzled and anxious, not knowing yet whether or
not to be pleased*): Has he told you . . . something about
me?

CINQUEMANI: Precisely! 'Something' about you.

LILLINA: And . . . and what did you say?

CINQUEMANI (*who doesn't want anybody—least of all his wife to hear*): Where's your mother?

LILLINA: Doing Class Five . . . but tell me, are you . . . glad about it?

CINQUEMANI: My child, I'm happy if you are. But there's your mother! And one never knows how she'll take it! Now go . . . the professor's waiting: go and hear what he has to say. He's not exactly in his prime—but he's got good sound commonsense! (LILLINA *looks puzzled.*) I know he's a bit eccentric—but he's got a heart of gold.

LILLINA (*suddenly happy*): So then . . . ? Oh, I was sure he'd talk to you.

CINQUEMANI: Why, did he tell you?

LILLINA: No, I just thought he would.

CINQUEMANI: Well, my child . . . (TOTI *appears in his doorway with his hat on.*) Oh, he's here. (*He picks up his watering can, broom etc. and exits to the left, pretending to be busy with his cleaning.*)

LILLINA: Professor, I'm so grateful to you. Oh, what a relief! I couldn't find the courage to tell Father myself. Thank you with all my heart. You are so good to me. (*She kisses his cheek.*)

TOTI (*moved*): Child . . . child. What are you saying? What good can I do you? Only the good . . . a father can do for his daughter. Nothing more.

LILLINA: Oh no—what you've done . . . is much more . . . . (*very sweetly*) my dear, kind Professor.

TOTI: I am not and can never be your dear one. Oh, if I were thirty—even twenty years younger, it would be different . . . but at my age . . . no, you must think of me only as a father.

LILLINA (*smiling*): Very well then—we'll think of you as a father, and we'll take good care of you, you'll see. I promise you you'll never have reason to regret what you've done for me.

TOTI (*profoundly moved*): Don't say that, my child, don't. You've suddenly filled my heart with joy. This is so much more than I expected. What is the little good I do to you compared with the good you'll be doing for me, just to see you laughing happily by my side.

LILLINA: Not only me Professor: you've made it possible for us both to be happy. (*With a sigh of relief.*) Oh, and we'll really be able to laugh at last.

TOTI: Yes, we'll laugh a lot together—you and I.

LILLINA: And Giacomino!

TOTI: Eh? (*He is startled.*) Giacomino? Who's Giacomino?

LILLINA (*laughing*): Did you expect him not to be happy too?

TOTI: I don't understand! Giacomino?

LILLINA: Of course. Didn't he ask you to speak to my father on our behalf?

TOTI: No, no child—you're making a mistake.

LILLINA: What do you mean?

TOTI (*taking his head between his hands*): I mean, I mean . . . Oh, I don't know what I mean.

LILLINA: What's the matter Professor, don't you feel well?

TOTI: I'm all right. Only it's a bit of a blow! Now, let me get things straight. I told you I wanted you to think of me only as a father didn't I?

LILLINA: Yes, that's what you said.

TOTI (*with a touch of anger and as if he forcing himself to accept a sudden reality imposed on him*): Father, yes, just a father. Now, don't lose your head, Agostino! Take a hold on yourself. (*He shakes himself as though he were freeing himself from an illusion, and swallows hard.*) Tell me, my child. Who is this Giacomino who you imagine asked me to talk to your father on your behalf?

LILLINA: Giacomino didn't ask you? But then—what did you say to my father about me?

TOTI: I simply told him that I am . . . an old man . . . who wants to make your future secure, by taking you . . . with me . . . as a daughter. That's all.

LILLINA: And do you want only me?

TOTI: Did you want me to take Giacomino as well? There are too many wicked tongues about as it is. What would people say to *that*?

LILLINA (*very simply*): But—didn't you say you wanted me—only as a daughter?

TOTI: Yes, but you must understand that if people are not to get the wrong impression, it's not enough for you just to come and live in my house; we must ... we must 'legalize' your position.

LILLINA (*naively*): Without Giacomino?

TOTI: Well—I don't say that Giacomino wouldn't be there, but you see, he can't leave my pension to you. In the eyes of the law, only I can do that.

LILLINA: Pension? But then ... I don't understand! My father told me that if I was happy about ... what you had said to him ... then he'd be happy too.

TOTI: Yes, my dear, but now there's a complication. I never expected a Giacomino to spring up like a Jack-in-the-box. I knew nothing about him. Nobody ever mentioned him to me before.

LILLINA: But you know him well, Professor. Giacomino Delisi.

TOTI: Delisi? (*Pleased*) Well, well, well ... of course I know him. Nice boy, nice boy. He was a pupil of mine, some years ago.

LILLINA: That's when I met him.

TOTI: And you've been courting since then?

LILLINA: Yes.

TOTI: Oh!

LILLINA: What's the matter? Don't you like him? You said you did.

TOTI: Very much. He often comes to see me.

LILLINA: I know, and that's why I thought he'd asked you to speak to my father about us. But now ... Oh my God what are we going to do? We're as badly off as before. And we must do something soon because I ... I can't hide it much longer. (*She buries her face in her hands.*)

TOTI: You can't hide what much lon . . . (*The truth dawns on him.*) Lillina! (*He suddenly feels a little weak at the knees at the realization and puts his hand on her shoulder to steady himself.*) Oh, poor child!

LILLINA (*sobbing*): For God's sake, Professor, help me. Help me.

TOTI (*gently*): How can I help you? What do you want me to do?

LILLINA: Talk to my father, tell him that you know Giacomino . . . that you know he's a good boy, and that you'll help to find him a job.

TOTI: Me?

LILLINA: Yes—so that he can earn enough for us to live on . . . And make my father understand that . . . that it has to be done at once, or else . . . Oh, help me, Professor. I beg of you.

TOTI: Well, yes—if it will help, my child. I will talk to your father. But will he listen to me?

LILLINA: Oh yes, he'll listen to you. You're a professor. The best professor here.

TOTI: What difference does that make? You've seen for yourself, that doesn't make him respect me. Besides, do you really imagine he'll seriously believe that I would be able to find a job for Giacomino?

LILLINA: Oh, please try all the same. I'm sure he'd listen to you.

TOTI (*shaking his head*): Money is all that matters to your father—and he thinks that I am rich. Besides, let's be reasonable; Giacomino is a good boy—I don't say he isn't—but he is very young; he hasn't got a position yet. How can he keep a wife? Love? (*He shakes his head.*) Even love needs to eat! And moreover there is a child on the way. The problem was difficult enough with this blessed Giacomino! . . . But now there is a Giacominino, and that makes two Giacominos! Do you want me to become a father and grandfather all at once?

LILLINA: Oh, we should never have done it. I am so ashamed of myself. And he too—poor Giacomino—he's so upset. But we neither of us know what to do; and there isn't much time. (*Breaking down.*) Oh please, please help us Professor. Now that you know everything you must help us.

TOTI: Oh very well then. I'll do what I can. (*Ruminating*) If fate has decreed that I should be a grandfather instead of a husband—well, that's what I'll have to be.

LILLINA: No . . . No . . .

TOTI: And yet, perhaps it's all for the best; (*almost to himself*) for now I can really say to my conscience that I am doing it only as a good gesture. Besides, I'll have a little grandchild, a Giacomin*ino*. I'll take him for walks . . . I'll play with him in the park . . . I'll tell him all about the earth, the sun, the stars, all the good things on this earth. No, I don't think I'd mind it at all. (LILLINA *stares at him with an expression which is a mixture of gratitude and wonder.*) Now, don't cry any more,—and don't be ashamed. Just think you've been confiding a secret in your father.

LILLINA: But Giacomino, Professor? What about Giacomino?

TOTI: Well, as for your Giacomino . . . (*He makes a gesture with his hand as if to say 'We'll hide him.'*) He'll be there, of course—but I mustn't know. I mean to say, of course I'll know—but it must seem as if I didn't. Do you understand? And I'll love him too—as if he were my son. Why not? Can't I love an old pupil of mine?

LILLINA: Oh no, Professor—not like that: Giacomino would never agree. It's very good of you to suggest it, and don't think I'm not grateful—but it would never work! No, there is only one way to help us: you must talk to my father and persuade him to let me marry Giacomino *now*. He'll find a job soon, you'll see; he'll earn enough to look after me. Please, Professor. (TOTTI *shakes his head dubiously.*) Now listen, I'm going into your lab. with the excuse that I must clean it—and presently Giacomino will be joining me.

TOTI: What? Giacomino? In there?

LILLINA: Yes. He comes almost every day at this time; through the window.

TOTI: Through the window?!

LILLINA: Meanwhile you go and talk to my father. Please, please, Professor . . . if you have any pity on me. (*She runs into the laboratory and closes the door.*)

TOTI *remains as if stunned, considering the heavy load* LILLINA *has burdened him with. He doesn't say a word, but his thoughts are clearly expressed in his face and gestures: will he succeed in persuading* CINQUEMANI? *How wonderful it would have been for him to have a little 'Giacominino' to play with and to love. He sees himself walking in the park, hand in hand with the boy, and he is happy; then he recalls that there is the other 'the older' Giacomino to be included in the 'entourage'. Himself, Lillina, Giacomino, the baby . . . four mouths to be fed on the Government pension! Too many, far too many! He scratches his head, wondering. Then he glances at the door of the laboratory and thinks that Giacomino is probably there at this moment with Lillina. For an instant he is cross; then he makes a gesture implying 'what on earth can be done? Why should I be mixed up in all this?' At this very moment,* CINQUEMANI *returns, cautiously and curiously, from the left, and surprises him gesticulating.*

CINQUEMANI: Are you talking to yourself, Professor? Where's Lillina?

TOTI: She's gone.

CINQUEMANI: Gone?

TOTI: I'm going too!

CINQUEMANI: Wait a minute. Have you spoken to her?

TOTI: Yes, I've spoken to her.

CINQUEMANI: And what did she say? (*Noting his expression.*) No? She refused? But why? She seemed so pleased.

TOTI (*resolutely*): Cinquemani, listen to me: The matter is not as easy as we thought.

CINQUEMANI: What do you mean?

TOTI: Well, there is an obstacle . . . (*He puts his hat over his belly.*) . . . a bump.

CINQUEMANI: A bump? What on earth are you talking about?

TOTI: Oh, Santo Dio, is it so difficult for you to understand? How shall I explain? Well, look . . . (*He removes his hat, pulls in his stomach and draws himself erect.*) Now—do you see that my tummy is perfectly flat . . . (CINQUEMANI *looks at it, unconvinced.* TOTI *also glances down.*) Well,—reasonably flat! Now, just imagine this is a straight road from here to here. Easy to walk on.

CINQUEMANI: To walk on?

TOTI: Yes. But if I put my hat on it (*he holds it against his belly again*)—it makes a hump . . . a mountain . . . and if you have to climb it, it isn't so easy. (CINQUEMANI *scratches his head and looks at* TOTI *as if to say 'The man's gone mad!'*) Don't you see, the road was straight—but it isn't any longer.

CINQUEMANI (*nods his head, then shakes it, trying to follow the story*): Eh?

TOTI: How the devil can I make him understand? Now look, when I speak of a woman, what can such a hump—such a mountain—mean? Surely, you see what I'm getting at.

CINQUEMANI (*it has suddenly hit him*): Do you mean . . ? Are you trying to tell me that my daughter . . . (*He grasps* TOTI *by the lapels of his jacket, menacingly.*) Mind what you say!

TOTI: Take it easy Cinquemani. Take it easy.

CINQUEMANI (*letting go of his jacket*): Who told you? Lillina? Answer me!

TOTI: Who else could have told me, God bless you!

CINQUEMANI: My daughter—dishonoured!

TOTI: Well, not exact . . .

CINQUEMANI: Yes—dishonoured! Who's the man? I want to know! I'll murder him!

TOTI: Come now: don't take it like that! You'll let her marry him . . . and everything will be all right.

CINQUEMANI: Let her marry him? When I don't even know who he is?

TOTI: He's a decent young man—I can assure you.

CINQUEMANI: Decent, you call him—after what he's done! And as for her . . . disgracing the family name! Where is she?

TOTI: Come now, Cinquemani—don't upset yourself so! You'll turn your blood sour!

CINQUEMANI: Tell me where she's gone or I'll . . . I tell you I won't be responsible for what I'll do. Oh, the shame of it!

At this moment, like an echo, from the laboratory comes MARIANNA's *shrill cry*: 'Shameful!' *followed by the voices of* LILLINA *and* GIACOMINO DELISI. *They have been surprised by* MARIANNA *who has seen them through the window on the other side of* TOTI's *room. Almost immediately the door is flung open and* GIACOMINO *and* LILLINA *are practically thrown out by* MARIANNA—*her clothes still disarrayed from having climbed through the window.* GIACOMINO *tries to bolt through the corridor, but* CINQUEMANI *catches him by the scruff of his neck.* MARIANNA *takes hold of* LILLINA *who falls to her knees. Professor* TOTI *is 'buffetted' from one couple to the other, trying to protect the youngsters and calm down the parents. The scene must go very rapidly the dialogue overlapping, all talking and shouting at once in great confusion and excitement.*

CINQUEMANI (*shaking* GIACOMINO *violently*): Ah, it's you, is it. You're the hero, eh? You filthy swine!

GIACOMINO: Forgive me. Forgive me.

CINQUEMANI: Forgive you? After what you've done to my daughter? Dragging our good name into the mud?

GIACOMINO: But I'm ready to make up for it. I want to marry her.

CINQUEMANI: Marry her? You expect me to give her to a starving good-for-nothing like you? (*Professor* TOTI *succeeds in freeing* GIACOMINO *from* CINQUEMA-NI's *hands.*)

CINQUEMANI: Get out of here! Get out before I murder you!

GIACOMINO (*to* TOTI *who is now between them.*) Professor, you tell him. I'm ready to marry Lillina. I'll find a job and work hard to support her.

MARIANNA (*simultaneously with the dialogue between* CINQUEMANI *and* GIACOMINO): So that's the way you clean the lab. every day, is it? I caught you at it this time, you shameless hussy! (*Hitting her.*) There! There! There!

LILLINA (*on her knees, trying to shield her face*): Don't hit me! Forgive me, mother. Forgive me.

TOTI: Don't hurt her, poor girl.

MARIANNA (*to* TOTI): Mind your own business! (*To* LILLINA.) Carrying on under my very nose!

LILLINA: Please mother, please . . .

MARIANNA: How far have you gone? What have the two of you been up to, eh?

LILLINA: He wants to marry me, Mother—can't you hear? He wants to marry me.

At this moment, the parents 'change over' as it were. MARIANNA *goes for* GIACOMINO *and* CINQUEMANI *for* LILLINA. *Poor* TOTI *is again 'buffeted' from one couple to the other, trying to keep the peace.*

MARIANNA: Marry? You think I'd give my daughter to you? You waster . . . you lout you! You've ruined my daughter, that's what you've done! Climbing through the window like a thief, to seduce my daughter!

CINQUEMANI (*simultaneously, to* LILLINA): Do you think I'd let him marry you? Look at him: he hasn't a penny to buy bread, and he wants to get married! I'll teach him he can't meddle with my daughter! (*He picks up a chair and goes for* GIACOMINO. TOTI *holds him back.*) Get out! Get out, or I'll murder you! (*With a*

violent jerk he frees himself from TOTI, *but* GIACO-
MINO *escapes down the corridor.* CINQUEMANI *tries to
follow, but* TOTI *bars the way. He turns to* LILLINA.)
And you too! Never put your foot in my house again! Get
out. Get out I say.

TOTI (*powerfully, dominating them*): Where do you want
her to go, you old fool? You take it out on her—when
you've only yourselves to blame for what's happened.
You who have let her grow up here among all these boys.
What else could you expect would happen to a pretty girl
in the midst of young rascals all the time? Boys are like
young bulls, idiots that you are: don't you know that?

CINQUEMANI (*to* LILLINA): Get out, I said. We don't
want you any more!

MARIANNA (*crying*): You're no longer our daughter!

TOTI: No longer your daughter? Very well then—from
now on, she'll be my daughter. I'll take her away with
me. Come, come, Lillina. Leave these two hard hearted
fools. (*He takes her head on his shoulder and caresses her
hair tenderly as they walk out together to the right.*)

MARIANNA (*attacking her husband*): It's all your fault!

CINQUEMANI: Mine?

MARIANNA (*softening as her tears overcome her*): Oh . . .
Cinquemani.

CINQUEMANI: Marianna . . . (*They fall into each other's
arms, weeping and consoling each other.*)

CURTAIN

ACT II

*The drawing-room in Professor Toti's house. The main en-
trance is in the centre of the back wall. There is another door
to the left. There are some toys of Nini's on the settee. At the*

rise of the curtain, SIGNOR DIANA *is discovered, standing, hat in hand. After a moment,* ROSA *enters from the left.*

ROSA: The Professor won't be a moment. Please sit down, Signor Diana. I'll take these toys out of the way.

DIANA: Don't worry, thanks. I can sit here. (*He indicates an armchair.*)

ROSA (*removing the toys from the settee*): Oh, the child's toys are all over the place. Do please sit here.

DIANA: Thank you. (*About to sit on the settee, he takes a Pierrot, half hidden under a cushion, and gives it to Rosa.*)

ROSA: Oh, thank you. I'm glad it's turned up. They really spoil him. Not a day goes by without him buying a new toy for the little one. Oh here is the Professor.

TOTI (*enters in his dressing gown. He looks worried*): Ah, my dear Signor Diana. (DIANA *rises.*) Please don't get up. Excuse me just a moment. (*He talks swiftly and quietly to Rosa.*) Rosa, I want you to run to my father-in-law's . . .

ROSA: Now?

TOTI: Yes immediately.

ROSA: And who'll look after the child?

TOTI: He's with his mother now. (*To* DIANA.) Please Signor Diana,—do sit down. (*To* ROSA.) Well, didn't you hear me?

ROSA: What do you want me to tell your in-laws?

TOTI: Tell them to come here at once—both of them. But don't frighten them: just say that their daughter doesn't feel well and that she wants to see them. Now, run along—quickly. (ROSA *exits centre.*) Please forgive me, Signor Diana. Let me take your hat. (*He puts it on a chair by the settee.*)

DIANA: I hope I haven't come at an inopportune moment?

TOTI: Oh no, not at all. It's just that my wife is a little . . . indisposed.

DIANA: Oh, I'm sorry to hear that. (*Rising as if to go.*) But perhaps you'd prefer to be with her . . .

TOTI: Oh no—that isn't necessary. Please, do sit down. I sent for her mother because—well, you know, women understand each other better. My wife won't tell me what's the matter with her—but I know what it is!

DIANA: Oh? (*Smiling*) Another happy event, perhaps?

TOTI: No, no! God forbid! One child is enough. (*Smiling*) I expect it's merely that just as April needs rain, young people need to shed tears every now and then. Ah, youth! Youth! (*Suddenly*) Have you any instructions, any orders for me, Signor Diana?

DIANA: Orders? Goodness me, you mustn't use that word . . . (*He smiles.*) Between us—

TOTI: Why not? It's true that my financial position has improved, and that I've been able to move from my garret to this comfortable flat, but you are still my headmaster.

DIANA: I have not come to talk to you as one of my teachers, but as a friend.

TOTI (*politely*): Your friendship greatly honours me.

DIANA: I am here to ask a favour . . . not for myself—although perhaps in a way it is for me too—however, a favour which I am sure will not be difficult for you to grant, in view of your recent good fortune, (*sweetening the kill*)—which was so well deserved, if I may say so.

TOTI: For heaven's sake, Signor Diana, don't say it was well-deserved. Merit had nothing to do with it. My brother was living in Rumania, and for years, neither of us knew whether the other was dead or alive. So I can't honestly say that he meant to leave his money to me. He left it simply because he couldn't take it with him, and it came to me simply because I was his only relative.

DIANA: And you don't call that a stroke of luck?

TOTI: I don't say it wasn't. (*Thinking*) Perhaps, in a way it was . . . But now the rumour has spread that I have goodness knows how much money hidden away in the house. Hidden indeed! Not a song! The entire inheritance—140,000 lire—went straight into the bank the moment it arrived.

DIANA: Quite a sum!

TOTI (*smiling*): It is. And, as you probably know, I agreed to become the largest shareholder in the bank, on condition that someone I trust is employed there to 'look after it.'

DIANA (*a little uneasy*): You mean Giacomino Delisi.

TOTI (*imperturbed*): Exactly! Giacomino Delisi. But believe me, Signor Diana, I was happier when I was poor. Then people just thought of me as a nobody and took hardly any notice of me,—but since my brother left me his money, little old Toti has become the man of the moment. Everybody wants to know what I do and what I don't, if I help one or befriend another, and whatever I say and whatever I do is discussed and criticized by everybody. But what do they all want from me? Aren't I entitled to do as I please, as long as I don't harm anyone? It makes me really angry Signor Diana, and believe me if it weren't for that little child there who will soon begin to toddle about the house, I wouldn't hesitate to withdraw those 140,000 pieces of paper from the bank and start a bonfire that would make history!

DIANA: I am sorry: I seem to have touched on a sore point. But will you allow an old friend to make an observation?

TOTI: Please, please do.

DIANA: In view of the malicious tongues of many people in our town, it seems to me that you are not doing as much as you could to protect yourself from the harm their gossip can do you.

TOTI: Signor Diana, gossip is a congenital disease of the wicked-minded—women especially are affected—and there is no cure for it. I have done nothing wrong. My life has been spent between my home and your school. School and home, home and school: that's my simple routine.

DIANA: Ah, my dear Professor, now we've come to the very reason for my visit: the school.

TOTI: Oh!

DIANA: Do you remember that some months ago, when you had just completed thirty four years of teaching, I advised you to retire?

TOTI: Of course I remember.

DIANA: You were not rich then, but now that you have been blessed with this substantial inheritance . . .

TOTI: Blessed my foot! I know what you're going to say: but you can continue to sing that song as often as you like and the Government can whistle it: I am not going to retire!

DIANA: Please; please, Professor—listen to reason.

TOTI: Reason? I have every reason for not retiring. Only God knows the price I pay for my determination. I love that little child; the hours I spend in your school which keep me away from him seem like centuries to me. My heart thumps for joy when the school bell rings at the end of the day, and I can run home to play with him, as if I were a child myself. And in spite of that, I am determined not to retire!

DIANA: Oh, you are obstinate! and illogical! You make your work seem a martyrdom, and yet . . . when you're asked to leave . . .

TOTI: It is a martyrdom! And for that very reason I intend to carry my cross to the very day when my wife and the child will be entitled to the maximum pension.

DIANA: But now your inheritance has altered the position. You're no longer in need of your pension.

TOTI: That's what you say. My pension may be hardly enough to buy a dozen handkerchiefs, but I have earned it honestly, with hard work. It has far greater moral value than the riches that have suddenly fallen on me from the skies—money which you've only to do this to—(*He blows on his open palm.*) and it blows away like the wind. Besides there are other reasons for my not wishing to retire.

DIANA: Oh?

TOTI: In confidence: if I didn't have the school, I'd be at home too much, playing with the child. I'm not exactly a youngster, (*smiling a little sadly,*) and—if you understand me—I'd be in everyone's way.

DIANA: But surely . . .

TOTI: That's enough Signor Diana, let's not talk about my resignation any more!

DIANA (*standing on his dignity*): I'm sorry, Professor, but we'll have to thrash this out once and for all!

TOTI (*with a twinkle in his eye*): Are you trying to force me to resign?

DIANA: Be patient, Professor, and try also to see my point of view. For the past few months—at school, in my home, even in the street, I have had no peace! The fathers, mothers, brothers, sisters of our pupils—even complete strangers—have come to me to protest against your remaining a teacher in my school.

TOTI: Oh, really?

DIANA: Yes. It's most unfortunate, but there it is! It has grown into an organized protest from the citizens of the town. They say your private life and your conduct are scandalous.

TOTI: Scandalous? And what do you say to that, Signor Diana?

DIANA: I don't wish to enter into a discussion as to whether they are right or wrong. I only say that as a private individual, if your conscience is clear, you may ignore the censure of others, but as a school teacher— you cannot! You are entrusted with a public position, and you, no less than I in my capacity as Headmaster, are obliged to take public opinion into account. That is why I have come to advise you once again to resign.

TOTI: And bow my head to a grave injustice?

DIANA: You must not put it like that.

TOTI: How else should I put it? As you are not prepared to, I must wait for someone else to come and discuss things with me, not as they *appear* but as they actually *are*. They will find my conscience clear. (*He rises*). Yes, Signor Diana, I accept the challenge of public opinion. I want to see who will have the courage to come and tell me to my face that I am not an honest man; and that what I am doing is not done for the best.

DIANA (*rises after a moment's pause*): Then there's nothing more I can say. I hope you will appreciate that I came here to advise you as a friend.

TOTI (*taking DIANA's hand in both his and shaking it warmly*): I do . . . I do . . . it was kind of you.

DIANA: I must warn you that they threaten to take their protest to higher authorities . . .

TOTI: Let them if they want to.

DIANA (*ill at ease*): . . . and that if the Minister of Education were to demand a report from me . . .

TOTI: You will tell him that you have requested my resignation but that I refuse to give it. (*He smiles.*) But don't worry, Signor Diana: we shall see what we shall see!

DIANA (*with a sigh of resignation*): My compliments to the Signora, and I hope she will soon be well again.

TOTI: Thank you. She'll appreciate your thought, I know.

DIANA (*goes to the door, then turns to him*): One last word—as an old friend: Think over what I have told you . . . and take my advice: resign.

TOTI: I'll see you to the door, Signor Diana.

DIANA *goes out, followed by* TOTI. *After a few moments,* LILLINA *enters left carrying Nini in her arms. She looks dejected, her hair is untidy and her eyes are red from crying.*

LILLINA (*calling*): Rosa . . . Rosa . . .

TOTI (*returning*): I sent her on an errand. She'll soon be back. You look tired, Lillina. Take a little rest and I'll look after Nini. Come Nini . . . (*He takes the child in his arms.*) Let's leave Mammina alone. She isn't well, poor little Mammina, and she's in a bad mood.

LILLINA: Nini's been very restless.

TOTI: No wonder when he sees you like that. Isn't that true, Nini? We can't bear to see Mammina in such a state. (*To* LILLINA.) For the last three days we can hardly recognize you.

LILLINA: That's because I'm not feeling well.

TOTI: I can see that. Come Nini! I'll take Nini to the other woman till Rosa comes back. (*He goes out with Nini. He comes back a moment later and he finds* LILLINA *much distressed. Suddenly realizing his presence,* LILLINA *addresses him anxiously.*)

LILLINA: Where's Nini?

TOTI: I handed him over to the other maid. (*Whimsically*) Really Lillina, the little rascal must be taught good manners . . . He must be taught to ask permission when he wants to be excused! But don't worry; now he is sucking his thumb and he is as quiet as a lamb . . . You instead seem to be more restless than before. (LILLINA *turns her head away*.) Come now, Lillina: Won't you tell me what's the matter with you? . . .

LILLINA: It's nothing really: just a headache. I can hardly keep my eyes open . . .

TOTI: . . . Shall I send for the doctor?

LILLINA: No.

TOTI: Very well, now listen . . .

LILLINA: Please! Please leave me alone! Don't worry about me; just be patient for a day or so. I'll be all right. It'll soon be . . . it'll soon be . . . (*She bursts into unrestrained sobs.*)

TOTI: Yes, yes—it'll soon be over! (*A pause. Then, very sweetly.*) Come my child: confide in me. Has anything happened between you and Giacomino?

LILLINA: No.

TOTI: Then why are you so unhappy? You still won't tell me? Then I will tell you. (*Firmly*) You are worrying yourself to death, and it's no use telling me that it's only a headache . . . that your eyes hurt. (LILLINA *shakes her head trying to deny it*.) Yes, Yes! You're worried by what people say about us. Don't deny it; don't shake your head.—It's true that people talk, laugh and even threaten.—They went so far as to send my headmaster

here, a few minutes ago you know!—But you and I know
that we do nothing wrong, and that's all that matters!
The important thing now is for us all to keep together.
We must have faith in ourselves until time will prove me
right. After I am gone, you'll be completely free to marry
Giacomino. Then the three of you will have a secure
future, secure from financial worries.—Do you understand? (LILLINA *nods her head*.) Well, that's enough
from me. Now you can speak. What has happened
between you two? Have you quarrelled?

LILLINA: I haven't quarrelled with anyone.

TOTI: Then why hasn't Giacomino been here for the last
three days?

LILLINA: I don't know.

TOTI: He hasn't even been to the Bank. The cashier told
me yesterday. Perhaps he's got 'a headache' too! Ah,
youth! Youth! You don't realize that time is on your side,
but for me every day I am unhappy because of you two,
is a precious day lost. I haven't heard you sing or seen
you smile for three days now! (LILLINA *bursts into tears
again*.) There, you see? And you say there's nothing
wrong. Something really serious must have happened.
(*The door bell rings*.) Ah, that'll be your parents. If
you won't tell me what it is, you'll surely tell your
mother.

LILLINA (*jumps to her feet. Between sobs*): You sent for
my mother? But I've nothing to tell her . . . I don't want
. . . Oh, don't torment me! Leave me in peace!

LILLINA *rushes out through the door on the left*. TOTI,
*down hearted, shakes his head as he gazes at the door through
which she went out. He waits a moment, then, as no one
enters, he goes to the centre door and calls.*

TOTI: Who is it? (*A pause*.) Rosa!

ROSA: Yes, it's me. (*She enters*.)

TOTI: 'Yes it's me!' I know it's you . . . But have you seen
my wife's parents? Are they coming?

ROSA: Yes. I expect they're on their way now. At first they wouldn't listen to me. They said they didn't want to be mixed up in your affairs.

TOTI: And who asked them to poke their noses into my affairs?

ROSA (*crossly*): I'm only telling you what they said!

TOTI: Did you tell them that their daughter isn't feeling well?

ROSA: Yes. And they didn't seem surprised.

TOTI: And then you had a nice gossip between you, *I* wouldn't be surprised! (*He looks at her searchingly.*) I have a kind of feeling that you know what's wrong with your mistress, and don't want to tell me.

ROSA (*snappily*): I know nothing. I'm only a servant here: I'm not a spy!

TOTI: Well there's no need to flare up like that!

ROSA: I have every reason to flare up! I'm a respectable girl I'd have you know—and I don't approve of what goes on in this house. I feel sorry for the Signora, and I'm fond of the child . . . but as for you—I'm not afraid to tell you to your face. I don't like what people are saying about you. You should be ashamed of yourself! A man of your age! And if you're not pleased with my services, then you can tell me to go—so there! (*The door bell rings again.* ROSA *makes a mock curtsy, holding up her apron with both hands.*) So there! (*She goes out.*)

TOTI: Wicked tongue! Wicked tongue!

After a moment, CINQUEMANI *and* MARIANNA *enter haughtily, without greeting* TOTI. CINQUEMANI *is wearing an old grey top hat (of the English Ascot type) and is carrying a thick walking stick with a horn handle.* MARIANNA *has a large veil over her face, and is wearing a pleated skirt with a pattern of green and black squares which shrieks of naphthalene from miles away.*

TOTI: My dear father and mother-in-law. Come sit down and make yourselves at home.

CINQUEMANI: (*gravely and with an ill-fitting-air of 'Grand Seigneur'*): This is hardly the place for us to make ourselves at home!

TOTI: At least take your hat off.

CINQUEMANI: I'll take nothing off.

TOTI: Well, you Signora Marianna—won't you remove your veil?

MARIANNA: Why should I? I like it!

CINQUEMANI: I only take off my hat in my own home—and as this is not my house,—it stays where it is! (*He sits down.*)

TOTI: This is your daughter's house. I can't help it if you never wanted to look on it as yours too!

CINQUEMANI (*rising*): Marianna . . . Pst! (MARIANNA *rises.*)

TOTI: One moment! Sit down there! I want to talk to you.

MARIANNA: Oh, do you? Well, you can just listen to what we have to say first! (*To* CINQUEMANI.) Come on! You tell him!

TOTI (*resigned*): Very well: Let's hear what you've got to say. But make it short.

CINQUEMANI (*in his most imposing manner*): Both me and my wife: *me* (*He points at himself.*) . . . and *my wife* . . . (*He points at her, stressing each word.*) Understand?

TOTI: Yes, well?

CINQUEMANI: I repeat that because I want to make it quite clear that . . .

MARIANNA (*finishing his sentence for him*): . . . That we really *are* married!

CINQUEMANI: Marianna—leave this to me! As I was saying; me and my wife have set foot in this house only once—the day you got married.

MARIANNA (*unable to keep still on the settee*): And only God knows what that cost us!

TOTI: Cost you? Why? I don't remember any present?

MARIANNA (*on the attack*): I meant the way people stared at us when they saw us coming here!

TOTI: Well, they stared at you . . . What then?

MARIANNA: It's the shame . . .

CINQUEMANI: Marianna! I'm doing the talking!

TOTI: Just a moment Cinquemani: I want to ask you something. Haven't I told you many times at school, to bring your wife here to see your daughter?

CINQUEMANI: Yes, you have.

TOTI: Then why didn't you come? What prevented you?

MARIANNA (*starting to her feet*): What prevented us, he asks!

CINQUEMANI (*also jumping up*): Marianna, shut up! I'm dealing with this. Professor, as you've brought up the school, I'd like you to know that when the other teachers and your pupils are there, I say 'good morning' and 'good evening' to you just out of politeness, and nothing more! You don't know the filthy things the boys scribble about you and my daughter on the lavatory walls . . .

MARIANNA (*shocked at his mentioning the word*): Oh, Cinquemani!

CINQUEMANI (*raising his hat*): Sorry my love—but a spade's a spade, isn't it? (*To* TOTI.) I have to scrub them off, because they're enough to make me blush with shame!

MARIANNA: And he asks us what stopped us coming here! Why, the whole town is talking about you!

CINQUEMANI: Yes, and I want you to know that my wife and I agree with what everyone says about you!

MARIANNA: Because we are decent people, and we can still blush! D'you understand?

CINQUEMANI: We have a sense of decency . . . even if *some people* haven't!

TOTI (*getting impatient*): Come, come . . . I think you've said enough. Do you want to know what you are? A couple of asses!

CINQUEMANI: Now look here: you'd better use more respect when you talk to me! Remember I'm your father-in-law!

TOTI: Father-in-law indeed! You know very well how and why I married your daughter.

MARIANNA: You took her because you wanted her.

TOTI: Yes, I did. With all my heart.

MARIANNA: Heart? Don't make me laugh! It certainly wasn't for our sake! As far as we were concerned she could have stayed at home—and it would have been far better. At least we could have hushed up the affair.

CINQUEMANI: Yes, but by doing what you've done, you've ruined her reputation—and ours!

MARIANNA: We feel so ashamed that we hardly dare show our faces in public.

TOTI: Well, they're not worth looking at anyway!

MARIANNA: Well! Of all the . . . There's no need for rudery . . .

TOTI: Have you quite finished?

CINQUEMANI: No, we haven't finished! You'll have to stomach a bit more yet. You even had the cheek to put that . . . that blasted Giacomino Delisi . . .

MARIANNA (*clapping her hands to her ears*): Don't you dare mention his name to me!

CINQUEMANI (*raising his hat*): Sorry my love. (*To* TOTI.) You've put him in a good position in the bank. What for? To make sure your money's safe?

TOTI: Ah—I see: so that's why you're so furious.

MARIANNA: No—that's only one of the reasons!

CINQUEMANI: Marianna, let me talk! Wasn't it enough that you let him come here to your house—in spite of the scandal it caused . . .

MARIANNA: And what a scandal!

CINQUEMANI (*to his wife*): Shut up! (*To* TOTI.) Did you have to let him look after your money as well? Couldn't you have left your pension and this fortune you've inherited to my daughter *without* all this fuss, and let her be free to live as she pleased with her baby? Why did you have to marry her? Hasn't she a father and mother who could have looked after her? (*His emotion gets the better of him and he takes a large coloured handkerchief from his pocket and starts to cry.* MARIANNA *follows suit.* TOTI *allows them to weep freely and comfort each other for a few moments before taking up the cudgel.*)

TOTI: Good! The crocodile is crying—Now's my chance to speak. Now tell me, how could your daughter inherit my meagre pension unless she was my wife? Tell me that? And as for the money my brother left me—who could have expected that? If it had come sooner, things might have been different. But in any case I would certainly have expected that Lillina—would have had the decency to wait patiently for my death before doing what she pleased with my money.

CINQUEMANI: Oh, we didn't come here to listen to all this stuff and nonsense! We only came because we knew that Giacomino had gone. It's all finished now.

TOTI: What do you mean?

CINQUEMANI: Just what I said. Giacomino's left her. It's all over—for good.

MARIANNA (*crossing herself*): Thank God.

TOTI: Giacomino's left Lillina? (*Almost to himself.*) Oh no! It can't be!

MARIANNA: Everybody says so.

CINQUEMANI: Why are you so upset? I thought you'd be pleased?

TOTI (*confused*): How is it possible that everybody should know about it but I? (CINQUEMANI *and* MARIANNA *look at each other in surprise.*)

TOTI (*almost to himself*): Oh—so that's why the poor girl's been crying her eyes out for three days now. (*He turns on them fiercely, his eyes blazing.*) What are people saying about it in the town? (MARIANNA *crosses herself.*)

TOTI: Oh stop crossing yourself: I'm still alive, you know—and I've plenty of fight left in me!

MARIANNA: Yes, but so has our Blessed Minister, thank God!

TOTI: 'Our Blessed Minister?'

MARIANNA: Yes. Didn't you know that *his* sister . . .

TOTI: Whose sister, Giacomino's?

MARIANNA: Yes. Rosaria Delisi—has got the church to take up the matter now.

CINQUEMANI: Yes, and Don Landolina is coming here himself, to talk to you today.

TOTI: Don Landolina? Who's he? Another nosey-parker?

MARIANNA (*shocked, crossing herself again*): A Sainted man!

CINQUEMANI: He's the priest of St. Michael's . . .

MARIANNA: . . . and her Father Confessor . . . that's who he is!

TOTI: I see! And you say he's coming to talk to me?

CINQUEMANI: Yes. He called at our house last night to find out if we approve of what goes on here between you three . . .

MARIANNA: And when we told him we did not . . .

TOTI: . . . He said he would come to talk to me! (*He rubs his hands as though he were glad of this*). Splendid. Splendid. Let him come! I'll give him a piece of my mind. You'll see! (*He turns to* MARIANNA.) But in the meantime, please go and speak to your daughter. She's in her room. (*He indicates the door on the left.*)

MARIANNA (*jumping up again*): No! I never want to see her again.

TOTI: Don't be silly. Try and find out as tactfully as you can what's happened between her and Giacomino.

MARIANNA: Have you gone mad? You expect me to talk about such things with my daughter? What do you take me for?

TOTI: For a good mother; whatever else you may be! I tell you it's a very serious matter. Please go in and talk to her.

MARIANNA (*to* CINQUEMANI): Shall I go?

CINQUEMANI (*after a moment's reflection,—gravely*): Yes.

MARIANNA: Very well; I'll go in—but I warn you I won't speak to her. If she cares to talk to me . . .

TOTI: All right,—but you'll see, as soon as she sees you, she'll throw herself into your arms, and tell you everything.

MARIANNA: Huh!

TOTI (*gently pushing her into the other room*): For Heaven's sake—be tactful. (MARIANNA *exits left.*) Now: you,

Cinquemani, you'll do something for me. I'll reward you for it.

CINQUEMANI: I will not be bribed, I'd have you know! Remember I am a Civil Servant! I've only a humble position, I know—still, I'm a Servant of the State: and I haven't forgotten that!

TOTI: No, you haven't—but you seem to have forgotten something else.

CINQUEMANI: Oh—what's that?

TOTI: That you're also a father—

CINQUEMANI: I'd like to know how many of us are fathers in this house!

TOTI: You least of all, I can assure you! But now, stop this bickering, and listen carefully to me. (*He pauses and puts his ear to* LILLINA's *door a moment to hear whether she is confiding to her mother.*) Come over here. I must talk quietly. I want you to go down to the Piazza . . .

CINQUEMANI: Yes?

TOTI: . . . and call at the bank. (*He tries to listen at the door again.*)

CINQUEMANI (*on his guard*): What for?

TOTI: Good heavens, what a face! Is that how you look when I ask you to do me a favour?

CINQUEMANI: Well, you haven't told me what you want me to do at the bank?

TOTI: Just see if Giacomino Delisi is there.

CINQUEMANI: What? That son of a . . .

TOTI: Now, now, Cinquemani . . . (TOTI *puts his hand over* CINQUEMANI's *mouth.*)

CINQUEMANI (*pulling* TOTI's *hand away*): If I see that scoundrel . . .

TOTI: You'll do like the hare before the hounds, you'll run for your life! But don't worry about that . . . It's more than likely that you'll not find him there. Instead you'll have a word with the cashier . . . You don't mind that, do you . . .

CINQUEMANI: No, I don't mind that . . .

TOTI (*jesting*): But don't pinch any money from him, eh?

CINQUEMANI: Oh, look here Professor: I am an honest man I'll have you know . . .

TOTI: I know, I know . . . I was only joking! You will only ask the cashier if he has any news of Giacomino, and then come back here as quickly as you can . . . (*The door bell rings.*)

CINQUEMANI: Oh Lord—if that's him, I'll . . . I'll . . . (*He is in a great panic and looks around for somewhere to hide.*) I don't want to see him, d'you understand? I just don't want . . . (*He stops as* ROSA *appears in the centre doorway.*)

TOTI: Yes, Rosa?

ROSA: It's Father Landolina. He says he'd like to speak to you.

CINQUEMANI (*relieved*): You see? I told you he was coming.

TOTI (*to* ROSA): Show him in. (ROSA *goes out centre.*)

CINQUEMANI: I'll be off. Thank Heaven some decent people are visiting this house at last. (DON LANDOLINA *enters.* CINQUEMANI, *centre, greets him reverently.*) Your Reverence. (*He goes out centre.*)

LANDOLINA (*unctuously*): My dear Professor Toti.

TOTI: Come in, Father. Do sit down please.

LANDOLINA: Thank you. You are very kind.

TOTI: To what do I owe the honour of your visit Father?

LANDOLINA: First I must ask you to forgive my interfering in a very delicate matter, which concerns me in as much as I am a Servant of God. I must call on your kindness and goodness—which are well known to everybody. I . . . (*He hesitates, trying to feel his 'ground'.*)

TOTI (*smiling*): Are you 'calling on my kindness and goodness' in order to make me swallow a bitter pill, Father?

LANDOLINA: Not exactly, I . . . it is a little difficult to explain.

TOTI: Well, if it will help you, Father—you may have just as much of my 'kindness and goodness' as is necessary to help you say what you have to say . . . (*changing his tone*) but no more!

LANDOLINA: I will come straight to the point. It is a question of conscience, Professor.

TOTI: Your conscience, or mine?

LANDOLINA: The conscience of a poor Christian soul. I will not dispute whether the person in question is right or wrong . . .

TOTI: You won't? Not even you?

LANDOLINA (*taken aback*): I beg your pardon?

TOTI: I should have thought that you of all people would have decided on that point before coming here.

LANDOLINA: I don't quite follow?

TOTI: Never mind. I was only thinking aloud. Please continue.

LANDOLINA: I was only saying that (I don't know whether rightly or wrongly)—that poor soul feels mortified, humiliated, insulted, by the rumours which have spread all over our town about . . . her brother.

TOTI: I understand. So you have come to me—on behalf of Giacomino Delisi's sister.

LANDOLINA (*not wishing to admit it*): I didn't say so! I . . .

TOTI: One moment, Father: if you wish to talk about Giacomino and my family, I think it's best that you take your gloves off, first.

LANDOLINA (*showing his un-gloved, white hands, with the faintest of smiles on his lips*): But really—I am not wearing . . .

TOTI: Come Father—I think you understand me. I may be blunt in my way of saying things, but that is because I have nothing to hide. I would prefer it if you too would be frank and honest.

LANDOLINA (*offended*): I must ask you to have more respect for my calling, Professor.

TOTI: Why—does your visit concern a secret told in Confession?

LANDOLINA: No, no: it concerns—as I told you—the mortification . . . the sorrow of a poor penitent who comes to ask advice and help from her Confessor.

TOTI (*nods his head*): Go on, Father.

LANDOLINA: I will be frank—as you have asked me to. Signorina Delisi is—as you know—very much older than her brother. Since he lost his parents as a child, she has been like a mother to him. Thanks be to God, under her guidance, he has grown up into a God-fearing, respectful and obedient young man.

TOTI: You have no need to tell me that Father. Do you think I don't know Giacomino? I know him better than you or his sister, I can assure you.

LANDOLINA: I merely wanted to point out that in my estimation, all these good points in his character are due to that excellent woman and the good education she has given him.

TOTI: Oh—how exciting to end up like a candle on the altar!

LANDOLINA (*missing the irony*): I don't understand?

TOTI: She burns and melts, Father! Oh yes an excellent woman, Signorina Delisi! But I agree, she has brought up her 'little brother' beautifully.

LANDOLINA: I'm glad you agree: and for that reason, one must look elsewhere for the cause of so much injurious gossip in the town. It is clear to me that it comes from the fact that he frequents your house too much. People find it . . . improper, that your wife—so young and so charming, if I may say so . . .

TOTI (*impatiently*): In short, Signorina Delisia has sent you to ask me to persuade Giacomino not to come here any more—in order to stop people talking! Is that what you want?

LANDOLINA (*with sad humility which has a spiteful sting to it*): No, Professor—not exactly.

TOTI: Then what else *could* you want from me?

LANDOLINA: Till now I have spoken only of Signorina Delisia, and of the suffering brought upon her by these malicious rumours which, I must point out, are harmful not only to the young man, but also to—(*He hesitates.*)

TOTI: If you mean me, Father, don't be afraid to say so.

LANDOLINA: Of course I know that *you* are above such shallow gossip,—but not so a poor woman; an elder sister who we must look on almost as a mother. She suffers,—weeps,—cries out for comfort and help. She is but a woman after all, and . . . well I'm sure you understand—

TOTI: Stop beating about the bush, Father, and tell me exactly what you want from me?

LANDOLINA: I will come to the point. I admit that Signorina Delisi did send me here, but it was only to implore you to have the goodness to—to let her have a few words in writing . . . a little 'statement' shall we call it . . . (oh, solely for her comfort and peace of mind, you understand) that there is and can be no truth whatsoever in all these ugly rumours.

TOTI (*after a moment's pause*): Is that all she wants? Nothing more?

LANDOLINA: Oh nothing more—I assure you!

TOTI: I see (*Very sweetly.*) And of course, Signorina Delisi feels certain that Giacomino will never again set foot in this house; because she—as a good sister—has persuaded her 'little brother' that it's for his own good if he stays away. Isn't that so, Father?

LANDOLINA: Yes Professor: I believe she has convinced him of that.

TOTI: And now she wants a little 'statement' from me? But certainly, certainly. I'll write one out for her.

LANDOLINA (*believing he has won his battle*): Oh thank you, thank you.

TOTI: Don't mention it. After all, what does it cost me? It's easily done: Only a few words: 'I, Professor Agostino Toti, in consideration of the ugly rumours etc, etc, etc . . .'

LANDOLINA: That's it . . . That's it!

TOTI: 'Do hereby declare and testify, etc, etc, etc . . .'

LANDOLINA: Wonderful! . . . Wonderful! . . .

TOTI: Is that the idea?

LANDOLINA: Oh that would be fine.

TOTI (*sweetly*): Yes, it would, wouldn't it? (*Abruptly*) Well, you may go now, Father. I'll write it out and send it.

LANDOLINA: Thank you, thank you, my dear Professor. I am truly moved by your generosity and your true Christian spirit. (*He rises.*) But—forgive me, could you not write it out now? Then I could take it straight to Signorina Delisi.

TOTI: No, I haven't time now. I have something rather urgent to do. But you may rest assured that I will see to it.

LANDOLINA: You'll send it to me, will you?

TOTI: No—why to you? I'll send it directly to Signorina Delisi.

LANDOLINA (*offering his hand*): Very well. Once again, my grateful thanks.

TOTI: Don't mention it. One, moment, Father. Tell me, did you know that Giacomino—that God-fearing, respectful, obedient—and I must add—idle young man, is at last working at the bank, where I found him a job?

LANDOLINA: Oh, do you imagine I was not aware of that, Professor? I know it only too well; and you must believe me when I say that his sister is full of gratitude to you.

TOTI: Is she? Really?

LANDOLINA: Of course, of course.

TOTI: Well, well . . . that's nice to know.

LANDOLINA: And now I must be going Professor. (*Shaking* TOTI's *hand.*) And once again—many, many thanks.

TOTI: Goodbye, Father. (LANDOLINA *is about to go, when* TOTI *recalls him.*)

TOTI: Oh, by the way, Father, I wanted to ask you something else: only a little thing which flashed through my mind just now. Tell me, what would you think of a young man who, after having seduced a girl and made a mother of her, suddenly declined all responsibility for her? And what would you say if that poor young woman accepted the help and protection of an old man who . . . (LANDOLINA *having understood* TOTI's *allusion right from the first, has begun to cough in order to cover his embarrassment.* TOTI *pauses in the middle of his sentence, stares at* LANDOLINA *for a moment, then smiles.*) You know, you have a very bad cough Father. You must get rid of it. You really must. A good hot poultice, with plenty of mustard! That's what you need.

DON LANDOLINA *exists precipitously, holding a handkerchief to his mouth and coughing.*

TOTI (*goes to the other door on the left and calls*): Signora Marianna! Signora Marianna! (*After a moment,* MARIANNA *enters.*)

MARIANNA: It's no use. She won't talk. She's lying on her bed and won't move.

TOTI (*resolutely and in haste*): Never mind . . . never mind. Please do me a favour and dress the child for me.

MARIANNA: Dress him? How would I know where his things are kept?

TOTI: Yes, that's true. Well, I'll do it myself. (*He goes off to the left.*)

MARIANNA *stares at him as he goes, wondering.* CINQUEMANI *enters centre. He notices his wife staring at the door through which* TOTI *left.*

CINQUEMANI: What's the matter? Anything happened?

MARIANNA: Anything happened? This seems to be a mad-house!

CINQUEMANI: You're telling me. I've just bumped into Don Landolina on the stairs,—tip-toeing as if he didn't want to be heard, and with his eyes starting out of his head. But what about Lillina? Did she tell you anything?

MARIANNA: Not a word, not a word.

CINQUEMANI: Oh well—let's be off.

MARIANNA: No, wait a minute. I don't think we ought to go just yet.

TOTI *comes in, still in his dressing-gown, with his hat on his head, and his jacket over his arm. He is carrying the baby in a little basket which he places on the table while he removes his dressing-gown and dons his jacket.*

TOTI: Now our little treasure is going out for a walk with his grandpa. Oh I'm longing to hear him call me Grandpa. (*He places the basket on a table for a moment and the other two—despite themselves—crowd round and beam at the child.*) Did you go to the bank Cinquemani?
CINQUEMANI: Yes, but they'd no news of Giacomino.
TOTI: Well never mind. We'll go out and find Giami, shall we, Nini?—(*To* MARIANNA) That's what we call his father—'Giami' . . . (*He picks up the basket and makes for the door.*)
CINQUEMANI (*stepping in front of them*): You're going to Giacomino's? You don't mean it!
TOTI (*pushing him aside*): Of course I mean it.
CINQUEMANI: For heaven's sake think what you're doing!
MARIANNA: What will people say?
TOTI: To hell with what they'll say.
CINQUEMANI: You'll only bring more shame on yourselves!
TOTI: You! Out of my way. (*He pushes them both aside and goes out, talking to Nini.*) Come along, Nini. A little walk'll do us good . . . and we'll see Giami.
CINQUEMANI: He's out of his mind! . . . Going to Giacomino's! (*He goes to the door and calls after him.*) Professor! Professor!
MARIANNA (*sinking into a chair*): God what a man! What a man! what a man!

CURTAIN

ACT III

The drawing-room in Signorina Delisi's house. There are two doors in the back wall, overhung with curtains. Between them is a large painting of the 'Madonna del Rosario' with a lighted lamp hanging beneath it. A door in each side wall, is also covered by curtains. The furniture is old and the room has a severe, almost monastic atmosphere.

DON LANDOLINA is seated on a sofa, sipping choco-late. ROSARIA DELISI is in a small easy chair just by him. As the curtain rises, they are both laughing.

LANDOLINA: Everything went well, believe me: exactly as I had hoped. I left him believing he had understood the motive of my visit. This chocolate is delicious.

ROSARIA: Is there enough sugar?

LANDELINA: Yes thank you. An excellent sufficiency (*Resuming*) 'Let us come to the point' he said . . . 'You've been sent by Signorina Delisi to ask me never to allow Giacomino to come to my house again. Isn't that so?' And I replied (*assuming his favourite expression and tone of humility and patient suffering,*) 'No, Professor—not exactly that!'

ROSARIA (*laughing*): I can just see his face when you said that.

LANDOLINA: He was dumbfounded! He never expected that. (*He rises to put his empty cup down. ROSARIA rises quickly and takes it from him.*) Thank you.

ROSARIA: Some more?

LANDOLINA (*he'd love it, but he must be polite*): N—no thank you.

ROSARIA: Sure?

LANDOLINA (*meaning yes please*): W—ell . . .

ROSARIA *puts the cup on the tray and sits down, obviously not intending to pour out a second cup. DON LANDO-LINA's expression sours a moment, then he continues.*

LANDOLINA: But when I told him that you and I had already persuaded Giacomino not to go there again, he hardly knew what to say. (*Imitating* TOTI.) 'What! How's that? But then . . .?!' (*He chuckles.*)

ROSARIA (*laughing*): Yes, yes: I can just imagine it! But Father it would have been better if you had got him to write out the declaration we want—in your presence.

LANDOLINA: I asked him to. But he said he hadn't time then, and I didn't think it prudent to insist further. It was wiser, having hinted what we wanted (and I flatter myself I found the best way of doing that)—to let him feel that such a document was required solely to put your mind at rest, and had no urgent or practical value, if you understand me?

ROSARIA: I do understand. But you know very well that I don't want it for myself: it's his young lady who insists on having that statement. Now I'm afraid the Professor may change his mind.

LANDOLINA: Oh I think there's no fear of that. He assured me several times that he would do it. In fact— (let us admit, it must have seemed to him a rather ingenuous request)—I had the impression that he was even pleased to be able to rid himself of so much trouble so easily.

At this moment, FILOMENA—*Rosaria's old servant—bursts into the room and announces almost in trepidation.*

FILOMENA: The Professor, Signorina! The Professor!

LANDOLINA (*rising—startled*): What?

ROSARIA: Here?

FILOMENA: Yes. I heard the bell ring and I was going to open the door, but luckily I looked through the window first to see who it was—and it's *him!* the Professor!—With the baby!

ROSARIA: With the child? Oh, my goodness!

LANDOLINA: The impudence! This is really going too far!

ROSARIA: Do you see? He agrees not to let Giacomino go to his house any more—and immediately he comes here himself!

FILOMENA: What shall I do? What do you want me to tell him?

ROSARIA: Don't let him in. Send him away.

FILOMENA: Very well, Signorina.

ROSARIA: Tell him Giacomino isn't in. You can talk to him through the window; don't even open the door.

FILOMENA: Very well, Signorina, I'll do as you say. (*She goes out.*)

ROSARIA: You see, Father? And you were only saying . . .

LANDOLINA: Believe me, Signorina, I am astonished at the man's impudence. Absolutely astonished.

ROSARIA: But what are we going to do?

LANDOLINA: Let us not be hasty. I am wondering—as we have to deal with such an obstinate man—whether it wouldn't be wiser to see him after all and to challenge him openly, rather than keep up this pretence . . .

ROSARIA: But who is to 'challenge' him? You?

LANDOLINA: Oh, no . . . not I. That would not be wise. Not that I'm afraid of him—please don't misunderstand me: but under the circumstances I think it best if a member of the family . . . yourself, Signorina . . .

ROSARIA (*gasps*): Me?

LANDOLINA: Why not? You are Giacomino's sister. And if you don't wish to, then Giacomino himself.

ROSARIA: Oh no . . . not Giacomino!

LANDOLINA: But don't you see: if Giacomino had the courage to tell him to his face that everything is over and that he must never dare to show himself here again . . . (FILOMENA *bustles in again.*)

ROSARIA: Ah, Filomena. Has he gone?

FILOMENA: No. He refuses to go.

ROSARIA: But didn't you tell him that Giacomino was not at home?

FILOMENA: I told him at least twenty times.

ROSARIA: And what did he say?

FILOMENA: He just laughed?

LANDOLINA: Laughed?

FILOMENA: Yes. He didn't seem to believe me, Now he wants to speak to you, Signorina.

ROSARIA (*nervous*): To me?

FILOMENA: I took the liberty of saying you weren't in, either.

ROSARIA: Good. And what did he say to that?

FILOMENA: He just laughed again, and said: 'Let me come in—I'll wait for her.' I even told him that the door was locked and you had taken the key with you, but he simply sat down on the doorstep and said he would wait for you there. Nothing will make him go.

LANDOLINA: Signorina, I advise you to receive him. (ROSARIA *is about to remonstrate.*) Believe me, it is for the best. Ask him in and try to keep as calm as possible. Be firm, but patient; you are the soul of patience, I know. (*As she still hesitates.*) Be advised by me, Signorina. Filomena, you may let him in.

FILOMENA: Very well Father. (*She goes out.*)

LANDOLINA: I will leave you now, Signorina—if you will excuse me. (*He goes towards the door on the right.*)

ROSARIA: You may go to Giacomino's room if you like, Father. He is there now.

LANDOLINA (*in his confusion, making for the wrong door*): Yes, yes, I'll do that.

ROSARIA: No, this way, Father.

LANDOLINA: Oh yes, yes of course, how stupid of me. (*He turns to the doorway.*) Remember, be firm but patient . . . (*correcting himself*) be farm but catient . . . oh dear, oh dear, you do understand . . . (*And he goes.*)

ROSARIA *looks round the room, worried, and decides to take out the tray of chocolate before the Professor comes. As soon as she has gone.* TOTI *enters slowly and proudly, carrying the basket, which he deposits on an occasional table by the sofa.* ROSARIA *comes back and he bows politely. She takes no notice but crosses to her chair and sits.*

TOTI: Good day Signorina. (ROSARIA *does not reply—a pause*.) I am glad to see you, Signorina.

ROSARIA (*cold and reserved*): Are you? May I ask what is the meaning of your visit, Professor? And why do you bring that child here?

TOTI: Well, it's such a beautiful day, and the poor little mite hasn't been out of the house for a few days now. He was crying so much, I said 'Come Nini, let's go out for a little walk together,' As soon as he breathed the fresh air, he stopped crying. You see, children are like birds; one minute they are cross, with their feathers all ruffled, and the next minute, the sun comes out—and they are lively and happy again.

ROSARIA: Couldn't you have taken him for a walk some-where else? Why just here?

TOTI: And why not here? We haven't seen Giacomino for a long time. I know he no longer goes to the bank, and I don't even meet him in the street these days. Nini began to miss him. I thought perhaps he wasn't well and we came to ask after him.

ROSARIA (*curtly*): He is perfectly well thank you, but he's not at home. Filomena must have told you.

TOTI: Forgive me, Signorina, you seem to be angry. Have I offended you or Giacomino by coming here? I'd be sorry if I had.

ROSARIA: As if you need to ask! Anyway I'm not angry . . . but I tell you again Giacomino is not in.

TOTI: Really?

ROSARIA: Yes, and I must ask you to save yourself the trouble of coming here again. If you have anything to say to my brother, he will meet you at your school or any other place you may care to suggest,—but not here . . . and certainly not at your home. I hope that is well understood.

TOTI (*shaking his head*): Such a harsh tone—yet you say you are not angry? I think I had best give you time to cool down a little. Perhaps there has been some mis-understanding?

ROSARIA (*scornfully*): Mis—under—standing!

TOTI: And if there has, it's as well to clear it up—frankly and openly . . . and *calmly*.

ROSARIA: I agree, Professor. Let us have it out once and for all.

TOTI: Good. Now we're getting somewhere. But first, let me sit down—and you go and call Giacomino.

ROSARIA: How many more times must I tell you he's not in?

TOTI: Forgive my asking, but is some—'Reverend' in the habit of conversing with furniture in your house?

ROSARIA (*taken aback*): Reverend? What do you mean?

TOTI (*picking up Don Landolina's hat, which he had left on a chair*): Your religious fervour is much talked of in the town. Perhaps you've been having a visit from your 'Spiritual Adviser?'

ROSARIA (*confused and irritated, snatching the hat out of his hands*): Give me that. It belongs to Father Landolina.

TOTI: And where is our dear Father? Busy giving 'Spiritual Advice' to Giacomino, no doubt.

ROSARIA: Nothing of the kind. He was here with me: now he's . . . in the other room with Filomena. (*She indicates one door. At this moment* FILOMENA *enters from the opposite side and quietly crosses the stage at the back to exit the other way.*)

TOTI: Really?

ROSARIA (*continues*): Anyway you have no business to pry into my private affairs.

TOTI: I don't pry: that is not one of my vices, Signorina! I leave that to others . . . to certain people who are forever prying into my private affairs. (*A pause.*) So, Giacomino is not in?

ROSARIA: No.

TOTI (*about to go*): Then you force me to return later.

ROSARIA: I told you that was not necessary. Giacomino will call on you at your school.

TOTI: You would trouble him to come all that way, when—as I am here and he is just upstairs—it would be so easy for us to talk and settle everything now.

ROSARIA (*at the end of her patience*): Very well: I see there is nothing for it but to call Giacomino and let him put an end himself to this monstrous and immoral situation for good!

TOTI: Take it calmly, Signorina. You may frighten the child.

ROSARIA: Oh! You are the devil himself!

TOTI: See now—you've woken him up.

ROSARIA: Oh! (*She flounces out—to the left—slamming the door.*)

TOTI: My poor Nini. The naughty woman has really disturbed your sleep. But you needn't worry—the old witch has gone. What? You want me to pick you up? But of course, of course darling. (*He takes Nini out of the basket.*) Perhaps if I rock him a little he'll go to sleep again. (*He sits down and begins to chant to him.*) Ah, ah . . . baby . . . Ah, ah, baby . . . (*He glances at the child.*) No, that won't do. (*He thinks it over a moment, then decides to try another way. He turns Nini over face downwards on his lap.*) I hope this is the right way to do it. (*He taps him gently on the back and resumes his chant.*) Ah, ah, baby . . . (*He then gently picks the baby up again.*) Ah, that's done the trick. (*He rises with Nini, and moves with him towards the corner. GIACOMINO enters and TOTI turns round to look at him. For a while they stare at each other.*)

GIACOMINO (*his clothes and hair are untidy. He is distressed, but tries not to show it.*): You wanted to speak to me, Professor?

TOTI (*sweetly and persuasively*): Yes, Giacomino. Oh, but let's have a smile first. Why, you would frighten Nini, with a face like that! Look at him . . . see how beautiful he is! (*GIACOMINO avoids looking at Nini.*)

Don't you want to look at him? Your child! . . . But what's the matter with you?

GIACOMINO (*bends down and pats Nini's head*): I don't feel well, Professor. I was lying down in my room: I have a splitting headache . . . A touch of 'flu perhaps . . . it wouldn't be fair to the child!

TOTI (*looks doubtfully at* GIACOMINO—*a pause*): Your sister said you weren't in . . .

GIACOMINO: Never mind what my sister said! I am here now. What do you want from me Professor?

TOTI: Just a moment. (*He puts Nini back in his carrier.*) Now you lie there quietly, like a good little boy. I felt somehow that you weren't well. And one can see it in your face.

GIACOMINO (*impatiently*): Professor, I . . .

TOTI: First of all, let's sit down on the settee, Giacomino. We'll be able to talk more comfortably then. (*They both sit down on the settee.*) There. I wanted to know whether the Manager of the Bank had spoken to you.

GIACOMINO: No. I haven't seen him lately.

TOTI: You haven't been to the Bank for the last three days.

GIACOMINO: I know. That was because . . .

TOTI: I don't want to know why. I met him on the street by chance yesterday. He mentioned something about your salary. I told him I didn't think you were getting enough, and we agreed that he would raise your wages.

GIACOMINO (*uneasy*): I'm much obliged to you, Professor . . . but I'd rather you didn't worry about me any more.

TOTI: Oh? Quite independent are we? We no longer need help from anyone, is that it?

GIACOMINO: It isn't that Professor, but . . . Oh, I wish you would understand . . .

TOTI: What am I to understand? You surely won't stop me from taking an interest in you?

GIACOMINO: But I don't want you to . . .

TOTI: You may not, but I do! . . . Huh! Would you believe it! He tells me not to worry about him! But who am I to worry about if not you?

GIACOMINO: Now listen Professor . . . (TOTI *stops him with a gesture.*)

TOTI: Let me finish and then you will talk! But without anger, please! (*A slight pause.*) You must know my son that my greatest desire is to see you and Lillina getting on well. And if I can help to make things easier for you, all the better . . . You know don't you, that I took to you from the first day you came to my school, just as if you were my son . . . (TOTI *interrupts himself for a moment to look closely at* GIACOMINO.) What's the matter? Are you crying? (GIACOMINO *is in fact trying to hold back the tears.*) Why? Why? (*He puts his hand on* GIACOMINO'S *shoulder.*)

GIACOMINO (*jumping up, his face bears a strange expression*): Leave me alone. Please!

TOTI: You look as though you're suffering, my boy.

GIACOMINO: Can't you see what you're doing. You're smothering me with all your kindness and goodness!

TOTI: I?

GIACOMINO: Yes, you! I don't want your affection! For God's sake leave me alone. Go away and forget that I ever existed!

TOTI (*stunned, quietly*): But why? Why? Giacomino—look at me.

GIACOMINO (*defiantly*): Well, if you must know, it's because . . . I must break off with Lillina. I . . . have become engaged to another girl, you understand? Another girl!

TOTI: En—ga—ged?

GIACOMINO: Yes, it's all over, with Lillina! Over for good! So there's no point in discussing it any more. Now, Professor, I must ask you to go!

TOTI (*almost without voice*): You . . . you are throwing me out?

GIACOMINO: Oh, no Professor,—but believe me, it's best for you to go. (TOTI *slowly picks up the carrier and starts to go*.) No . . . don't . . .

TOTI: You told me to go . . .

GIACOMINO: But . . . Nini . . .

TOTI: Nini, eh? You didn't think of him when you decided to desert his mother, did you? (GIACOMINO *buries his face in his hands*. TOTI *puts down the carrier again*.) I can see what torments you . . . It's a terrifying conflict between your heart and your mind . . . But tell me: you said you have become engaged to another girl. When did that happen?

GIACOMINO: A month ago.

TOTI: And yet you kept coming to my house . . .

GIACOMINO: Only for a few days . . . It wasn't easy for me to do otherwise . . .

TOTI: Who is the girl?

GIACOMINO: A friend of my sister . . .

TOTI: I see! And so you simply made up your mind to forget your past and with a shrug of your shoulders to leave it all behind you; Lillina, your responsibilities . . . everything . . .

GIACOMINO: What else could I do? . . . Oh, can't you see that you made me the slave of an impossible situation?

TOTI: I made you a slave? I who made you master in my home! . . . How can you say such a thing? . . . This is sheer ingratitude!

GIACOMINO: But . . .

TOTI: No, no, my boy! It's you who made the situation impossible! Don't you see? It's immaterial whether you are legally or illegally married to Lillina; by taking her you've made her your wife, and of course you are the father of her child . . .! What I did for you and Lillina was not for my benefit. Indeed, what have I derived from it? Nothing but mockery and insults, for no one, not even you seem to appreciate the feeling of an honest man who only wanted to provide a comfortable living for Lillina and yourself . . . You blame me for what you've only to blame yourself! My conscience is clear! What about yours? (*For a moment* GIACOMINO *seems to be crushed by the logic of Toti's argument*—TOTI's *mood suddenly changes.*) No . . . I cannot believe you're responsible for such an abominable action! I am sure that it's your sister and her Spiritual Adviser who have turned your mind . . .

GIACOMINO (*fighting his own feeling*): Nobody has turned my mind! Oh, you don't want to understand! I know you mean well Professor, but we can't possibly carry on as we have been doing . . . Don't you realize Professor, that . . . certain . . . certain situations can only exist if nobody knows about them. They have to be hidden; you can't do things openly for everyone to laugh at.

TOTI: So! it's because people laugh! But my boy, it's not you: it's me they're laughing at . . . me! And only because they don't understand. The truth is they envy you because they see you in a good position, with a secure future, and because they know that you will inherit my money!

GIACOMINO: Money!!! If that's the case, then for heaven's sake don't concern yourself about me any more, Professor. There are scores of other young men who'd be only too glad of your help.

TOTI (*deeply wounded, takes hold of him by the lapels of his jacket and shakes him violently*): What did you say? Lillina is young, but she is honest, by God! And she has always been loyal to you. And you dare to insult her? What do you take her for? Do you imagine she is the sort of girl who can be thrown from one man to another? . . . Oh! (*He pushes him away with disgust.*) And to think that I am the cause of all this. I who protected you; I who took you into my home, spoke up for you; I who took from her every doubt, every scruple, so that she could love you wholly and without fear. And when at last she felt secure in your love,—you . . . the father of her son . . .

you want to . . . (*With great determination.*) But you'd
better think it over, Giacomino! Mind what you're doing,
for now—I am capable of anything! Think it over,
Giacomino! I'll have you thrown out of the bank! and let
you starve!

GIACOMINO: It won't make any difference!

TOTI: I'll go to your fiancée—right now . . . and I'll take
Nini with me!

GIACOMINO (*afraid*): My god, you wouldn't do that!

TOTI: Oh, wouldn't I?! Who's to stop me? (*He takes Nini
out of the carrier.*)

GIACOMINO: You've no right to . . .

TOTI: No right? I have every right to protect the family I
have helped to create! . . . I'll go to your fiancée and to
her people, and show them this child who you find it so
easy to abandon. Your son Giacomino! Look at him!
Have you the heart to leave him? (*He holds Nini out
towards* GIACOMINO. GIACOMINO *can no longer
keep up his pretence of indifference and clasps Nini tightly
to him.* TOTI *laughing and crying at the same time.*) I
knew—I knew you were not really bad at heart . . .
Thank God! You've listened to the voice of your heart.
(*A short pause.*)

ROSARIA's *and* LANDOLINA's *voices are heard from off
stage.*

TOTI: Let's leave this house quickly, before these wicked
people turn your head again. They pretend to have left
us alone. It's my bet they're listening at the keyhole—
come, we'll go back to Lillina . . . all three together. (*He
leads them towards the door, when the other door on the
right flies open and* ROSARIA, LANDOLINA *and*
FILOMENA *rush into the room and try to hold* GIA-
COMINO. *They all talk at once.*)

LANDOLINA: We heard what he said, Giacomino don't
go . . .

ROSARIA: Did you hear Giacomino: don't go . . .

GIACOMINO: I must go Rosaria; I must . . .

LANDOLINA: It's a mortal sin, . . . a mortal sin, Giacomino . . .

TOTI (*placing himself between* LANDOLINA *and* GIA-
COMINO): Mortal sin!!? You with your hypocritical
morals, would have broken up a family! . . . I with the
principles which you call immoral, have kept it together
and saved it! . . . Get thee behind me, Satan!

TOTI *goes out after* GIACOMINO *and Nini, leaving* RO-
SARIA *and* LANDOLINA *at the door, shouting:* 'Giacomino . . . Giacomino . . . don't go!'

CURTAIN

THIS TIME IT WILL BE DIFFERENT

Come prima, meglio di prima

1920

Translated by
Felicity Firth

CHARACTERS

FULVIA GELLI (also known as FLORA and FRANCE-
SCA)
SILVIO GELLI, her husband
LIVIA, their daughter
MARCO MAURI
AUNT ERNESTINA GALIFFI
BETTY, a housekeeper
THE REVD. DON CAMILLO ZONCHI, a priest and
schoolmaster
MRS NÀCCHERI, a widow, his sister-in-law
JUDITH, her daughter
ROGHI, a farmer
CESARINO ROTA, a music teacher
BARBERINA ROTA, his wife
A SHOP ASSISTANT
JOHN, a gardener
A NURSE

The first Act takes place in a village in the Valdichiana; the
second and third in a villa near Lake Como. Time: the
present.

ACT I

A large sitting-room in the 'Pensione Zonchi.' It is a ram-shackle old house and the new whitewash on the walls does nothing to disguise the fact. A large high glazed door dominates the back wall, through which we glimpse a dim little entrance-hall. Beyond this a small open door leads out to steps going down to the garden. The small balcony at the head of these steps has a faded green wooden railing, and beyond the railing can be seen a clear stretch of sky. The house is set high on a hill and the balcony commands a view of a vast open valley and of the road which winds its way twice round the hill as it climbs towards the house.

When the glass door is closed the entrance hall is hidden by a net curtain, sky-blue in colour and brand-new, which strikes a discordant note. This is crudely hung from rods fixed across the glass at eye-level.

The furniture in the room is that of a typical old-style provincial pensione, arranged with meticulous symmetry: a porcelain stove; an antiquated sofa; upholstered chairs and armchairs; home-made cushions and hand-embroidered anti-macassars; an equally antique mantelpiece with a huge roco-co gilt-faced mirror covered by a piece of gauze, once blue and now yellow, to protect it from flies; little vases full of paper flowers; a corner cupboard stuffed with china orna-ments; cheap oleographs on the walls, black with age; and an ancient pendulum clock with a distant weary chime which marks the passing of every half-hour.

Doors right and left. A bright sunny morning towards the end of April.

As the curtain rises we see the Revd. DON CAMILLO
ZONCHI; ROGHI, *a local estate-manager;* MRS NÀC-
CHERI, *known as the* WIDOW NÀCCHERI, *and her
daughter* JUDITH. *These last two are upstage on the balcony overlooking the garden and are scanning the valley
beyond.* MRS NÀCCHERI *is looking through binoculars
while* JUDITH *is shading her eyes with her hand. Both are
searching the distant road for any cabs coming towards the
hill from the direction of the railway station. Inside the room,*
ROGHI *is seated on a chair beside the sofa, while* DON
CAMILLO ZONCHI *is standing.* MRS NÀCCHERI *is
aged about fifty and wears a curious little wig stuffed into a
hairnet; it is tightly crimped with a row of little curls peeping
out along her forehead. Her gaunt, angular face, with its
deep-set, lashless, pale-blue eyes, is like a mask. Thickly
coated with white powder and crudely daubed with colour, it
is gruesomely reminiscent of a painted skull. Her clothes are
too young for her and rigorous corseting distorts her ageing
body into a comic conformation of unnatural hollows and
bulges. She snaps at her brother-in-law as if by right; keeps
her daughter at a distance (she is jealous of her); and
addresses others with the languid hauteur often adopted by
impoverished gentry. Her daughter* JUDITH *is twenty-eight.
Abandoned by her husband she now neglects her appearance
and takes a back seat. Her lank hair, sallow complexion and
hollow cheeks all combine to give her the lost air of a poor
creature rescued from the Dogs' Home.* DON CAMILLO
ZONCHI *is fifty-four; a school-teacher and a minor canon.
He is swarthy, jaundiced-looking, irritable, and has malicious
little beady eyes. He endures his sister-in-law's outrageous
bossiness, while inwardly seething with shame and humilia-
tion. He owns the boarding-house, but* MRS NÀCCHERI
*runs it for him, so that his apparent rôle there is that of guest.
He does not wear a cassock, but a black twill frock-coat and
breeches, clerical bib and dog-collar, with woollen knee-socks
and silver-buckled shoes. The farmer,* ROGHI, *is a big heavy
fellow with a sad face. His unkempt beard shows signs of
several days' neglect. He is wearing a shooting-jacket, a*

disreputable old white hat, and hefty country boots complete with spurs.

DON CAMILLO (*expectantly, to the two women looking out from the top of the steps*): Still no sign?

ROGHI (*after a moment's pause*): It's still too soon.

DON CAMILLO (*irritably, still waiting for his answer*): Eh! Judith! I'm speaking to you!

MRS NÀCCHERI (*entering furiously from the balcony, spitting venom*): Surely I am the one to ask! (*She shows the outsize binoculars and stresses every word.*) If there's anything to be seen, of the two of us, I imagine that with this I am likely to see more than Judith!

DON CAMILLO: Don't upset yourself, Marianna. Maybe not! I mean, even with these (*shows her his glasses and settles them on his nose*) I still don't see as well as Mr Roghi.

ROGHI: Aye, the gift of sight is something to be thankful for . . .

MRS NÀCCHERI. Yes indeed, Mr Roghi, how I agree! I myself have absolutely no need of spectacles! Not for reading, not for sewing, not even for certain goings-on in this house, which God knows, need to be seen to be believed!

DON CAMILLO: Marianna, please! We are not concerned with domestic matters now! For heaven's sake let's keep to the task in hand and watch the road for cabs coming from the station.

JUDITH (*still looking out*): Here they come! Here they come! I can see two! But they are going the other way! Down the hill! (MRS NÀCCHERI *runs to have a look through the binoculars.*)

DON CAMILLO. Down the hill? Why should they do that? Are you sure?

JUDITH: Yes. Here's another! Now that one's Dodo's!

MRS NÀCCHERI: That's not Dodo's! Dodo's is in front!

JUDITH: No, mamma! Take a good look! It's the third one.

MRS NÀCCHERI: It's the one in front!

DON CAMILLO: But if they're going the wrong way . . .

MRS NÀCCHERI (*snapping angrily in her brother-in-law's direction*): It's the front one!

ROGHI: I don't see how it's possible to tell at this distance. From up here they must look minute, about this big. (*He gestures.*) And as for Dodo—I hate to say this, Mrs Nàccheri, but I saw for myself he was the last to leave the square.

MRS NÀCCHERI: That doesn't prove anything. He and that dreadful horse of his are two of a kind. It will get there first even if it was the last to leave.

JUDITH (*still watching, to her mother*): You're right! Look! Look! It has overtaken the second one and now it's overtaking the first one! Of course it's him! (MRS NÀCCHERI *gives a shrug and comes back into the room.*)

DON CAMILLO: For some reason they all seem to be late this morning. Usually by this time . . . (*The clock strikes eleven.*) There! It's eleven! They are usually back by now and you can see them at the second bend coming up. Which reminds me, Judith . . . (*He breaks off, embarrassed, checking himself.*) Well, I mean . . .

MRS NÀCCHERI (*her hackles rising again, sharply to* JUDITH *who is still outside*): Judith! Come on then! Hurry up! Come and see what it is your uncle wants to ask you!

DON CAMILLO (*still confused*): It really doesn't matter. (*Pulling himself together with an effort.*) It was just a little thing I thought she might know the answer to, whereas perhaps you might not.

MRS NÀCCHERI: Well, then, come on! Let's hear it!

DON CAMILLO (*to* ROGHI): Before the Professor left I taught him the little dodge of getting the cab to stop just below the garden. Then you can take a short cut, walk up through the garden instead of having to drag the horses all the way round by the road.

MRS NÀCCHERI. Well?

DON CAMILLO: Well, I just wanted to ask Judith if she had remembered to open the garden gate.

MRS NÀCCHERI: Is that all? (*She turns to her daughter who is hanging back from the conversation covered in confusion.*) Come on! Answer your uncle's question! Did you remember?

JUDITH (*looking away in exasperation*): Yes, yes. It's open.

MRS NÀCCHERI (*with an ironic nod towards her brother-in-law, as if speaking for her daughter*): You see, it's open! Uncle's orders! It would have been much more like her to have forgotten! Pity she couldn't have done as much for her husband! If she had obeyed him a bit more she wouldn't now be hanging round my neck like an overgrown schoolgirl.

ROGHI: Don Camillo, are you sure the Professor is coming back here this morning? I don't want to wait if he is not.

MRS NÀCCHERI: I shall have something to say if he does not! I have had had enough, I can tell you!

DON CAMILLO: Patience, Marianna, please!

MRS NÀCCHERI: I'm sick to death of the whole business!

DON CAMILLO: Calm down, come on! He will be back . . . But I have to say quite frankly, Roghi, dear chap, I can't really see him agreeing to your request. It's unlikely, if not impossible.

ROGHI: You don't think he would do just a brief consultation?

DON CAMILLO: I doubt . . .

ROGHI: It would be enough for me if he would just take a look at my poor baby!

DON CAMILLO: Ah, well! If you could get him to come and see her! The thing would be as good as done. He would operate and save her.

ROGHI: God! If only he would! I would fetch him in the car! At any time he chose!

JUDITH: As a man he is kindness itself!

DON CAMILLO: I know. But he can't. Don't you see what will happen? What he did here was a miracle, so . . .

MRS NÀCCHERI (*interrupting*): And he has to choose our house to go and do it in!

DON CAMILLO (*giving her a grim look and cutting through her interrupting*): Once news of it got around, everyone would be wanting him!

ROGHI: But look at yesterday. There was an emergency so he went to Sarteano. I mean, today, couldn't he . . .

DON CAMILLO: He simply can't. He has at least twenty people clamouring for him already.

MRS NÀCCHERI: Well, he needn't think he is going to disrupt this household for another month dispensing charity to all and sundry!

DON CAMILLO: After all he's got a daughter in Merate and affairs of his own. His original idea was to come here for one day.

MRS NÀCCHERI: Which has turned into six whole weeks!

JUDITH: While the daughter, I gather, knows nothing at all about what has been happening.

ROGHI: Really? She doesn't know her mother is here?

DON CAMILLO (*with a meaning look and a gesture towards the door, right*): Keep your voices down! . . . She is getting up. (*Mysteriously to* ROGHI.) Roghi, my dear chap, it's a wonder we haven't all gone out of our minds!

ROGHI: Because of that judge, you mean?

DON CAMILLO (*with some heat*): Judge? What judge? . . . He's no more a judge than I am!

JUDITH (*very quietly and unhappily*): Madman would be nearer the mark.

DON CAMILLO (*pressing his point*): The man needs a strait-jacket!

JUDITH (*very distressed*): It was terrible to see him!

DON CAMILLO (*more fiercely still*): He was a devil! He was possessed! Don't make me think about it!

MRS NÀCCHERI (*who has been staring at the pair of them, uncle and niece*): Just listen to them, Mr Roghi, won't you? Did you ever hear anything like it?

DON CAMILLO (*puzzled*): Why? What do you mean?

MRS NÀCCHERI: Your voices! One all milk and water . . . (*She imitates Judith, producing a nasal whine.*) 'It was terrible to see him!' And the other as plummy as a fruit-cake . . . (*She takes off Don Camillo's voice.*) He was a devil! He was possessed!

ROGHI (*laughing in spite of himself*): Oh, Mrs Nàccheri, you like to have your joke!

DON CAMILLO: Indeed . . . It hardly seems the time . . . But you must admit he was the very devil!

MRS NÀCCHERI: It doesn't seem right to be talking of devils in a priest's house. He was more like an earthquake. And let me tell you, Mr Roghi, he certainly made Uncle Camillo and little Judith jump out of their skins. It would have been a laugh if it hadn't backfired on me—thanks to their meddling.

DON CAMILLO: If one could only see these things coming!

MRS NÀCCHERI: It hardly helps being wise after the event!

DON CAMILLO: How was I to know the husband would turn up here?

MRS NÀCCHERI: Well, of course you knew! You asked him here yourself!

DON CAMILLO: I did not! That is simply not true! I wrote to him at Merate in my capacity as priest, as soon as I had heard her confession.

ROGHI: After the lady shot herself?

DON CAMILLO: Exactly. She wanted to make her confession. She wanted to die at peace with the world. She wanted her husband's forgiveness for the wrong she had done him. So I wrote to him. Well, of course the Professor could have sent his answer by letter. But oh, no, he chose to come and do his forgiving in person.

ROGHI: And when he got here he found the other chap had beaten him to it?

DON CAMILLO: Oh, the other chap got here first . . . arrived at dawn. From Perugia. Only hours after she had shot herself. At first, what with all the upset, we hadn't even noticed him.

JUDITH: As for her, we didn't even know who she was ...

DON CAMILLO: And there was this fellow, beside the bed, sobbing his heart out. He couldn't stop! I've never seen anything like it!

ROGHI: Must have been her lover.

MRS NÀCCHERI: Lover? Some lover! One of dozens. The latest one.

ROGHI: Are you saying that this lady ... do you mean she was a bad lot?

MRS NÀCCHERI: Oh, shocking! As bad as they come!

JUDITH: Keep your voice down for pity's sake!

MRS NÀCCHERI: Oh, beg pardon I'm sure! Good heavens girl, what does it matter?

DON CAMILLO: Yes, but think of the Professor!

MRS NÀCCHERI: ... who of course will be paying the bill. Not that he can possibly compensate us for the nuisance of it all. Nearly two months of it now.

DON CAMILLO: What a way to talk! (*To* ROGHI, *in tones of simulated concern*.) The lady had abandoned the married nest some thirteen years earlier you understand, and ... (*He breaks off, and with half-closed eyes, rounds off his statement with a gesture indicating priestly compassion*.)

MRS NÀCCHERI (*pulling a pious face and parodying her brother-in-law's gesture*): and ... and ... (*Suddenly investing her tone with a cutting edge*.) Dear Mr Roghi, imagine the effort it has cost us trying to live up to all this kindness and tolerance! I just hope the good Lord is taking note up there, because down here, I can tell you, everybody is laughing at us.

DON CAMILLO: That's not true.

MRS NÀCCHERI (*very emphatic still*): My point is there are dozens of villages in the Valdichiana. The place is a spa! It is crawling with small hotels. But she has to go and choose this one, doesn't she! She has to fetch up on our doorstep! And it's *his* fault (*meaning Don Camillo*)! Well, his and hers (*meaning Judith*)!

JUDITH: Everything is always my fault . . .

MRS NÀCCHERI: Well, whatever your uncle says or does you treat him as if he were God! And then when trouble comes I am the one who suffers. Mind you, there's nobody here capable of taking an adult decision. It's like dealing with a bunch of children! (*She hums a nursery rhyme.*)

DON CAMILLO: I was here the night she arrived. She came by cab. Dodo's in fact. All by herself, very down in the mouth, with one small suitcase. I was on my way home from school . . .

MRS NÀCCHERI: I was not here, myself!

JUDITH: Honestly, mamma, we made it perfectly clear the place wasn't open for visitors.

MRS NÀCCHERI: Well then, you shouldn't have let her in!

DON CAMILLO: It was dark! A woman on her own . . . She was very insistent that it was only for one night . . .

JUDITH (*gesturing in the air with her hands*): And, that night . . .

MRS NÀCCHERI: There was a bang in the middle of the night, Mr Roghi, which practically flung me out of bed.

ROGHI: But was she actually aiming for her stomach?

DON CAMILLO: What! She was aiming for the heart . . .

MRS NÀCCHERI: That's his theory!

DON CAMILLO: Oh, yes! Being a woman, not used to guns you see, she pulls the trigger . . . the barrel slips . . . gets her in the stomach.

JUDITH: We rushed to her room, and there she was poor woman, on the bed . . .

MRS NÀCCHERI: Some poor woman!

ROGHI: By now she was, surely!

DON CAMILLO: White as a sheet, of course, but smiling, apologizing. Kept saying it was nothing . . . Judith went straight off for the doctor.

ROGHI: Doctor Balla?

DON CAMILLO: . . . and you know what *he's* like.

ROGHI: Don't I, though! He's the one who has given up on my daughter, poor little mite!

DON CAMILLO: Same thing here. He said there was nothing he could do. Yet when the Professor got here, he said if only she had been operated on straight away there wouldn't have been any kind of risk. Whereas, when *he* operated four days later, when the husband did it I mean, infection had set in. She was actually dying. Past cure, beyond hope.

JUDITH: And that lunatic wouldn't have it . . . tried to stop him operating.

ROGHI: Who? The lover? The lover didn't want the husband to operate?

DON CAMILLO: He raised hell! He wanted to carry her away in his arms, this dying woman. He didn't want anyone to touch her!

ROGHI: He *what*?

DON CAMILLO: He kept saying that if the husband saved her, *he* would lose her.

JUDITH: He would rather have her die!

ROGHI: But what about the husband? Didn't he find it quite intolerable having the other fellow there in his wife's bedroom?

DON CAMILLO: Oh, he blamed me for that!

MRS NÀCCHERI: And quite right, too!

DON CAMILLO: Ironic, when I had been the one who had tried to get rid of the chap—tried to get him out before the husband arrived. But there was simply no shifting him. Just refused to budge. Even after Dr Gelli got here, and I mean, this was the woman's own husband! (JUDITH *goes out onto the balcony again to look for the returning cabs.*)

MRS NÀCCHERI: He put up a good fight! Quite a performance!

ROGHI: Well!

DON CAMILLO: He made the point, you see, that a death-bed is no place for displays of jealousy, and that anyway her husband could hardly object to his presence when he hadn't seen his wife for thirteen years, especially after what had happened. In the end he had to be forcibly removed by the police.

JUDITH (*from the far balcony*): They are here! They are here! The cabs are back! (MRS NÀCCHERI *waddles over to look.*)

DON CAMILLO: At last!

JUDITH (*crying out in horror*): Oh, my God! But it's him. *He's* back again!

ROGHI: Who do you mean?

DON CAMILLO: The lunatic lover? He's come back?

MRS NÀCCHERI: It's him all right! He's back! Here we go again!

DON CAMILLO: What the dickens can he want here now?

JUDITH (*drawing back in terror*): He is running up the hill! He has jumped over the garden wall!

ROGHI: He's got a damned cheek!

DON CAMILLO: And once again, Dr Gelli's not here! Wait till he gets back and finds him here!

MRS NÀCCHERI: He is looking very jaunty. He's waving his arms about! (*She demonstrates.*) He's going like this!

DON CAMILLO: Now, back me up, Roghi, old chap! He must not be allowed in here with Mrs Gelli. Come on, we had better all go through there! (*He points to the entrance hall and hustles them all out of the room.*) We'll shut this door! We'll shut this door! (*He closes the glass door and goes off with* ROGHI, MRS NÀCCHERI *and* JUDITH.)

Almost at once the door on the right opens and FULVIA GELLI *appears, looking bewildered, frightened and very pale as if snatched this very moment from the jaws of death. There is a sombre look in her eyes and her face is set, as if petrified, in a grim and black despair. Having come here empty-handed and expecting to die, she has risen from her sick-bed with nothing to wear but her travelling clothes. These strike a jarring note, out of keeping with the desperation conveyed by her face. Even more incongruous is the magnificent and unruly mass of hair, dyed a brilliant, brazen shade of tawny-red, which frames the desperate face like tongues of fire. She has not had the strength to fasten her bodice properly, with the result that her breast is half-uncovered. The effect is*

*coldly provocative, coldly because she quite evidently feels a
deep-seated loathing and scorn for her own beautiful body.
She regards it as something no longer belonging to her,
something she is not even very familiar with, for she has never
shared, except with occasional intense disgust, the pleasure
that others have derived from it. She takes a few steps into
the room towards the closed glass door. Beyond it can be
heard the agitated voices of the two women and of* DON
CAMILLO *and* ROGHI *in their effort to stop* MARCO
MAURI *from coming in. He, however, suddenly breaks free
of all of them with a violent wrench, flings open the door, and
hurls himself at* FULVIA, *whom he calls* FLORA, *and
embraces her, clasping her frantically to him. He is about
forty, dark and thin, with bright, darting, rather mad-looking
eyes which contain a kind of suppressed hilarity even when he
is at his most agitated and violent. Above his rounded,
gleaming brow his hair, parted in the middle, curls as closely
as a negro's, but is already touched with grey. He has very
bushy eyebrows. His words and gestures are delivered with
such passionate excitement that the effect is theatrical. This
is because, while he is perfectly warm and sincere, he will
suddenly seem to be looking at his own performance and will
then burst out in angry gestures of remorse, or will counteract
his vehemence by suddenly lowering his voice and adopting a
confidential tone, often disconcerting his listeners by his
sudden, totally unexpected, change of manner.*

FULVIA's *response, at first, is to push him away, as if
finding his embrace loathsome; but then, shocked and overwhelmed by his frenzy, and dazed and still weak from her own
recent sufferings, she faints and collapses in his arms as if
dead.*

MAURI (*extricating himself and throwing open the door*):
    Go away all of you! Go away! (*Rushing back to* FULVIA
    and embracing her as above.) Flora! My Flora! Flora!
    Flora! I'm free! I'm free! I have got my freedom and I
    have come back to you! I am free of my family, my
    situation, everything! (*Then seeing the abandonment with*

which she lies supine in his arms.) My Flora!

At this cry, DON CAMILLO, ROGHI, MRS NÀCCHERI *and* JUDITH, *who have followed him into the room and, stunned by his violence have hung back flabbergasted, gaping at the frantic embrace, now come rushing forward shouting at him and threatening him all at once.*

ROGHI: Good God! Can't he see she can't even stand!

DON CAMILLO: What the devil's got into him?

JUDITH: She has fainted! She has fainted!

MAURI: Fainted? No, no! . . . Flora!

DON CAMILLO (*hectoring*): Let go of her! Come on, now! Leave her to us, now, will you! And just go! Right away from here!

MAURI (*without listening, still holding* FULVIA): My Flora . . . Flora . . . Flora . . .

DON CAMILLO (*to the women*): Get her away from him, can't you? (JUDITH *and* MRS NÀCCHERI *try to comply.*)

JUDITH: Let me have her . . . her, let me have her . . .

MAURI (*vehemently threatening*): No one's to touch her!

DON CAMILLO: She's not your property!

MAURI: She is! She belongs to me!

DON CAMILLO: That, I am afraid, is not the case! Her husband is here.

MAURI: All right, then, where is he? Let him try and take her if he can. He'll have to use force.

ROGHI (*seeing* FULVIA *inert in* MAURI's *embrace and looking ready to fall at any minute*): Well at least put her down on the sofa for goodness' sake! (*Points to sofa.*)

JUDITH (*hastening to help* ROGHI *support* FULVIA): Come on, over here! Over here! It's all right, I've got you!

MAURI (*carrying* FULVIA *over to the sofa*): It's nothing! I assure you, it's nothing! Look! She's coming round!

JUDITH: I'll get the smelling-salts. (*She hurries off, left.*)

MRS NÀCCHERI (*to* DON CAMILLO): Come on now, do something! You're supposed to be master here!

ROGHI: It *is* your house!

MAURI (*rising to face them as one possessed and loudly enunciating his words*): This place, gentlemen, is a hotel!

DON CAMILLO (*taking the offensive*): I beg your pardon? Where . . . when . . . whoever said it was a hotel? Is this written somewhere?

MAURI: It's over the door, downstairs. It says 'Pensione Zonchi'!

DON CAMILLO: Ah, yes! But that's in the summer. It's out of season, now. Do you understand? This is simply my house and I decide who comes into it.

MAURI (*shouting*): Don't you shriek at me!

DON CAMILLO (*almost at a loss for words*): Do you hear that? So I'm the one who's shrieking!

MAURI: It won't get you anywhere. I'm not leaving.

DON CAMILLO: Oh, yes you are! And I'll tell you why. . .

MRS NÀCCHERI (*interrupting*): *I* will tell you why—because this is not your house!

DON CAMILLO: . . . and you have no business here, not now! Understand?

MAURI's *only reply is to take the smelling-salts from* JUDITH, *who has just returned with them, and offer them to* FULVIA, *lying on the sofa.*

MAURI (*to* JUDITH): Here! Let me!

DON CAMILLO (*to* ROGHI, *indicating* MAURI): You see how determined he is?

MAURI (*bending over the recumbent* FULVIA): Flora, my own, I am here . . . Come on, now . . . You're all right, you're better . . . And I am free, now—I'm free, do you realize? And I am going to take you away with me!

DON CAMILLO (*stepping in, decisively*): Oh no, you are not. That is one thing you can be sure of. You are not taking anybody away!

MAURI: Are you going to stop me?

ROGHI (*stepping forward*): You'd be reckoning with me as well, if need be.

DON CAMILLO: No need, Roghi. Her husband will be here any moment now.

MAURI: He is the one I came to speak to!

DON CAMILLO: He will soon send you on your way!

MAURI: I shall want to see him! The point is, she didn't kill herself because of him, she killed herself because of me. And in my turn, I have left my job for her, and my family! I've left my wife, I've left my children! (*He looks round at all of them, and then turns to* ROGHI.) Be reasonable! How can anyone possibly separate us now!

DON CAMILLO (*catching sight of* FULVIA *who, propped up by* JUDITH, *is regaining consciousness, and looking about her in bewilderment*): She'll be the one to do it! . . . Look . . . now . . . she will send you away herself!

MAURI (*turning quickly to look at her, then hurrying to her side*): You won't do that, will you, Flora? You won't send me away? (FULVIA *lifts a hand to hold him at a distance and then turns to* DON CAMILLO. *She still seems stunned, but the grim look has crept back*.)

DON CAMILLO: You must believe me, Mrs Gelli, he forced his way in here, at a time when he knew the Professor would be out.

FULVIA (*rising and addressing him with the utmost formality*): What is it you want from me, Mr Mauri?

DON CAMILLO: There you are! What did I tell you?

MAURI (*astounded*): Flora! . . . Oh, my God! What's all this 'Mr Mauri'?

FULVIA (*shrugging irritably*): But I scarcely know you!

DON CAMILLO: I happen to know that you have lied to this lady!

MAURI (*very violently*): You shut up, you old fool!

DON CAMILLO: You practised a gross deception on her. She told me.

MAURI (*to* FULVIA): Why do you say you scarcely know me? It's me, Flora, me! I have given you my whole life!

FULVIA (*sickened*): Oh, do stop talking like that!

MAURI (*growing pale*): God! Talking like what? It was you, Flora, you who . . .

FULVIA: My name is not Flora.

MAURI: It's Fulvia. Yes, I know it's Fulvia! And it was you who wanted me to call you Flora.

FULVIA (*crushingly*): Why not tell them more? I am sure these people would love to hear all the details!

MAURI (*mortified*): No! I . . . God, do you despise me that much?

FULVIA (*sitting down again, wrapped in her own thoughts and muttering to herself in a dark abstracted way*): I don't despise anybody.

MAURI (*persisting*): Is it because I misled you?

FULVIA: No, no . . . (*Exasperated*) No!

MAURI (*turning again to* DON CAMILLO): Is that what you have against me? That I deceived her? But didn't I admit it, here, out loud, in front of everybody? I shouted it, I yelled it for everybody to hear, that I had this extra burden on my conscience. I even yelled it in your husband's face. Didn't I? Didn't I? When I told him he was a fraud? A fake and a fraud! Claiming that he had come here to 'forgive you'. *He* forgive *you*! He should have begged you for forgiveness, begged you on bended knee, as I am doing now! (*He falls before her on his knees.*) Look! Look at me! Here! I am on my knees! (*Then, very loud and clear.*) Because we are all guilty of deceiving this woman!

FULVIA (*gets up quietly from where she is sitting and speaks in a quiet, cold, desperately tired voice*): God in heaven! I find these histrionics completely nauseating.

MAURI (*as if seeing himself now with her eyes; still on his knees, unable to get up*): Nauseating . . . yes, I suppose so. You are right. I can see it . . . I can see *me*. (*He covers his face with his hands and speaks through tears.*) But it isn't me. What you see, Flora, is my passion. It's my passion making all this noise, not me. I nauseate myself if I stop to listen; but I can't help myself! I mean to keep quiet, and I find myself shouting! (*He gets up at last, with a determined air, as if he had suddenly regained command of himself.*) I came here to try and show you that I never lied to you really. What I told you was the truth: it was the truth for me. Because there never was anybody else in my life, not really, not for me. There was only ever you, and that was just for a few days—how many was it? Twenty . . . not more than twenty. Twenty days out of a lifetime.

FULVIA: All right. Twenty days, then. And they are over . . . Over. Finished.

MAURI: No! How can you say that? You can't say that now! Now that all the dishonesty's behind us!

FULVIA: Dishonesty? What dishonesty are you talking about?

MAURI: Mine, of course. I lied to you! But that's all in the past, that's behind us! I have my freedom . . . I am free, now.

FULVIA (*she stares at him darkly for a while, as if distracted by some idea forming slowly in her mind, before focussing her full attention on him*): Free in what way?

MAURI: To do as I like! I have left everything! My job . . . I have resigned from my job. I have left my wife. She actually showed me the door, told me to go. She's delighted.

MRS NÀCCHERI: There, now!

MAURI (*hurrying to explain*): She has never loved me! She has never known what to do with me. She lives her own life. She has her own money—and property, farms and things. Some fiendish impulse must have got into her that day, to make her go to Perugia, seek out Flora and tell her . . . (*He turns to* FULVIA, *who has sat down again, but seems far away once more and lost in her own thoughts.*) . . . What did she tell you? What *did* she tell you? . . . I still don't know. (FULVIA *does not reply, so he turns to the others.*) Perhaps, do you see? . . . she may have thought she was doing us a favour, patching up our family life, by getting out and coming here. (*He approaches* FULVIA *joyfully and starts to say something else but appears to have some difficulty in saying it; finally he summons up enough courage to blurt it out quite baldly. The effect is both painful and ridiculous.*) There's going to

be no more pretence between us any more! And imagine
. . . yes, of course I can tell you . . . my wife . . . she actually gave me . . . handed me in person . . . a sum of
money to go away.

FULVIA (*looking up and speaking promptly to forestall any
exclamations of amazement from the others*): And so?
What next?

MAURI (*stunned by the unexpected question*): What next?
What do you mean!

FULVIA: What will you do next?

MAURI: What shall I do next? . . . Oh! . . . What shall I
do next? But if I've got you, that's everything! I shall do
all sorts of things! I could . . . I mean . . . I can give
concerts . . . not in the big cities, of course.

FULVIA (*in an odd, cold voice, as she gets up*): Perhaps
you will be good enough to repeat all this to my husband
when he returns.

MAURI (*overjoyed, while the others are thunderstruck*):
You want me to tell him? Really? Tell him all this?

FULVIA (*interrupting him and addressing* DON CAMIL-
LO, *her tone icy*): He should be here by now.

DON CAMILLO: Yes . . . I wonder . . . it's getting on . . .

MAURI: Oh, what a joy to tell him this! You can't
imagine what a joy! Now that you are . . . Oh, my love, I
am so happy!

FULVIA (*annoyed*): Please . . . I beg you . . .

MAURI: But in the beginning, Flora, you have to admit,
I wasn't the one who took our affair seriously. It was you
who took it to heart, doing what you did, if I may say
so! . . . Oh, yes . . . And all because of that dreadful old
cow!

ROGHI (*unable to stop himself laughing*): That's a bit
strong!

MRS NÀCCHERI (*raucously cackling, and speaking at the
same time as* ROGHI). Ah! ha! ha! Who's the old cow?
Does he mean his wife?

DON CAMILLO (*at the same time as the other two*): I told
you he was mad!

MAURI (*with perfect seriousness*): An old cow is exactly what she is. She's a peasant, quite uncouth, and nine years older than I am. (*Then, referring to* FULVIA.) *She* has seen her! I married her because she had a piano.

MRS NÀCCHERI (*laughing helplessly, as above*): Ah! ha! ha! (*The laughter catches on, and spreads to* ROGHI *and* JUDITH.)

MAURI (*nettled*): Excuse my saying so, madam, but this really isn't a laughing matter.

ROGHI (*still laughing*): Sorry, lad, but it has got its funny side!

MAURI: You laugh because you have no idea what it means to find yourself stranded, at the age of twenty-five, still full of dreams for the future, in a rotten little one-horse village even worse than this one here if I may say so . . . and to just sit and rot too, for years, not four or five, but ten interminable years, as the local magistrate!

ROGHI (*to* DON CAMILLO): There you are you see! He *is* a judge!

DON CAMILLO (*with total conviction*): He's mad!

MAURI (*seriously, at once*): I resigned. It was a life such as you cannot possibly imagine! A life that none of you people rotting away in here can have any notion of! Not even you, Flora, honestly, and you have known life at its most horrible. But horror, God knows, is at least horror! This was a life made up of nothing . . . Nothing! . . . Gloom . . . Silence. The silence of time which refuses to pass . . . There wasn't even any drinking water. The water came from a cistern; it was gritty and foul-tasting. Though that wouldn't have mattered! It's the silence! . . . That silence! Do you know, from inside that house you could hear the pulley squeaking on the cistern in the square below whenever a breath of wind rocked the rope. While inside the house . . . well, imagine a sticky dusty table-top strewn with legal papers and a fly buzzing about on top of it, and that fly me only life to be seen for miles around, so you sit and watch it for hour after hour after hour. So then, imagine how it felt one day to hear a piano; suddenly, in that silence, a piano! The only one in the village. It was rain in the desert! I made straight for it! And yes, yes I did, I married that woman so much older than I was, and she seemed very beautiful and very intelligent, all because she had a piano . . . Because music . . . music, you see, was what I studied. I never studied law. I am a musician! And yet, from the moment I married her, she called me Judge. And so do the children. All four of them, all illiterate . . . brought up by her in the sticks . . . and they all call me Judge. Not Daddy, not Papa—and actually not Judge, more like Jerdge, like their mother. Is the Jerdge in? No, Jerdge bain't in, 'e's down the Court! (*They all burst out laughing except* FULVIA.)

ROGHI (*laughing*): I can't help laughing!

MAURI: Of course you laugh. Of course you do. I hope to see the funny side myself, now. Now that I'm out of it at last, thank God! And on amicable terms. She even kissed me good-bye. Personally, I felt like strangling her.

DON CAMILLO (*who has seen* SILVIO GELLI *in the distance approaching through the garden gate, and who now appears on the scene, evidently disconcerted by all the laughter*): Professor Gelli, here you are at last! Thank heaven for that!

SILVIO GELLI *is aged about fifty. He is tall, bony, powerfully built, and wears gold-rimmed spectacles. He is cleanshaven. The top of his head is almost bald, but long, pale, colourless locks hang untidily down over his forehead and at his temples. He smooths them back from time to time, and quite often his hands then stay clasped over his head, in a meditative gesture of his own. He wears the bewildered frown of someone undergoing a severe crisis of conscience. This he tries to conceal. Consequently, he quite often stands about looking stupid and inert, with a cold vacuous smile fixed on his lips: in such moments he involuntarily betrays an old streak of cruel mockery born of dark ambiguous passions,*

*long controlled, but which still smoulder inside him. If inter-
rupted in one of these bouts of vacuous abstraction, the
chinks in his moral armour, he glowers: his inane smile gives
way to a taut grimace of pain, as if pain to be authentic must
be physically expressed. When his features recover from this
contortion, they recompose themselves into a sober, weary
semblance of an uninterrupted lifelong rectitude, the expression of a man untouched by such storms of passion as those
which have all too recently beset him.*

When he enters FULVIA *rises to her feet with a graceful
feline movement. She is in exactly the frame of mind which
thirteen years earlier was the cause of her downfall. This
moment for her will be the supreme test. Her whole bearing
evinces her determination to face it boldly, a determination
which has been obscurely forming in her mind throughout the
preceding scene. She means to match her conscience nakedly
with his as in a test of strength, whatever it may cost her in
dignity. Her singleness of mind is brutal; she is ready even to
exploit the presence of her mad lover to gain her ends.*

SILVIO (*noting all at once the general mood of hilarity, the
    elatedness of* MAURI, *and his wife's unmistakeable air of
    challenge, to* MAURI): You're here again, are you?
MAURI (*cutting in*): Sir! Yes! I came to . . .
FULVIA (*magisterial, immediately interrupting him*): I'll
    speak if I may. (*To her husband.*) Yes, he is here. Ask all
    these people to leave us alone.
DON CAMILLO: Of course, Mrs Gelli, at once. First I
    must just explain to the Professor . . .
FULVIA (*hastening to cut him off*): . . . that this gentleman
    broke in here uninvited. That is so!
MAURI (*to* DON CAMILLO, *with a nod in* FULVIA's
    direction): But we have reached an agreement!
MRS NÀCCHERI (*to* DON CAMILLO): That's not true
    for a start!
SILVIO (*to* FULVIA): Did you ask him here?
FULVIA: I did not. That is one of the things we must talk
    about.

SILVIO: This agreement you mention . . .

FULVIA: There's no agreement. It isn't true!

MAURI: It was my own idea to come.

FULVIA: Wait until you are spoken to!

DON CAMILLO: Come on! We'll go! We'll leave you to it. (*He shepherds* ROGHI, JUDITH *and* MRS NÀCCHERI *out of the room.*)

MRS NÀCCHERI (*turning as she leaves*): Yes, yes, of course . . . but first I think we should explain our position to these good people. We . . .

DON CAMILLO (*apprehensively*): No, wait, Marianna! What are you saying?

MRS NÀCCHERI: I am saying that it's already the end of April for goodness' sake, and that in May as you perfectly well know the summer visitors start coming to take the waters.

SILVIO: For myself, madam, I plan to leave as soon as possible.

MRS NÀCCHERI: I dare say you prescribe Valdichiana water for your own patients, Doctor. The point is we start getting the hotel ready about now!

DON CAMILLO: But I shouldn't like the Professor to think . . .

SILVIO: I have my own urgent reasons for getting out of here as soon as possible, as I think you know.

ROGHI: If you're not actually planning to leave today, Professor Gelli, I'd appreciate it if . . .

SILVIO (*with a look towards his wife*): Now if you don't mind . . .

ROGHI: Of course, of course! My dear Professor, you must see to your affairs. I'll wait . . . I'll wait . . . I'll come back . . .

DON CAMILLO: Let us remove ourselves, shall we? Come along! (*He pushes* ROGHI, MRS NÀCCHERI *and* JUDITH *out through the door. He is the last to leave. He bows and closes the glass door behind him.*)

FULVIA (*quickly and nervously*): Look, Silvio. This gentleman here, whom I hardly know . . .

MAURI (*cut to the quick*): Don't say that, Flora!

FULVIA: Let me do the talking please!

MAURI: But you can't say things like that!

FULVIA: How long I've known you, dear, doesn't make much difference to people in my profession! (*Turning to her husband.*) Did you hear him call me Flora? He calls me Flora!

MAURI (*reproachfully*): Fulvia!

FULVIA (*quickly*): No, no, it's Flora. Flora. I am Flora. (*To her husband.*) People call me by my first name straight away. I am on intimate terms with all.

SILVIO: What I wish to know is how, and why—after all that has happened—this gentleman is here again at all.

FULVIA: Yes, well, this gentleman, Silvio, is firmly convinced that I wanted to kill myself because of him. Which is not true.

MAURI: Not true?

FULVIA: Not true. I did it for my own reasons. Tell him how you met me, and where. That should make it clear.

SILVIO: But I have no wish to know.

FULVIA: I had been arrested.

MAURI (*immediately protesting*): Nonsense! You hadn't been arrested!

FULVIA: I had been summonsed to appear in court. I had been involved in a very sordid case.

MAURI: Don't believe a word of it! She was acquitted!

SILVIO: I tell you I don't want to know anything about it!

MAURI (*carrying straight on*): She was only a witness for heaven's sake! I should know! It was in Perugia, just a month after I had been transferred there. I was there, in the Coroner's court. A colleague of mine was examining the case . . . the murder of a man called Gamba.

FULVIA: I was living with Gamba in Perugia.

MAURI: He was a painter . . .

FULVIA: Painter! He was a wretched little mosaic-worker from Murano.

MAURI: He had come to Perugia to restore some mosaics . . .

FULVIA: He was a bastard. He was always drunk.

MAURI: He hit her, you know! He used to hit her!

FULVIA: He was found dead one night. Lying in the street with his head bashed in. (SILVIO GELLI *smooths back his hair with both hands. He stands clasping his head.*)

MAURI (*quick to note* GELLI's *disquiet*): Horrible, isn't it? To think she had sunk to that? So now perhaps you'll be good enough . . . to release her!

FULVIA: Oh! Spare us the theatricals!

MAURI (*carrying straight on, but more quietly, to* SILVIO): Her case shows that the real problem, the real test, is whether one can ever possibly shed the social stigma. You just try it. Take off that silly smile and try it.

SILVIO: I am not smiling.

MAURI: Oh, you were smiling. And I suggest you try it. Try stealing a five pound note one day and make sure you're caught. You'll soon know what I'm talking about. But of course you don't steal . . . Fine! And do you suppose this poor girl would ever have done what she did if it hadn't been for you, her husband . . .

FULVIA (*fiercely interrupting*): That's enough! I forbid you to go on!

SILVIO (*calmly and quietly*): Now I simply came here . . .

MAURI: To forgive her! yes, we know.

SILVIO (*serious, firm and unhesitating*): No. To acknowledge all the wrong that I have done to this lady in the past. It didn't occur to me that anybody else would be presuming to stand in judgement.

MAURI (*challengingly*): And are you going to make it up to her?

FULVIA: Hold on! You don't know what you are talking about!

MAURI: No, Flora! I ask if he is willing to make reparation! And I ask it to his face! I mean, I have done you wrong as well. You have forgiven me, but now I must make reparation! That is what I must do!

FULVIA (*her tone indicating that she wants no discussion*):
Very well. What I was going to say to you, Silvio, was
simply this: Mr Mauri is prepared . . .

MAURI (*with an air of intense defiance*): To make reparation! Indeed I am!

FULVIA (*turning on him in exasperation*): All this talk
about reparation! It's a joke! When I don't even acknowledge that you have done me any wrong! All right! So you
lied to me! Everybody lies to me! It makes no odds to me!
(*To her husband.*) And what about you? Having rescued
me from death, do you feel an obligation towards me?
Because you needn't! I want nothing from you, nothing!

SILVIO (*astounded*): What? I . . .

FULVIA (*returning swiftly to her argument*): And tell me,
did you come here in your capacity as doctor? Were you
expecting to operate?

SILVIO: No.

FULVIA: But you operated just the same, even though
nobody asked you to.

MAURI: I tried to stop him! I did my best!

FULVIA (*taking no notice of* MAURI): And I certainly
never asked you to!

SILVIO (*embarrassed, cornered, not sure where all this is
leading*): No . . . I mean, I did it . . .

FULVIA (*coming quickly to his aid, her eyes curiously
bright*): You really couldn't help yourself, could you?

SILVIO: It was seeing you like that . . .

FULVIA: And so? . . . I was as good as dead. The miracle
astonished you as much as anybody. It has certainly
made me believe in miracles.

SILVIO: What are you driving at with all this?

FULVIA: Nothing. Well, this. It was hardly your doing,
your 'bringing me back to life'. You don't need to have
any fancy notions about being responsible for me because of it. You are under no obligation of any kind. I
find the idea quite unacceptable. Neither you, nor anybody, owes me a thing!

SILVIO: And what do you intend to do?

MAURI: She's coming away with me!

FULVIA: My God! What a situation to be in! Forced to choose between a totally unfounded sense of duty, and an equally imaginary remorse.

SILVIO: You are just the same!

FULVIA: Ah, well, I'm pleased to hear that! I am glad to think that my dyed hair and this face I've got now don't stop you from recognizing the girl I once was.

SILVIO: Looking at you now, at this very moment, I see the old you. I haven't seen you look like this in all the time I have been here!

MAURI: It is because I am here!

FULVIA (quickly, to MAURI): Your presence means nothing. I thought I told you not to speak! (She turns back to her husband.) So you think I look like I did in the old days? Is that why you have seemed so . . . I don't know . . . unsettled?

SILVIO: Unsettled?

FULVIA: Yes, you look anxious, puzzled . . . regretful perhaps. Something like that!

SILVIO: What should I regret?

FULVIA: Perhaps you are wishing that you hadn't taken it upon yourself to do rather more than you meant to.

SILVIO: Oh, no! I don't regret that!

FULVIA: And you seriously think that you are a changed character?

SILVIO: The fact that I am here at all should tell you that.

FULVIA: But things haven't turned out quite as you expected?

SILVIO: I should say not! Most certainly not! I would never have come!

FULVIA (contemptuously): Well then, perhaps you should go!

SILVIO (with great restraint): I think it is really too bad of you to subject me to all this is front of him . . . (meaning MAURI.)

MAURI: But I know all about you anyway! I know everything!

SILVIO: What do you know? You know what she has told you! You know that I wronged her. You know nothing about what I suffered as a result.

FULVIA: Suffer a lot, did you?

SILVIO: I suffered wretchedly. That is why I am here. But you are not going to make me say all this in front of a stranger.

FULVIA: Oh no, you don't get out of it that way! It's for your edification, dear, that I want him here, not for mine!

MAURI: Anyway I am not a stranger to *her*!

SILVIO (*answering* FULVIA): He's here for my edification. How's that?

FULVIA: Oh dear, it hardly seems right saying this about an important professor; it's really quite embarrassing. But if I am here now, with this man, or with any man come to that—you must know that it is because of you, because of you, and how you treated me all those years ago! What do you expect. All I can remember about that time when I was eighteen, is how you victimized me, played with me like a cat with a mouse. It amused you to see how far you could push me. Well, now you can see exactly how far you pushed me . . . And you say you have suffered. I'd be interested to know just how much you have suffered.

SILVIO: I told you how much.

FULVIA: No, you didn't. What you said was that you couldn't suffer.

SILVIO: I told you I felt numb, cut off from my suffering; and from yours. That is what I said.

FULVIA: Ah! Emotionally emptied, I suppose.

SILVIO: You don't understand. You can't. There are some things one can't explain.

FULVIA: Were you alone? Did you have nobody? (*She is thinking of their daughter and her expression is indescribably desolate.*)

SILVIO: I felt inept.

FULVIA: Unworthy perhaps?

SILVIO: Unworthy certainly. Because I realized that it was my fault that you had gone away. That's why I could never manage to fill the void.

FULVIA (*scathingly*): And yet you say you have suffered on my account.

SILVIO: Not perhaps in the way you think. Not that, even now. I have suffered because of life, because of the way things are . . .

MAURI: Oh, I know what you mean! You're so right! Take me, for instance . . .

SILVIO (*paying not the slightest attention to him. To FULVIA*): There's no answer. You can kill yourself like you did, or go mad I suppose, but there's no rational answer.

MAURI (*muttering to himself*): Life is brutal! Don't I know it!

SILVIO (*continuing to ignore MAURI*): I come rushing down here, saying to myself, 'She's dying; she wants peace; she wants to have done with it all; hurry! hurry!' And now I am here the reality is so different from what I had imagined that my feelings are thrown into confusion.

FULVIA: What do you want to do now?

SILVIO: You took the offensive the moment I arrived, pushing this gentleman at me. You don't want duty, you don't want reparation . . . I don't know. You seem to have your mind made up. But God knows what you're after.

FULVIA (*with a complete change of tone as if struck by a sudden revelation*): You have no idea how devious you still look sometimes, when you look through those half-closed lids.

SILVIO (*astonished*): Do I?

FULVIA: Yes, yes, you do.

SILVIO: Devious?

FULVIA: Devious. Deviousness personified. Just now was a perfect example. You turned and looked at me like this. (*She imitates the look.*)

SILVIO: Impatience, probably, or tiredness.

FULVIA: Deviousness. There's no mistaking it. I recognized it of old. You still have to do it, even now, don't you? Put on an act for me? Of one sort or another? All you men do it! You forget that women have seen you in certain little moments when you are rather more natural, if you know what I mean. That's why women find men funny. You're always putting on an act of some sort. When it's not funny, it's pathetic, or disgusting . . . Not that it matters now.

SILVIO: This business of freeing me from any sense of obligation, is that a test, to find out whether I really have changed?

FULVIA: Lord, no! But my goodness . . . how's that for deviousness?

SILVIO: I'm serious, Fulvia. It's just that on that particular score I'd find it very hard to give you proof.

FULVIA: I'm not asking you to! Haven't you grasped the fact that I don't want you to feel tied in any way? I am now . . . what I am . . . I'm not going to cash in on your having come here to tie you down, just because you have given me back my life. What my life is going to be now, what I am now, what happens to me now . . . these things don't interest me in the least. You'd be a fool if you gave them a second thought. You came running because you were sure I was going to die. Well, too bad, I didn't make it!

MAURI (*with intense feeling*): But I'm here, Flora!

FULVIA (*with crushing flippancy, pointing him out to her husband*): Oh my dear, yes of course, I meant to tell you. He's here.

MAURI (*as above*): I am . . . and I am all yours.

FULVIA (*feigning terror*): For Christ's sake don't start talking about love! (*To her husband.*) You see? Ready and willing to carry me off!

MAURI: Stay with me forever!

FULVIA: That's nice, dear! The voice of love's young dream.

MAURI (*with passion*): No! . . . Nobody means it as I do!

FULVIA (*explaining to her husband, as above*): He has left his wife and children for me . . . And your job, too, isn't that right?

MAURI: Everything!

FULVIA: It's a good life he's offering! He's going to give concerts in the country! It's a pity my voice has gone . . . The result of my wicked ways, no doubt! We could have done a double act with me singing and him at the piano! (*She laughs stridently.*)

MAURI (*deeply hurt*): So I'm just a joke?

FULVIA (*quickly*): Oh, no, no. I really do believe in your piano-playing.

SILVIO (*irritated*): But none of this is serious!

FULVIA: Are you finding it upsetting? I'm not, not in the least. Just stop worrying about me, the pair of you! How many times do I have to say it! Don't make such heavy weather of it! For years now, Silvio, I have lived one day at a time. I am perfectly used to doing without necessities, and to not knowing what the next day holds in store. It doesn't worry me. Fate can indulge in whatever whims it likes where I'm concerned. I have become Fate's thing . . . (*She goes up to her husband and gives him an extraordinary, lurid wink, playing up to her reputation as a 'fallen woman'.*) You used to have a few little whims of your own, once. Know what I mean?

SILVIO (*blanching*): What? Did I?

FULVIA (*between laughter and tears, perilously near hysteria, which increasingly threatens to erupt as she tries to fight it down with her self-tormenting, self-degrading line of talk*): Oh, yes! Don't you remember the little whims you went in for when I was . . . practically a child! . . . Things you taught me, things that to me were unspeakably revolting!

SILVIO (*trying to bring her to her senses*): Fulvia!

FULVIA: Oh! Such things are part of my life now.

SILVIO: Fulvia! Fulvia!

FULVIA: I am famous for them.

SILVIO: You just enjoy tearing yourself to pieces.

FULVIA: If so, it's with your hands! I taught those tricks to *him*, you know? That is why he is so desperate to have me back! (*At the height of her agitation, she breaks off to cry out.*) Horrible! Horrible! Horrible! (*She gives a great neighing shudder of disgust, clasping her hands round her head in a gesture of total withdrawal, her face hidden in her arms. She cries out again.*) God, it was revolting! (SILVIO *and* MAURI *rush to her side, concerned and shocked. While her agitation subsides in a fit of shivering, they address her in tones of extreme consternation.*)

SILVIO: You can't go on like this!

MAURI (*abjectly pleading*): How could you, Flora! I have always thought of you as somehow holy! As a kind of saint!

FULVIA (*suddenly, rising to her feet, still shaken, but once again resolute. She lays both hands on* MAURI's *shoulders*): *Yes*, it's true, yes, you have, yes! (*Quickly thinking better of this, she adds briskly.*) Yes, that's quite true, but now please, keep out of this, will you?

MAURI (*happily, trying to seize her hand to kiss it*): Oh, Flora! Thank you!

FULVIA (*snatching her hand away in a fit of repugnance*): No . . . no . . . no . . .

MAURI: For me it's enough. If you return my love with pain, just pain and nothing more, for me even your pain is sweet, so sweet that it will be enough.

FULVIA (*quickly*): Yes. All right. (*She turns to her husband.*) Look, I have decided . . . I am going with him . . . You can leave now, Silvio, with a clear conscience. You have done your good deed.

SILVIO (*his eyes full of the atrocious pain he is suffering, as, struggling to contain his emotion, he solemnly begs her*): Fulvia, please, I beg you, I cannot take any more of this situation.

FULVIA: Well, I am being quite straight. Your coming here was a good deed. As for the other thing you did, more or less in spite of yourself, I am quite sure that *that* wasn't part of your original intention. You did me a bad

turn there. But in all conscience I can't and shan't hold
you responsible for it. So you can go home with your
mind at rest . . . Or, at most, I suppose if you like . . .
seeing that I have nothing of my own, and that coming
from the gutter I am not above asking . . . you could give
me some money. (*Then, indicating* MAURI.) Like *his*
wife. She paid him off! (*She bursts out laughing.*)

MAURI (*vehemently*): No! No money! No, Flora! I'm not
taking any money from him!

FULVIA: You are stupid. Don't you see? It's not for us!
It's for his own sake! The more he gives us the better he
will feel. It is quite clear (*then, emphasising her words
meaningfully*) that in spite of all my efforts, he still feels
a lingering remorse. I'm proposing that he settles the
account in hard cash.

SILVIO (*unable to contain himself any longer, and speaking
with great resolve*): That's enough now, Fulvia! There's
something I must speak to you about.

FULVIA (*with scarcely contained fury and a dangerous glint
in her eye*): Oh, no, you don't. Don't you dare! I can tell
from your eyes what you want to talk about.

MAURI (*sneering to himself*): The daughter! He wants to
talk about the daughter!

SILVIO: I do have to talk to you about her!

FULVIA: It will be the worse for you if you do! Don't you
understand that for the last hour I have been besmirching
myself with as much dirt as possible just to stop you
mentioning her?

SILVIO: Don't you want me to tell you about her?

FULVIA: No!

SILVIO: You are trying to provoke me!

FULVIA: Earlier on it was you who wouldn't mention her!

SILVIO: I am talking about her now!

FULVIA: Don't you dare! You can't (*she puts an arm round*
MAURI's *shoulders*) now that I have decided to go with him!

SILVIO: Very well. I shall go . . . As long as it's clear that
this way you forfeit the right to bring any kind of
accusation against me.

FULVIA: Accusation? (*Turning to* MAURI.) Have I accused him of anything? (*To* SILVIO.) I have sung your praises, thanked you, told you you may go. But still you stay. What's keeping you? You want to go on talking, dragging up excuses that I certainly haven't asked for!

MAURI: He is using you as a mirror.

SILVIO (*truculently*): What do you mean, mirror?

MAURI (*calmly, almost with a smile*): In any conversation . . . we prop people up in front of us, like a mirror. We don't know we're doing it. We think that someone else is speaking to us. But it is really just us, talking to ourselves . . . I know.

SILVIO: Well, that may be your experience!

MAURI: It's equally true of you.

SILVIO (*to* FULVIA): Why do you persist in belittling my remorse, which I have proved to you is absolutely genuine?

FULVIA: I don't belittle it; I want to relieve you of it.

SILVIO: You think that 'besmirching yourself with dirt' is the right way to go about it?

FULVIA (*in a different voice, desperately sincere; sounding now so deeply dispirited that she can no longer sustain the rôle she has been playing*): My God, I have spent all these days with him . . . I was like my old self . . . even he said so . . . but waiting with my heart in my mouth for him to say something . . . my old heart as it used to be, in the days when I had a home and was a mother . . . and I've been waiting, for days on end, for him to mention my little girl . . . I kept thinking 'Hold on! . . . hold on! He is different now! He's good! . . . he has come all this way . . . he will talk about her now, he's sure to!'

SILVIO (*loudly and resonantly, hoping to quell her agitation*): But I couldn't talk about her!

FULVIA (*quickly, vehemently, changing tone herself*): So why do you choose to do so now?

SILVIO: Because I have to tell you *why* I couldn't.

FULVIA: I no longer want to know. Your reasons are your own affair.

SILVIO: They are not my reasons! I am thinking of what is best for her, for *your* daughter!

FULVIA: And thinking of my daughter meant you couldn't talk to me about her?

SILVIO: I was solely thinking of her good.

FULVIA: I know what it is! She thinks I'm dead! That's it, isn't it? It has been done before! Who told her? Did you tell her I was dead?

SILVIO: I never said so . . .

FULVIA: She thought of it for herself, then, and you let her believe it! Is that it? Very well. All right, I guessed it. What you are saying is, that as far as she is concerned, you can never bring me miraculously back to life.

SILVIO: Well . . . you tell me! What do you think? Do you see that as a possibility? I have done nothing but think about this for a month. It has been on my mind from the moment I thought you might recover. You have been waiting for me to talk about it . . . Well, this is why I haven't. What is to be done? You tell me! Can you just pop up at home again? Just like that?

FULVIA (*horrified*): No . . . no!

SILVIO (*driving home his point*): I mean, where are you supposed to have been all this time? And what was our motive in letting her think you were dead?

FULVIA: No, of course it's impossible.

SILVIO: Well . . . now you see it for yourself.

FULVIA: And there again, do you think I really mind? I was all set to die, after all . . . But I didn't die. And there's more to it than that! You don't yet know, my dear, the full extent of the miracle you have brought about. I can scarcely believe it myself! You could say that I am in a state of grace. Restored by one moment to what I was all those years ago . . . My dear, you may not be able to bring back a mother, live, to your daughter, but you have certainly brought a living child to me!

SILVIO (*stunned and dismayed*): What are you saying? What child? What . . . ?

FULVIA: One child or another . . . inside my body . . . it's the same child to me!

SILVIO: Fulvia, what are you saying?

MAURI: What! Do you mean you . . . ?

FULVIA: Why do you think I am so light-hearted?—Now you know! Don't you see that I don't care about anything any more?

MAURI: You let him take you to bed?

SILVIO (*finally throwing off all indecision and anxiety, his mind irreversibly made up*): Well, if that's the case—there are no two ways about it!

FULVIA: What do you mean?

MAURI (*under his breath*): You betrayed me with *him*!

SILVIO: I had already thought . . . before you told me this . . . that perhaps there was a way, one way only, to set things right!

FULVIA: What way? You have told her I am dead!

SILVIO: No—there is, there is a way! And now, you have no choice, you have to take it, however hard it may be, both for you and for me.

FULVIA: And what is it?

SILVIO: You are coming with me.

MAURI: No, Flora! Don't do it! Don't do it!

SILVIO: She will do it, now.

FULVIA (*to* MAURI, *reassuringly*): Wait! (*To* SILVIO, *as if challenging him.*) *Where* are you taking me?

SILVIO: Where? Home, of course!

FULVIA: But how?

SILVIO (*without hesitating*): As my wife! As my wife!

FULVIA: But she's there and she thinks I'm dead.

SILVIO: There is that. It's a tough one. Insuperable, really. We shall have to get round it in the only way left to us.

FULVIA: I don't understand what you are saying.

SILVIO: You will come as my wife even though officially, and for her, you won't be her mother.

FULVIA: Your wife but not her mother . . . Oh! You mean a 'new' wife?

MAURI (*immediately*): But that's monstrous! Monstrous!

FULVIA: But I'm not a 'new' wife!

SILVIO: No! But that's how it has got to seem! And you will still *be* her mother.

FULVIA: And she will think I'm her stepmother.

MAURI: Don't do it, Flora! Don't do it! It's monstrous!

SILVIO (*to* MAURI): There is no other way. If this solution is monstrous, tell me a better one. Is your offer any better?

MAURI: Far better! A million times better! Oh, Flora, you'd be much better off starving with me! Think of the agony of having your own child regard you as an interloper.

SILVIO: If you can bear it . . .

FULVIA (*immediately, with some hauteur, although she is already apprehensive*): That's not it. I can bear anything! . . . And my daughter *is* my daughter . . . I am not in fact an interloper . . . I am still her mother. (*She rises to her feet, and as if she were only just beginning to understand the implications of* SILVIO's *offer, she asks.*) So you would take me back with you?

MAURI (*horror-stricken*): You're accepting it?

FULVIA (*ignoring* MAURI *and speaking rather to herself than to her husband*): How do we do it? . . . As we are married already, I suppose we don't need to do anything!

SILVIO: The second marriage would be just a front . . . simply for her!

MAURI (*to himself*): The treachery of it! Going back to him! To his bed!

FULVIA (*still half to herself*): She will be sixteen now . . . She certainly won't remember me at all.

SILVIO: She was only just three . . .

FULVIA (*with a quick grimace*): . . . When I died, you mean. (*She recollects herself.*) But what about all the others! They will recognize me!

SILVO: Not where I live now. There's nobody. It's in the country, really. That's not a problem. And we could always move.

MAURI (*with persistence*): And me, Flora? Is it all over for me? Are you really doing this? Is it possible?

FULVIA (*shrugging with irritation*): What do you want now!

MAURI (*in a terrible voice*): What do I want? What am I to do now? If I lose you, what is left?

SILVIO (*approaching him*): You must realize it's too late now for that kind of talk.

MAURI (*as above*): I have smashed up my whole life to be with her!

FULVIA (*coming between them, to her husband*): Wait a minute. Let me have a word with him . . .

MAURI (*embracing her in a frenzy*): I don't want words! You belong to me. I shan't let you go!

SILVIO (*bodily attempting to wrest her from him*): Do you think you can keep her by force?

FULVIA (*struggling to free herself*): Let me go!

MAURI (*still frenzied*): I shan't let you go! I shan't let you go!

FULVIA (*extricating herself and pushing him away from her*): Let me go, I say!

SILVIO: Out! Get out of here! Go on, out!

MAURI (*bursting into desperate sobs*): Have some pity at least!

FULVIA (*trembling with anger*): Why should I have pity? I broke it off with you, remember?

MAURI: But I didn't! I didn't!

FULVIA: For God's sake stop snivelling! It's the last thing I need!

MAURI: My whole life . . . As if I weren't somebody too! You annihilate me . . . You say I am the last thing you need! (*He sits down heavily, as if she really had killed him, still desperately sobbing.*)

SILVIO: Come on now, let's have done.

FULVIA (*addressing SILVIO as she goes over to MAURI*): Have a heart . . . have a heart . . . I must try to do this kindly.

CURTAIN

ACT II

A room in SILVIO GELLI's *house, near a village on Lake Como. The room is large and bright and seems filled with the blue of the sky and the green of the surrounding countryside.*

It is furnished in delicate, distinguished colours. The furniture is not new, for FULVIA *must recognize it as the same furniture she left behind, thirteen years ago, in another house. There is a verandah at the back, with steps leading down into the garden. Two doors in the wall, right. On the left, a door leading out to the front entrance.*

Four months have elapsed since Act I. It is August.

The curtain rises to reveal FULVIA, *the housekeeper* BETTY, *and a draper's* ASSISTANT. FULVIA *is wearing a clearly expensive, brightly-coloured summer housecoat. Her hair is still the colour of fire but gathered into a neat coiffure. Her face no longer has the grim pallor it had in the previous Act: she seems cheerful. The housekeeper* BETTY *behaves almost like a social equal and stands with the others at a small table, examining samples of material through a lorgnette, and testing the feel of the stuff between her fingers. There are dozens of samples, white, pale blue, pink and lilac, and an assortment of lace trimmings, which the draper's* ASSISTANT *has produced from a large canvas case with leather straps which sits on a chair beside the table.*

ASSISTANT: Of course! If Madam wishes to have all the inconvenience . . .

FULVIA: What! It won't be an inconvenience!

ASSISTANT: Naturally, not . . . Forgive me! . . . For a mother-to-be . . . but it will be a long job, if I may say so, making an entire layette by hand . . .

FULVIA: Oh, it will help to pass the time!

ASSISTANT: Of course. I mentioned it because we have a large variety of ready-made infants' wear in stock—some fabulous things, you know? All matching and complete . . . Some really beautiful work . . .

FULVIA (*to* BETTY, *who is looking at a sample*): What do you think of this one?

BETTY: Too flimsy! Much too flimsy!

ASSISTANT: That one, Madam, is mousseline! Very, very fine. They are using a lot of that now. Or nainsook.

BETTY: You can call it nainsook if you like! I call it flimsy.

ASSISTANT (*annoyed*): Begging your pardon, Madam, that one, as I said, is mousseline.

BETTY: Mousseline, then. It's still flimsy.

ASSISTANT: Oh no, I do assure you. It's very soft and fine—well it has to be, doesn't it, next to Baby's skin? But it's ever so hard-wearing. That I can guarantee.

FULVIA: Yes, perhaps. It's not, actually, what I was looking for. There used to be a material, fine like this and soft, but much stronger.

ASSISTANT: Is Madam perhaps thinking of cambric?

BETTY: There was nothing like the old muslins.

FULVIA: No, not cambric.

ASSISTANT: Linen batiste? Cotton batiste?

FULVIA: I don't know. I'd like to show it to you. Be a love, Betty, and pop upstairs. You know that old chest, where Livia still keeps . . .

BETTY: I know.

FULVIA: . . . some of her old baby-clothes. I saw them there.

BETTY: Yes, Madam. I'll go and look. (*She starts to go.*)

FULVIA: No, wait! I have a better idea. Don't say anything to her. Just ask her to come down here a moment.

BETTY: Yes, Madam. (*She goes out through the second door, right.*)

FULVIA: You'll see. You'll see how soft it is, and at the same time how strong.

ASSISTANT: I do have to say, this nainsook comes up with a lovely close weave once it's washed, Madam. And for softness of course, there's nothing to touch the mousseline.

FULVIA: Anyway, we have agreed on these pastel batistes. If only you had a paler lilac . . .

ASSISTANT: We would certainly have that in stock, Madam. Though I think this one here is a lovely shade ...

FULVIA: But the Valenciennes I think not, no, definitely not. It doesn't go.

ASSISTANT: I agree, madam. We have a terrible time with wholesalers these days.

Enter LIVIA *from the second door, right. She is an awkward girl, just turned sixteen; serious, stiff, confused whenever she has to bring herself to look someone in the face. She is dressed today in deepest mourning. At first* FULVIA *is unaware that she has entered the room.*

LIVIA: Did you send for me?

FULVIA (*hardly turning her head*): Oh, yes, Livia. Come here. (*Seeing her black clothes, she pauses.*) ... Er ... Why are you dressed like that? (LIVIA *lowers her eyes and dares not answer.* FULVIA *suddenly remembers the reason for the mourning.*) Ah, yes! Of course! I am sorry, so sorry. (*Realizing the moment is not suitable.*) No, well, never mind, it was nothing.

LIVIA (*coldly*): What did you want?

FULVIA: No, really, nothing. Are you off to church this minute?

LIVIA: In a bit. The priest said he couldn't do it until eleven.

FULVIA: You will be late finishing. Three requiem masses ...

LIVIA: I asked for only two.

FULVIA (*in a tone of gentle reproach, she is clearly hurt*): No, Livia. That will only upset your father. Not to mention me!

LIVIA (*still coldly*): It was so as not to upset you that I changed it to two. (*She says this as if her apparent consideration for* FULVIA *had not been a cloak for a deliberate wish to hurt.*)

FULVIA (*bitterly*): But what could upset me more than this? I mean, your thinking that I would mind? There have been three masses every year: you must have three masses this year, too. Is Papa coming with you?

LIVIA: I don't know whether he will want to.

FULVIA: He will come. Of course he will. I shall tell him to come. (*Changing the subject.*) I was just choosing the material for the baby-clothes.

LIVIA (*stiffly, as if this were something that did not concern her*): Oh . . .

FULVIA (*finding it impossible not to notice* LIVIA's *attitude*): Now, do go. I really didn't need your help. (*Then, seeing the readiness with which* LIVIA *is prepared to leave, she adds, irritably, with a sudden change of mood and tone.*) I wanted you to lend me the key to that chest where you keep all those old baby-clothes of yours.

LIVIA: Fine. I'll send someone down with it. (*She leaves through the second door, right.*)

FULVIA (*to the draper's* ASSISTANT *who has been folding all the samples and trimmings and putting them away in his case*): I'm so sorry . . .

ASSISTANT: Oh, Madam, please!

FULVIA: Look, I'd like to settle this. Let's say I'll have the nainsook.

ASSISTANT: Very good, Madam. Believe me, you couldn't do better.

FULVIA: I think I told you how many yards.

ASSISTANT: Certainly. I have got it all down. I'll have it all delivered today. My respects to you, Madam.

FULVIA: Goodbye. (*The draper's* ASSISTANT *leaves through the outside door, taking his case of samples with him. At the same time* BETTY *re-enters through the second door, right. As soon as* FULVIA *sees her, she says rather scornfully.*) So you have a mass said too, do you, for the soul of the dear departed?

BETTY (*slyly*): Oh, Madam, I do beg pardon. It's what we've always done, you see. Each year, on the anniversary . . . oh, I do beg pardon.

FULVIA (*indignant and severe*): Why should you beg my pardon?

BETTY: Well, perhaps this year we should have kept it from Madam.

FULVIA: Does that mean you think there's something wrong in it?

BETTY: Oh no, Madam. We do it for the poor child's sake.

FULVIA: Ah! You do it for her! Not for yourself then, and not really for your dead mistress?

BETTY: Oh, for myself too, of course, and for my dead mistress. It's what we've always done, as I explained.

FULVIA: Every year since she died?

BETTY: Every year, yes, Madam. Each of us has a mass said. Miss Livia has one, and I have one, and the Doctor has one.

FULVIA: And Livia has always had a mass said, right from the start?

BETTY: She thought of it first!

FULVIA: No, look, that can't be true. You must have got it wrong, Betty. Livia must have been tiny at the beginning, much too small to think about masses for the dead. Unless you thought of it for her, or her father did.

BETTY (embarrassed): Yes ... you are right ... It must have been her father ...

FULVIA (laughing): Dear, oh dear! What a complicated business! You really should remember, you know! You have been here all along! After all, your first mistress died in your arms.

SILVIO GELLI, who has been talking to LIVIA outside the room, comes in at this point through the first door, right. He overhears the tail-end of FULVIA's words and calls out to her in horror, afraid she is about to reveal their secret.

SILVIO: Fulvia! (He is immediately struck speechless at having blurted out her real name.)

FULVIA (she turns round at once, and takes a malicious pleasure in remedying his blunder): What did you call me? Fulvia? Dear God, I know it's her anniversary, but do

you actually have to go so far as to call me by her name?
It seems a bit much!

SILVIO: I'm sorry . . . yes, you are quite right . . .

FULVIA: That's all right, darling! It's natural enough. It's
awkward when someone decides to change their name.
You see, Betty, I used to be called Flora. Horrid name!
A dog's name, really. So he re-named me Francesca,
which is my second name. (*To her husband.*) You really
must try to remember it, darling! (*She looks at him and
sees that he is still looking upset and anxious.*) Whatever's
the matter? I think it's really rather nice of me to try and
cover up your gaffe.

SILVIO (*impatiently, trying to convey that this is not the
reason for his anxiety*): Oh . . . yes, thank you . . . But . . .

FULVIA (*understanding*): Not at all. We were just talking
about today's three masses . . . (*To* BETTY.) Did Livia
give you something for me?

SILVIO (*quickly*): Of course. That's what I came down for.

FULVIA (*suddenly worried*): Doesn't she want to give me
the key to the chest?

SILVIO (*to* BETTY): You can go, Betty. Actually, I think
Livia wants you upstairs.

FULVIA: I suppose she's crying now because I asked her
for it?

SILVIO (*to* BETTY *who has not moved an inch*): That will
be all, thank you, Betty. (BETTY *leaves through the
second door, right.*)

FULVIA (*immediately giving vent to her anger*): This is
becoming quite impossible!

SILVIO: Let me explain.

FULVIA: It was my idea to have all our old furniture
moved out of our bedroom into hers—because I saw she
was upset about it. I had it moved and I gave her the
keys.

SILVIO: I know you did.

FULVIA (*with increasing feeling as she states her case*): I
needed that stuff! I really needed to have those things
around me!

SILVIO: But think . . .

FULVIA (*quickly, emphatically*): I do think! I think of everything! But this is too much! Dear God! I made those baby-clothes with my own hands before she was even born!

SILVIO: Yes, I know.

FULVIA: Do you remember you didn't like me doing it? You used to take the stuff out of my hands to stop me. I can't tell you what it was like, finding those things again—put away with all my old clothes from those days. It was extraordinary. I held those things against my face and took deep breaths of their purity, my purity once; I took great life-giving gulps of it—I could taste it—I cried into those baby-clothes and washed my soul in them. (*Then abruptly.*) So. I gave them to her. I deliberately deprived myself . . .

SILVIO: You have to understand . . .

FULVIA (*quickly*): It's because I do understand that I did it . . . But just now the salesman was here, and I wanted to show him the stuff of one of those frocks. Surely that's not wrong! Surely I'm allowed to do that!

SILVIO: That's not the point!

FULVIA: Well, what *is* the point? Just because she has worn them, does that mean I'm not allowed to copy them for the new baby? (*Her face clouds dangerously.*) She had better look out! All right, I know I'm the new wife, and in that capacity she can think what she likes of me! But as a mother, that's different! As a mother, she is going to have to respect me!

SILVIO: She does respect you . . .

FULVIA: I don't mean as *her* mother! I mean as mother of the new baby! She's going to have to be very careful! The reason I'm so protective of this baby is that it is the one thing that makes me feel alive in this place.

SILVIO: Please don't excite yourself like this.

FULVIA: I'm not in the least excited . . . When I think of the lengths you have gone to to finish me off! . . . (*There is a pause. Then slowly, quietly, shaking her head.*) Even deciding the exact date of my death.

SILVIO: No, no . . . She simply asked me, once . . .

FULVIA: So, hey presto! You produced a date. And three masses . . . Now, tell me the truth. It must have been you who told that dozy old dormouse . . .

SILVIO: All right, all right! I told you! Betty repeated the story to Livia so many times, to put herself in a good light probably, that in the end the silly old fool came to believe it.

FULVIA: That I died in her arms? (*She laughs.*) Ah, ha, ha, ha! And she will actually go with you to hear masses for the repose of my soul!

SILVIO: The business of the masses was Livia's idea. She asked me once and I didn't like to say no.

FULVIA: But you went with her to the church every time.

SILVIO: It made her happy. You know I'm not a church-goer.

FULVIA: And are you going today?

SILVIO: No, not today.

FULVIA: I want you to go!

SILVIO: No. No, I'm not going.

FULVIA: Don't deprive me of this spectacle. At least it gives me something to laugh at! A bit of entertainment for the corpse! (*With a change of tone.*) I have already told Livia that you'll be going.

SILVIO: And I have just told her that I am not.

FULVIA: Do you do it on purpose?

SILVIO: What?

FULVIA: To make her hate me even more?

SILVIO: Even she must understand, and I think she does in fact, that by now the masses are just a token of respect.

FULVIA (*bursting into a fresh paroxysm of laughter*): A token of respect from you to me? Ah, ha, ha, ha!

SILVIO: That makes you laugh . . .

FULVIA: Of course it does, my dear. Far better it should make me laugh! (*She laughs again.*) Because it must feel ridiculous to be you, all dressed up in black, in church with a long face, because of me (*still laughing*), while I'm here at home, alive and kicking and cocking snooks at the lot of you!

SILVIO: But it's not like that. I don't do it for myself . . .

FULVIA (*in a different voice*): But look, does this respect of yours extend to me, here, now?

SILVIO: What are you getting at?

FULVIA: It's just that none of it seems to do *me* any good!

SILVIO (*emphatically*): My attitude to you in this house has always been one of respect!

FULVIA (*quickly*): It's not me you respect, dear, it's your precious fiction! Your lie!

SILVIO (*solemnly*): Oh, no, please! You must believe I am sincere.

FULVIA: Oh, I believe that all right! I believe you are sincere! That is the horrible thing about you: the sincerity with which you lie! The way you . . . oh God, don't make me talk about it!

SILVIO: No, go on, say what you have to say!

FULVIA (*in a quite different tone*): Do you really want to do something to help me?

SILVIO (*disconcerted by this new departure*): What? Of course I do!

FULVIA (*quickly and coldly*): Then stop showing me any respect at all!

SILVIO: What do you mean?

FULVIA: I mean try treating me like dirt . . . like some ghastly stray bitch you've picked up in the street which has followed you home and you can't shake off.

SILVIO: Ah, well, that seems a great idea.

FULVIA (*distantly, as if talking about somebody else*): Yes, that's right. Like a dog you can't get rid of so in the end you give in and bring it home with you. Perhaps if she thought it was more like that; if she saw me treated as a nuisance and despised and rejected, and also saw me putting up with it patiently and humbly, she might . . .

SILVIO: I couldn't do that!

FULVIA: Oh, I know, it's too late now! You have done the opposite! There's an odour of sanctity in this house, and it comes from that dead woman . . .

SILVIO: She missed having a mother! It seemed to me the kindest thing, to hide the truth and let her think of her mother as a sort of saint. Kinder to her and kinder to you as well.

FULVIA (*her first words are uttered violently, but she quickly regains control*): Not kinder to me! Don't ever say it was kinder to me! Don't ever think you did it for me! You did it for yourself, to quiet your own beastly conscience. Not that you succeeded. You can't pacify a conscience with lies.

SILVIO: I have asked you not to use that word!

FULVIA: Look, first you made me die, and then you sanctified me! You sanctified me, you sanctified yourself, you sanctified every damn thing in this place! (*With another change of tone.*) I can accept that my death might have been a necessary fabrication. She was, after all, a very young child. And she only had you to turn to as life began to unfold before her. I can see how it happened . . . as soon as she was big enough she will have asked about her mother . . . But, for heaven's sake, you were lying anyway, couldn't you perhaps have given some hint that your marriage was unhappy?

SILVIO: Well, yes! I can see that now, of course!

FULVIA: She would have loved you all the more; she would have had nothing to regret!

SILVIO: But how could I possibly have imagined that this would happen! It's odd, to say the least. You speak as if you were jealous of someone . . .

FULVIA: I am. There's another woman in my daughter's heart.

SILVIO: But that's you, yourself, don't you see?

FULVIA: It's not! It's not! You think that's me? No, I have sensed it, I have felt it—in her mind I am dead! Well and truly dead! I stand looking her in the face, and I am dead! Her mother is not me, this person here, this living person; her mother is someone entirely different . . . beyond recall, dead! Sometimes I'd like to grab hold of her and give her a good shake. I'd like to look her straight in the eye and say: It's not how you think! Believe me, my dear: just because she's dead . . . The dead can do no wrong, and that's why, after a time, people only remember their good side. So you see, dear, even death can be a lie! (*She breaks off, trembling with emotion, her face like that of one possessed.*) Have you any idea how often I have wanted to do that?

SILVIO: For pity's sake, Fulvia!

FULVIA: Oh, don't worry! I am very careful, more so than you! (*She pauses.*) Well, obviously! After all those years you spent honouring her mother's sacred memory, naturally when you turned up like that with me, it was bound to seem a betrayal. (*Another pause.*) Before that, yes, she will have thought about her mother . . . once a year, maybe. (*With a change of tone.*) But no! No, that's not right. People forget. People get used to anything. The situation now is completely different. Now she *is* jealous, jealous on her dead mother's behalf. (*Pause*) It will have struck her—how could it not?—the moment I came on the scene. Before that she was simply herself. But once I was there beside you she became her mother's champion. It was natural. She wanted to defend her territory. She wanted all her mother's things . . . her furniture, everything. I had to hand the stuff over myself. It seemed quite fair. That's the extent to which the lie has taken over in this house, for all of us: it is the element in which your daughter lives. *Your* daughter, mind. I don't feel as if she is my daughter at all, now. I really don't. Have you every heard of anything so inhuman? This lie has got to be obliterated. It has got to be done away with, because I am alive . . . do you see? . . . I'm alive!

SILVIO: Please, Fulvia, please! You agreed we should keep quiet—it was for your sake, if you remember!

FULVIA: For my sake? You're only interested in protecting the dead mother's memory!

SILVIO: But that's you!

FULVIA: Nonsense. For her I am simply—this person—
and I can never be her mother! I have reached the point
of believing it myself! To me, now, she has become that
other woman's daughter. It is a nightmare. From the
very first moment when I saw her and had to stop myself
flinging my arms round her. I wanted to hold her close
and make her mine again. She was so stiff and formal
that I had to be stiff and formal too, and now that
formality has become entrenched, it has become real, it
is part of what I am! I look at her, I see her doing that
shrug of hers and I simply no longer believe, I no longer
feel, that those eyes and that mouth could ever have been
made by me. It's as if somebody else had been here and
given birth to her without my knowledge. And ironically
enough, without her knowing either! A ghost-mother, a
ghost who has since turned real. Only too real! Real
enough to kill any maternal instinct I may have for her.
More than ever now, now the instinct is stirring again for
somebody else. But I must stop this . . . I don't want to
think about it any more. She can keep her dead mother.
Just as long as she leaves me in peace to live my life and
wait for my new baby.

SILVIO: Don't talk like that! You have only had four
months together . . .

FULVIA: Four months of smiling at her; four months of
slow torture. My God, I have had enough! Let's just
leave it. (*She settles herself at full length on a reclining-
chair.*) We have had a good chat . . . Now let's forget
about it. (*Long pause.*) Last night I suddenly woke up. I
started thinking, very calmly. And I thought yes, there's
this pain I have got, this horrible thing in my life. But
there again . . . well, there's always sleep! And if I wake
up, I can look at my hands against the light of the pink
lamp . . . (SILVIO, *drawn towards her at this point, approaches and stands looking down at her.*) What? Just that
. . . like this . . . I look at my hands . . . and the bed . . .
and the new bedroom furniture . . . Life goes on . . . and

there are lots of things in it to think about apart from my pain. (*With a little shrug.*) It needs to be said; it is just not true that when you are suffering, you can't think of anything else. You think of all sorts of things. Last night I was thinking—guess what?—I was thinking of happiness, of the kind of happiness that I should like to have! And it made me think that after all I'm not . . . you know . . . the lowest of the low.

SILVIO (*who has drawn nearer and nearer to her, unable to take his eyes off her*): For heaven's sake, what are you saying! (*He tries to take her hand.*)

FULVIA (*pulling her hand away*): No, you don't. It's my hair, isn't it? When I wear it like this it never fails . . .

SILVIO: No, Fulvia. It suits you, yes of course . . .

FULVIA: It excites you!

SILVIO: Fulvia, please, don't say that . . .

FULVIA (*angered that the motive for his present closeness should be her own dubious and unintentional sexual attraction*): Well, this isn't the kind of happiness I am looking for! (*At this point BETTY enters, in a state of great excitement, from the direction of the front door.*)

BETTY: Doctor Gelli! Doctor Gelli!

SILVIO (*hurrying to his feet, disconcerted at this interruption of an intimate moment*): What is it?

BETTY: It's Aunt Ernestina. Aunt Ernestina is here!

SILVIO (*horrified*): What? Here

FULVIA (*surprised and delighted*): Well, good heavens! Aunt Ernestina! Is she still alive?

SILVIO (*to remind her that she is now his 'second' wife*): Francesca! (*He turns to BETTY and goes out with her towards the hall.*) Where is she? How did she come?

BETTY (*answering him*): By cab. She's just paying the cabby now.

SILVIO: Go to her quickly and stop her coming in here! Take her straight upstairs to Livia!

BETTY: Yes sir, of course! Miss Livia will be pleased! (*She hurries out into the hall.*)

SILVIO: We could certainly have done without this!

FULVIA: But why send her up to Livia? She's my aunt. She's bound to know the whole story!

SILVIO: She'll know it, but she also knows the line to take with Livia.

FULVIA: She's in the conspiracy then?

SILVIO: You know what she's like . . .

FULVIA: I can guess. She will have been mortified, horrified, all her sensibilities outraged . . . but not averse from accepting a little hush-money.

SILVIO: But what do we do now? If she sees you, she'll give the game away! . . . We have got to get rid of her at once! . . . I thought I had seen the last of her . . . and damn it she's back!

The voices of BETTY *and Aunt* ERNESTINA *are heard in the hall, and the next minute* FULVIA'*s aunt comes in and heads straight for* SILVIO, *her arms raised tragically. She is a skinny little old woman, embittered by early disappointment rather than by poverty; as stupid as a hen and with the permanently dazed air of the deaf. She is not deaf, however, and possibly only pretends to be dazed. Her hair is dyed with some horrible red pomade. She is dressed in deep mourning.*

BETTY (*offstage*): No, just a minute! Not that way! Not that way!

ERNESTINA: Let go! (*She enters, as described, followed by* BETTY): So she's dead? My poor niece really is dead this time?

SILVIO (*furious, afraid that* LIVIA *may overhear*): Be quiet, will you? Just don't say anything! (*To* BETTY.) Run upstairs, and at least make sure that Livia doesn't come down. (BETTY *hurries off through the second door, right.*)

ERNESTINA: She must be really dead if you have been able to marry again! I wrote to you but you didn't write back.

SILVIO (*angrily, to stop her saying more, and indicating* FULVIA'*s presence*): She's here! But don't say a word!

ERNESTINA (*thoroughly dazed now, noting* FULVIA's *presence, but not recognizing her, and take her to be in fact* SILVIO's *newly-acquired second wife*): Oh, forgive me. I didn't see you, Mrs Gelli. I am the first Mrs Gelli's aunt. (LIVIA *bursts in from the second door, right, and runs to* AUNT ERNESTINA *with open arms.*)

LIVIA: Aunt Ernestina! Aunt Ernestina!

ERNESTINA: Livia! (*They clasp one another tightly and at length.*)

LIVIA: Dear, dear Aunt Ernestina!

ERNESTINA (*in tears*): My motherless baby! My poor motherless child!

SILVIO (*very angry, attempting to separate them*): That's enough, now! There is no need to make an exhibition of yourselves!

ERNESTINA: Yes, of course . . . you are right . . . we must have consideration for . . .

SILVIO: It's not a question of consideration. I would simply remind you that your niece has been dead for thirteen years. (*He stresses his words meaningfully, to remind her that in* LIVIA's *presence she must keep up the established fiction.*)

ERNESTINA (*completely mystified*): Ah yes . . . yes . . . but for me, you see . . . I have only just . . .

SILVIO (*quickly coming to her rescue*): Your grief probably still seems fresh to you, but do remember that for Livia as well as for you, the tragedy isn't something that happened yesterday, nor even four months ago.

ERNESTINA (*still not recognizing* FULVIA): Yes, of course! It must be more than four months . . . Do forgive me, Mrs Gelli . . .

LIVIA (*coldly, offensively, supposing her father's harsh manner to have been assumed out of regard for her new stepmother*): Let's go upstairs, shall we, Aunt Ernestina? Come!

ERNESTINA (*promptly*): Oh yes, my child . . . my poor motherless pet . . . yes . . . yes . . . you're wearing black too, I see . . . (*They leave the room through the second door, right, their arms round each other's shoulders.*)

FULVIA (*as if frozen*): She didn't recognize me.

SILVIO: It's my fault. It's my fault. She did write to me. She wrote asking . . .

FULVIA: But did you see? She didn't recognize me . . .

SILVIO: So she must believe . . .

FULVIA: . . . that I am really dead?

SILVIO: Because she thinks I have remarried! I should have answered her letter, warned her, explained. I really never thought she would turn up here after all these years. I was so exasperated I turfed her out quite brutally!

FULVIA: It's her she has come to see of course!* (*She gives an upward glance to show she means* LIVIA.) Now she knows she has an ally, someone to defend her against you—and against me.

SILVIO: Oh, no! That's not right!

FULVIA: Are you sure *she* didn't actually write and invite her?

SILVIO: Heavens, no! You must have seen how suprised she was!

FULVIA (*as if to herself*): Aunt Ernestina . . . Good God! . . . And she didn't even recognize me . . .

SILVIO (*as he makes towards the second door, right*): Well, she's going back now where she came from!

FULVIA (*calling him back*): No! What are you doing?

SILVIO: I'm sending her packing!

FULVIA: And play into *her* hands? Didn't you see the insolent way she stood there? . . . just waiting for you to upset the old lady for my benefit?

SILVIO: I'll take it upon myself—I'll tell her *I* want her to go!

FULVIA: She will still think it's because of me! Can't you see, that whatever you do, it is going to make me look bad?

SILVIO: So what do you suggest I do?

---

* TRANSLATOR'S NOTE: It may be felt that Fulvia should, for clarity, refer to Livia here by name. In the original text she seems to avoid doing so wherever she can.

FULVIA: The way she hugged her! All that stuff about
dear, dear Aunt Ernestina . . . And the stupid old woman
going 'Poor motherless child!' . . . I could almost laugh if
I didn't feel like crying . . .

SILVIO: Well. I shan't have a moment's peace as long as
she's here! She has got to go, this very minute!

FULVIA: Do something for me, will you? Go to church
with Livia and send the old girl down to me. I am going
to tell her who I am.

SILVIO: Then will you get her to go? Straight away?

FULVIA: We'll see. We'll see.

SILVIO: No, no. I am not going to have that woman in
the house! She's going!

FULVIA: She might be a help . . .

SILVIO: How the hell could she be a help! (SILVIO *goes
out through the second door, right.*)

FULVIA (*alone—after a pause—abstracted*): Aunt Ernestina . . . I thought she was dead . . . (BETTY *re-enters from
the hall, lugging two huge suitcases belonging to* AUNT
ERNESTINA, *one in each hand.*)

BETTY: These cases weigh a ton . . .

FULVIA: Do those belong to Aunt Ernestina . . . I mean
to Miss Galiffi?

BETTY: She has brought a trunk as well!

FULVIA: So she thinks she has come to stay?

BETTY: Well, judging by her luggage . . . Shall I take it up
to the spare room?

FULVIA: Yes, yes . . . for now . . .

BETTY *goes out through the second door, right. Shortly
afterwards Aunt* ERNESTINA *enters through the same
door, very confused and unsure of herself, rather like an
elderly chicken escaped from the coop.*

ERNESTINA: May I come in?

FULVIA (*closing the door behind Aunt* ERNESTINA,
*she is determined to get some fun out of the situ-
ation before disclosing her identity*): Come in, won't

you? Do sit down. Has Livia gone? She must have been
late . . .

ERNESTINA (*acutely uncomfortable*): Yes . . . She went
with her father . . .

FULVIA: Sit down. Sit down.

ERNESTINA: Thank you . . . She has gone to church . . .

FULVIA: What did you say?

ERNESTINA: I said she has gone to church, with her
father.

FULVIA: Yes, of course, to hear the masses. Perhaps you
would like to have gone with them . . . because of
course, you know, today . . . (*confiding, in a hushed tone,
with a meaning look*) for his daughter . . . it's the anniversary . . .

ERNESTINA: Oh . . . you know about it, then?

FULVIA: My goodness me, how should I not know!

ERNESTINA: Well, I don't know anything at all! So, she
must have died fairly recently, did she? My poor niece?

FULVIA (*staring at her and struggling to conceal the icy
chill of her astonishment before she speaks*): Not all that
recently, to tell the truth.

ERNESTINA: I haven't been here for about six years. I
was her only relative. They could have let me know . . .
How did she die? Do you know how she died?

FULVIA (*shaking her head gloomily*): Yes, I know.

ERNESTINA: Was it bad?

FULVIA: Very bad, yes! (*A pause, then.*) They killed her.

ERNESTINA (*startled*): What! Killed her! Who killed
her?

FULVIA: Sh! Keep your voice down, for heaven's sake.
(*Mysteriously*) Nobody knows about it.

ERNESTINA: Killed her! But how? Where? There was
nothing in the papers.

FULVIA: Well, you know . . . there are some crimes the
newspapers won't touch. (*She gives Aunt* ERNESTINA
*another mysterious and meaning look and then says in
hushed tones, confidentially, to reassure her.*) Now, you
are not to worry!

ERNESTINA (*stunned*): Not to worry! (*Completely flummoxed.*) And how do you know about it? Did your husband tell you?

FULVIA (*nods and frowns grimly, and resumes her confidential tone*): He told me all.

ERNESTINA (*dumbfounded*): What did he tell you? Dear Lord in heaven, what a terrible thing!

FULVIA (*as before*): Don't worry! Don't worry! I can hold my tongue. (*She places a hand on the old woman's hands as if swearing an oath.*)

ERNESTINA: But Mrs Gelli, I know nothing at all of this! Dear God! What was his part in it? Don't forget, I am the victim's aunt!

FULVIA: A nice aunt you must have been! Now, please! You might as well come clean! I have told you—I know everything.

ERNESTINA: What do you mean—'come clean'?

FULVIA: Well, weren't you the accomplice?

ERNESTINA: I? The accomplice?

FULVIA: Yes, you. You, my dear!

ERNESTINA: What are you saying? Accomplice in what?

FULVIA: You need to ask? In the killing of course!

ERNESTINA: Me?

FULVIA (*unable to contain herself any longer at the sight of the old lady's terror and astonishment, and bursting into peals of frenetic laughter*): Ah, ha! ha! ha! (*The next instant she approaches her aunt very closely, draws her hair back from her forehead and temples, and forces the old lady to look her squarely in the face.*) Now tell me the truth, Aunt Ernestina! Take a good long look! Don't you recognize me?

ERNESTINA (*practically fainting, staggering backwards, her hands held out in self-protection*): What? . . . What? . . .

FULVIA: It's me! Do you really not recognize me?

ERNESTINA: Fulvia? Is it you?

FULVIA: Sh! I am Francesca now!

ERNESTINA: But why?

FULVIA: Ah, why! I have told you why!

ERNESTINA: Heaven help me! . . . I must be losing my wits . . . You? You, back here, in this house?

FULVIA (*wagging a finger to contradict her*): No, it's Francesca, Francesca.

ERNESTINA: Why! . . . Fulvia . . .

FULVIA (*as above, spelling out the syllables*): Fran—ces—ca!

ERNESTINA: I really am going mad.

FULVIA (*suddenly embracing her*): Poor Aunt Ernestina, no you're not! But it is true you know that you were his accomplice. He told me so himself!

ERNESTINA: No . . . no . . . I swear I never . . .

FULVIA: Well, then, who has Livia gone to church to pray for?

ERNESTINA (*assailed by fresh confusion*): Well . . . I . . .

FULVIA: You see? And look at your black clothes! That's an accomplice's outfit if ever I saw one!

ERNESTINA: That's because this time I thought you really were . . .

FULVIA: Ah, yes, of course. Well, this is me, now. Mrs Francesca Gelli.

ERNESTINA: Let's have a look at you . . . My sight is not as good as it was, you know.

FULVIA: It's hair-dye that does that! (*She points to the old lady's dyed locks.*) It's bad for the eyesight . . . you'll have to take care. I'm in the same boat. (*She points to her own hair.*) They told me. You can lose your eyesight altogether.

ERNESTINA: Nonsense, it's old age! . . . Yes, you see, with your hair that colour I just didn't know you!

FULVIA: All right, but what about my voice?

ERNESTINA: What do you expect after thirteen years? Also I am going a bit deaf. And then, having been told for a fact that you . . . which heaven forbid, my dear! . . . But tell me, tell me what has happened? You have got together again, have you? And for the child's sake you have concocted this new tale . . .

FULVIA: Yes, At least, I thought . . .

ERNESTINA: You think they've guessed? Oh no, Livia
believes it, Livia certainly believes it.

FULVIA: Oh, everyone believes it!

ERNESTINA: What then?

FULVIA: The trouble is, I have come to believe it myself,
just as Betty has done!

ERNESTINA: What? Now, don't go and confuse me all
over again!

FULVIA: No, the point is I am now quite used to it. And
you have got to believe it too, Aunt Ernestina, really believe it, I mean . . . as truly as you believe in
yourself.

ERNESTINA: Yes, I see. For Livia's sake, you mean? And
for the neighbours and so on?

FULVIA: No, I mean for your own sake, for yourself, as
her aunt!

ERNESTINA: As Livia's aunt?

FULVIA: No! As the aunt of the niece who is dead!
(*Enigmatically*) A fine niece she turned out to be! (*She
pauses.*) You colluded with Silvio for money, I know; but
I am telling you, you had every reason to be really
ashamed of your niece!

ERNESTINA (*shocked*): What?

FULVIA: She was the worst kind of woman imaginable.
Vicious and depraved. (*She breaks off, seeing the expression on her aunt's face.*) And knowing that, do you still
want to go on protecting her memory?

ERNESTINA: But it's yourself you're talking about, isn't it?

FULVIA: No, my dear Aunt, it is not! I keep telling you,
I am Mrs *Francesca* Gelli, and you cannot imagine what
pleasure it gives me to smear the name of your other
niece, Fulvia, with as much dirt as I possibly can—seeing
as how she has been promoted in this house to the
company of the saints and has special services held for
her in church—to which everybody goes, even the skivvy!
(*Then, with a sudden joyous exclamation.*) You know I'm
to be a mother again?

ERNESTINA: A mother?

FULVIA: A mother . . . a mother! Like last time! Like I was before! The mother *she* never knew! Oh, Aunt Ernestina, you don't know what this means to me! It's a rebirth for *me*! This feeling of being a mother . . . do you know I feel exactly the same now as I did when I was expecting *her*. But exactly! And now, because I'm alive again, like I was then, I feel that it's me, and just me, that they should be calling holy; I am the saint, because of all I have suffered: the misery of those years and now the sheer martyrdom of these last four months with her. If you knew what I have been through! God, if you only knew!

ERNESTINA: Oh, I can well imagine. But she didn't know what she was doing to you, poor little thing . . .

FULVIA: No, she didn't know, but God she was fierce! Cool, too. It was the gentlest, purest spite. (*She suddenly seems profoundly distressed. She stands up and holds a clenched fist in front of her eyes.*) Heaven help me if she looks me straight in the eye!

ERNESTINA (*disconcerted*): What?

FULVIA: Nothing. I was thinking of something I said earlier on to her father, but it's a thought I mustn't allow myself! (*With an effort she resumes her normal manner.*) Believe me, Aunt Ernestina, I have done all I can—I don't mean to get her to love me . . . I'm not thinking of myself—but to make her feel that I . . . how can I put it? . . . For instance, even the way she snubs me, at times, I have found touching, and I have had a little smile to myself. Once or twice she has caught me smiling, and then you should see her expression! But yes, it has been torture. I have only been able to bear it because of how I feel now, this extraordinary feeling of being eighteen again and waiting for my baby. (*She breaks off as if struck by a sudden idea.*) By the way! You must do something for me, Aunt Ernestina. I'm sure you will help.

ERNESTINA: Oh? What's that?

FULVIA: You can suggest it to her as a way of getting
back at me! Get her to appear one day in that dress of
mine she keeps in her cupboard, the white muslin with
the tiny roses.

ERNESTINA: No! What can you be thinking of?

FULVIA: Oh go on, do! I should so love to see myself
again, in her, to see how I looked when I was her age!

ERNESTINA: What an idea! Certainly not!

FULVIA: I admit she doesn't look much like me . . .

ERNESTINA: She would never do it! She'd refuse!

FULVIA: So as not to contaminate her dress by exposing
it to my view? You may be right.

ERNESTINA: And think of me! Have you thought?
Have you thought what a muddle I am going to be in
now?

FULVIA: My word . . . don't you dare give anything
away! Silvio is worried out of his mind . . . He keeps
on about it . . . In fact he wants you to leave immediately.

ERNESTINA: What, now? Right away?

FULVIA: Poor Aunt Ernestina . . . come all this way to
help your little great-niece to plot against the interloper!

ERNESTINA: Oh, no! What are you saying?

FULVIA: Didn't she send for you? Tell the truth!

ERNESTINA: I swear to you she didn't! I simply came to
find out . . .

FULVIA: . . . bringing your trunk? (*She laughs.*)

AUNT ERNESTINA (*caught out*): Yes, I brought the
trunk . . . But I never imagined . . .

FULVIA: Never mind; never mind. Actually, from my
point of view, now . . . But you will have to be able to
pretend—really convincingly—you won't have to slip up,
ever . . .

ERNESTINA: Heavens above . . . How shall I manage . . .

FULVIA: You have managed for years!

ERNESTINA: Possibly, but not in front of you!

FULVIA: Well the thing to do will be to concentrate your
thoughts on my shady past.

ERNESTINA: I couldn't do that!

FULVIA: Why not?

ERNESTINA: I never think about that when I am with Livia.

FULVIA: Exactly. Well, you can start now!

ERNESTINA (*horrified*): With you there, too? Ouf!

FULVIA: Don't be silly! I am not your shady niece, remember! Though you will notice that Livia treats me as if I were. I can see it in her eyes. God knows what abominations she suspects me of.

ERNESTINA: What nonsense! She's a complete innocent!

FULVIA: Hatred makes her knowing. She has tasted the forbidden fruit.

ERNESTINA: What fruit?

FULVIA: In the Bible, Aunt Ernestina. The fruit of the tree of knowledge . . . the serpent . . .

ERNESTINA (*quite at sea*): Ah . . . yes . . . (*Then*) And your husband? What about him?

FULVIA: What about him?

ERNESTINA: What is he like with you now?

FULVIA (*shaken, she looks at her aunt for a moment, uncertain how to reply: then, with a frown*): He tolerates me.

ERNESTINA: But now that he has become such a . . .?

FULVIA: Oh, don't tell me! I know what he has become! But with me, you see, it's another story! He wants the fallen woman all right . . .! The special pleasure, in private, is to have the saintly wife back from the grave, using her newly-acquired techniques (*she makes an ambiguous gesture with her hands*) to get to work on his moral fibre . . .

ERNESTINA (*shocked but very curious*): I don't understand . . .

FULVIA (*nauseated*): He likes to have it torn to shreds so that he can put it together again the next morning, a little crumpled maybe, to wear for his daughter. He hasn't changed. Except that in the old days he wasn't fifty, nor did he make a profession of high moral rectitude, and nor did I understand him as I do now! Forgive me, dear

Aunt Ernestina: you can't possibly be expected to understand.

ERNESTINA (*her sense of decency affronted, she returns hastily to the earlier topic*): So. I shall have to avoid looking at you. I shall have to avoid *you* as much as I can.

FULVIA: You mean, so as not to give yourself away?

ERNESTINA: Of course . . . But my dear, don't you think it would be possible, somehow, to break it to her sort of gradually . . .

FULVIA: No! Absolutely not! I keep telling you! Those thirteen years actually took place. And with this present resentment she feels . . . it would be terrible for her! . . . One just couldn't! I am so sure of it I don't even think about it any more . . . and (*breaking off suddenly she whispers insistently.*) Sh! (BETTY *comes in from the hall.*)

BETTY: The piano-teacher's here, Madam. Mr Rota.

FULVIA: Oh heavens! Livia won't be having a lesson today and that's for sure! I should have let him know! I shouldn't have let him come all this way . . .

BETTY: That's right, Madam. As Madam knows, they will be expecting . . . (*She indicates with a gesture that they will be expecting lunch.*)

FULVIA: Has Mrs Rota come as well?

BETTY: Yes, Madam. They are out there shaking the dust off themselves and dripping with perspiration, Madam.

FULVIA: Oh, poor things! Show them in. (*Exit* BETTY. FULVIA *whispers in Aunt* ERNESTINA's *ear*). Now, take very great care, Aunt Ernestina, I beg you!

Enter CESARINO ROTA *and his wife* BARBERINA. *They are comic types: he is very slight, bald, but with a great mane of white hair sticking out all round his bald pate and over his ears. His face is crimson after his walk in the hot sun. He is lost in a vast new suit of raw silk far too big for him and clearly made for him by his good wife. He has rolled up not only his trouser bottoms but also the sleeves of his jacket, several times over, because of the heat. He has a large handkerchief in his hand, soaked with sweat. His wife BAR-BERINA is stout and stupid. She lives in a state of permanent apprehension thanks to her husband's mercurial effervescent temperament. She is wearing a gaudy dress, its brightness jarring with the heavy dullness of her dark and homely colouring. A jaunty little straw hat on the side of her head completes the picture.*

BARBERINA (*from the hall*): May we come in?

FULVIA: Come in, come in, dear Mrs Rota.

BARBERINA: Good morning, Mrs Gelli.

CESARINO (*bowing, with a flourish*): My dear lady . . .

FULVIA: Allow me to introduce you. Mr Cesarino Rota, Livia's music master, and Mrs Barberina Rota, his wife. Miss Galiffi, Livia's great-aunt (*Nods and bows all round.*) Do please sit down.

CESARINO: But it's so hot, so hot, dear Mrs Gelli! How delightful it is in here! The dust was terrible!

BARBERINA (*in horror trying to draw her husband's attention to the fact that he has come into the room with his trouser-legs and sleeves still rolled up*): Cesarino! Really!

CESARINO (*not understanding*): What?

BARBERINA: Dear me! You can't come in like that . . .

CESARINO (*immediately trying to put things right, starting with his trousers*): Oh dear me, yes . . . I'm so sorry! (*As he rolls down his trouser-leg a whole lot of dust falls out onto the carpet.*) Oh, look at the mess . . .

BARBERINA: Go outside, for goodness' sake!

CESARINO (*getting up at once and going out*): Yes, of course . . . Excuse me, excuse . . . (*He goes out.*)

BARBERINA: I am so sorry, Mrs Gelli.

FULVIA: Don't worry. It doesn't matter a bit.

BARBERINA: He is ever so absent-minded. You can have no idea!

FULVIA: It's the artistic temperament!

BARBERINA: Coming along the main road, you see, it was really . . .

FULVIA: Yes, I am so sorry that you . . .

CESARINO (*coming back in*): There we are then! (*He instinctively starts rolling up his sleeves again.*) And my pupil? Where is my pupil?

FULVIA: I was about to say, Mrs Rota. Unfortunately Livia . . .

CESARINO: Is she unwell?

FULVIA: No, she has gone to church with her father . . .

CESARINO (*suddenly worried, as he is the church organist*): What day is it? What service is it? Should I be playing the organ?* Oh heavens! Oh, dear! Barberina!

FULVIA: No, no! Don't worry! It's a private service. Today is . . . (*She turns to Aunt* ERNESTINA) . . . Tell me, Miss Galiffi, is it twelve years or thirteen now?

ERNESTINA (*off her guard and at a loss*): What? What did you say? I don't . . . um . . .

FULVIA: I was talking about the anniversary . . .

CESARINO (*promptly, as he remembers*): Ah, yes! Her mother . . .

BARBERINA (*apologetic at not having realized*): Of course, yes! Her mother's death!

FULVIA (*feeling apologetic herself now, and with a nod towards Aunt* ERNESTINA): And of course she was Miss Galiffi's niece . . .

AUNT ERNESTINA (*brightly, in an effort to regain her composure*): Yes . . . yes . . . today . . . it's the anniversary.

FULVIA: The thirteenth anniversary—is that right?

ERNESTINA: Yes, yes, the thirteenth . . . the thirteenth.

CESARINO: Oh, well then . . . well then . . .

BARBERINA: We didn't realize. We do beg your pardon. We would never have come.

FULVIA: Of course—but nobody thought to let you know.

---

*TRANSLATOR'S NOTE. 'Should I be playing the organ' is not in the original text, yet Cesarino's meaning is hardly clear without it.

BARBERINA: I am so sorry. (*She is about to get up.*) In that case . . .

FULVIA (*quickly*): No, no. Do please stay. (*To Aunt ERNESTINA.*) I don't suppose, do you, Miss Galiffi, that Livia . . . oh, no, no piano . . . she certainly won't be playing the piano today . . .

CESARINO: What! Surely after thirteen years . . .

BARBERINA (*shrilly*): Cesarino! Have some respect for . . . (*She nods towards Aunt ERNESTINA, who doesn't know how to take all this.*)

CESARINO: Dear me, I'm so sorry, so sorry!

BARBERINA: She is still in mourning, can't you see?

FULVIA: Yes, she was *very* fond of the first Mrs Gelli . . . she loved her like a daughter.

CESARINO: Of course, of course . . . one can see that. And now she has come to visit her little great-niece.

ERNESTINA: Yes, yes . . . I've come . . .

CESARINO: On purpose for this sad occasion?

ERNESTINA (*not knowing what to say*): Yes . . . yes . . .

BARBERINA: Well, then, it will be much better if we . . .

FULVIA: No, look, I was going to say, *I* don't think Livia will mind in the least if we invite her teacher and his wife to eat with us, as usual. Especially as it was really up to her to warn you not to come. I am sure you'll agree that her aunt is the person to ask . . . Miss Galiffi, what shall we do?

ERNESTINA (*stumped*): Do? Do about what?

FULVIA: You are in far the best position to know what the child's feelings are likely to be . . .

ERNESTINA (*stumbling over her words and getting hold of herself with great difficulty*): Yes, but my dear—I mean my dear Mrs Gelli, you must realize that I too . . . I too . . . am here as your guest.

FULVIA: Ah, well! In that case I, for my part, shall not allow the Professor and Mrs Rota to go back home in this heat in the mid-day sun.

CESARINO: It's one o'clock already!

FULVIA: Is it? Then they will be here at any minute . . .

CESARINO: Ah, yes! The magic of the motor-car . . . how lovely that must be! Indeed, I have to say, my dear Mrs Gelli, that if we were to go home on foot at this moment, we should certainly collapse . . .

FULVIA (*rising to her feet*): No, of course not. No, go and make yourselves comfortable. (*They all rise.*) Use that room if you wish (*indicating first door, right.*)

BARBERINA: Thank you. In that case I will take my hat off, if I may.

CESARINO: And I hope I have your permission . . . Well, I was going to tune the piano today.

BARBERINA: Oh, no, Cesarino! Didn't you understand? There's to be no piano today!

CESARINO: Tuning isn't playing!

FULVIA: You can always do it later, Mr Rota, after luncheon.

CESARINO: Splendid, splendid! Well, perhaps we could go and freshen ourselves up a bit, then!

BARBERINA: You'll excuse us. (*She gives a little bow and they both go off through the first door, right.*)

ERNESTINA (*desperately, like one possessed*): Ah, no, no, no, no, no! I'm going! I'm going! I can't take this!

FULVIA (*smiling*): Poor, dear Aunt Ernestina. It's awful for you . . .

ERNESTINA: My dear! It's altogether too much! I'm going this very minute! (*At this point* BETTY's *voice is heard coming from the front entrance.*)

BETTY (*offstage*): They are back!

AUNT ERNESTINA: I shall go upstairs! I shall go upstairs! I'll go and get my things and then I'm off! (*She leaves in a great flurry through the second door, right. Almost at exactly the same moment* SILVIO GELLI *enters from the hall.*)

SILVIO (*anxious to know if Aunt* ERNESTINA *has gone yet*): Well?

FULVIA (*with a glance towards the hall*): Is Livia back?

SILVIO: She came in the other way. I expect she's upstairs. What did you do?

FULVIA: She's going. She made up her own mind to go . . .

SILVIO: Today as ever is?

FULVIA: Probably. Today or tomorrow . . . She saw for herself the impossibility of staying.

SILVIO: Good. I shouldn't like it for instance, if today at luncheon . . .

FULVIA: Well, luckily there's the piano teacher and his lady.

SILVIO: Are they in there? (*Pointing to the first door, right.*)

FULVIA: Yes. See to them now. Quick as you can. We'll be having luncheon at any minute. (SILVIO *goes out.* LIVIA *then enters from the second door, right, and approaches* FULVIA *with an air of determination and a fierce frown.*)

LIVIA: Did you tell Aunt Ernestina to leave?

FULVIA (*grieved to see* LIVIA's *attitude and answering very gently*): No, my love. I didn't . . .

LIVIA: Well who's making her go then, the minute she has got here?

FULVIA: I don't know. Nobody . . . it was her decision.

LIVIA: It can't possibly be her decision!

FULVIA: I can only tell you what she said . . .

LIVIA: But for heaven's sake—she told me this morning when she arrived—she said she had come for a good long stay with me!

FULVIA: I know. Apparently she has even brought a trunk . . .

LIVIA: Well, then . . .

FULVIA: I give you my word, Livia, that as far as I am concerned she can stay as long as she likes. I told your father I'd like her to stay.

LIVIA: Did *he* do it, then? (*She gives* FULVIA *a fierce, hard look, straight in the eye.*) Why?

FULVIA: Not on my account, Livia, believe me! I know you suspect me.

LIVIA: Suspect? I don't suspect! It's perfectly obvious!

FULVIA: No, listen. Let me remind you that once before—when I was not even here—he didn't want her here and he sent her away. He told me so himself . . . I imagine it's true . . .

LIVIA: Oh, then! Yes, it's true. But this time it's different.

FULVIA (*still very gentle and sorrowful*): Because I'm here now, you mean. Do you realize I actually told your father this would happen? I told him you would blame me.

LIVIA: I don't know about that. He may have told you to say it, but you told her to go!

FULVIA: I certainly did not tell her to go. Nobody did! . . . How can I convince you? If she decided to leave, suddenly, just like that, it must have been because . . . oh, I don't know . . . perhaps it was talking to me that did it; perhaps she took a dislike to me. This seems to be my effect on people here, whatever I do . . . And if you could just be even slightly fair towards me, you would see it for yourself. Believe me, I couldn't have been nicer to her. But I was told she was a cantankerous old thing . . .

LIVIA: I happen to love her!

FULVIA: I imagine you do. And that's the reason, I would have you know, that I was so nice to her. I can't make it out . . . we even had a bit of a laugh. I can't think what upset her. (*She then attempts to introduce an intimate, humorous note into the conversation, pointing out the funny side of Aunt* ERNESTINA.) I say, you don't think . . . (*She leans her head towards* LIVIA *with a smile, showing her a lock of hair and adding.*) Look, my hair . . .

LIVIA: What do you mean?

FULVIA: Well, hers is dyed, too, as you know. I saw her give my hair a fairly steely look. I just wondered if it bothered her that mine looked so much better than hers. Of course you are too young to know about these little weaknesses.

LIVIA (*in a tight, clipped voice*): Yes. I am. Thank goodness.

FULVIA (*realizing that this last barb is directed at her and not at her aunt*): But my dear! Do you know *why* I dye it? Out of consideration for you!

LIVIA (*nauseated*): For me?

FULVIA: Yes, for you. Your father suggested it.

LIVIA: I don't understand.

FULVIA: No, I know you don't. Well, my natural hair colour is exactly the same as yours! Exactly the same!

LIVIA: Well?

FULVIA: You could well think you had inherited your mother's hair colour.

LIVIA (*placing her hands over her head as if to protect her mother's hair, and backing away from* FULVIA): Yes, I have. I know.

FULVIA: Did your father tell you? Well, that's why he advises me to carry on with this different colour. I would really rather stop, I assure you. (*With sudden tenderness, her voice full of anguish and longing at the memory of herself at the age her daughter is now.*) I am looking at these tiny soft ringlets on your neck . . . I'd love to touch them, take them between my fingers and gently, gently unwind them . . . oh! not so as to hurt! (LIVIA *shudders with instinctive revulsion.* FULVIA *notices her reaction, and smiles an indefinable smile of sorrow, perhaps for herself.*) It gives you the shivers, doesn't it, just hearing me say that?

LIVIA (*pushed to the limit, snapping*): No!

FULVIA: Is it disgust at the thought of my touch? . . . It's understandable. I can imagine that when you were tiny your mother must have stroked your hair in just that way.

LIVIA *buries her face in her hands and bursts into tears.* SILVIO, *who has evidently been awaiting his cue, enters from the first door, right.*

SILVIO: Livia, whatever is it?

FULVIA (*quickly*): It's nothing, honestly! She's crying because Aunt Ernestina's going. You will simply have to make her stay.

SILVIO: Yes, well. We'll see.

FULVIA: No, she must stay. She really must stay.

SILVIO: All right, then. She can stay. But Livia knows perfectly well (*He moves to put his arms round her.*) that Aunt Ernestina isn't worth all these tears . . .

LIVIA (*clinging tightly to her father, her body convulsed with hatred and disgust*): That's not why I'm crying! That's not why I'm crying!

SILVIO (*with LIVIA still clinging to his breast, the full severity of his gaze on FULVIA*): What, then?

FULVIA (*her eyes distant; her arms opening in a desolate shrug*): I don't know. (*BETTY enters after a brief pause, from the first door, right and hesitates in the doorway.*)

BETTY: Luncheon is served, Madam. (*She withdraws.*)

SILVIO: Come on now, Livia! There we are! Come, let's join the others, shall we? Don't let them hear you crying . . .

LIVIA (*pulling herself together*): Yes . . . yes . . .

SILVIO: Let's dry these tears . . . (*He moves off with his arm round LIVIA, then pauses, and looks back at FULVIA.*) Coming? . . .

FULVIA (*with another open-armed shrug and a sigh*): Coming.

CURTAIN

ACT III

The same as Act II. Six months later. An evening in February.

LIVIA *and* ERNESTINA *are in the Gellis' drawing-room. They are no longer dressed in black. LIVIA is very nervous and restless. She is sitting at a small table littered with books and magazines. She picks one up, flicks through it and flings it back on the table. Aunt* ERNESTINA *is walking about, trying to keep warm. The daylight is gradually fading.*

ERNESTINA: I thought we were going to have it fine for their homecoming; now it looks as if we are in for another cold snap. (*Pause*) Brrr . . . it's chilly in here. (*Pause*) Aren't you cold?

LIVIA (*rudely, slamming down a magazine*): No!

ERNESTINA: Well, you're very lucky! (*Pause. She rubs her hands together.*) February . . . February! It's a bitterly cold night to be travelling with a new-born baby. (*Pause*) And by the way, where has Betty disappeared to?

LIVIA: I don't know.

ERNESTINA: She has been out for over four hours! I do think she might have got things a bit ready for them. Nothing's been done!

LIVIA (*crossly, standing up*): Everything's perfectly ready! (*A pause.*) I find it maddening that it should bother you so much!

ERNESTINA (*with a sentimental smile*): Well, you know how it is! I keep thinking of how thrilled we all were when you were born!

LIVIA: I don't see what I've got to do with it?

AUNT ERNESTINA: Well, dear! She is your little sister . . .

LIVIA (*no longer able to contain herself*): You stupid woman! (*There is a long pause. LIVIA, shaking with rage, hurls a book she has picked up across the table. She turns once or twice towards her aunt as if about to say something, but her feelings of hatred and resentment are too strong for her and she is unable to speak.*)

ERNESTINA (*sighing*): Oh, dear, dear! I can see tears ahead!

LIVIA: It's unbelievable! How can you! How can you! Talk about my birth and the joy it gave my mother? It's unbelievable! It's quite unbelievable!

ERNESTINA: A new little life beginning . . . Exactly what this house needs!

LIVIA: There's just one thing I am waiting to find out and then I've done! You'll be able to keep your precious new life all to yourself—since you've changed sides!

ERNESTINA: What are you waiting to find out?

LIVIA: That's my business!

ERNESTINA: And why all this mystery all of a sudden? What do you mean 'I can keep it all to myself'? You're not thinking of running away?

LIVIA (*irritated*): For goodness' sake, Aunt Ernestina! I don't want to talk!

ERNESTINA (*after a pause*): And there's your father to think of. He loves you so much . . . he thinks the world of you . . .

LIVIA (*losing her temper*): Stop it, can't you! I don't want to hear this stuff!

ERNESTINA: I shan't say another word. (*There is a long pause, but the need to have her say is irresistible.*) But you've got some wrong ideas, you know. (*Another pause.*) You've got a bee in your bonnet, I'm telling you . . .

LIVIA (*with a snort of anger*): God, can't you drop it!

ERNESTINA: You tell me I have changed sides! . . . I came here for *you*!

LIVIA: Oh yes . . . to take my side, wasn't it!

ERNESTINA: Of course it was!

LIVIA: And now you're on hers!

ERNESTINA: I am not on her side! I am being fair, that's all! It's clear to me that you're the one who is refusing to patch it up.

LIVIA (*with another aggressive outburst*): Have you any idea what sort of a woman this is that my father has brought into our house?

ERNESTINA (*shocked*): What . . . sort of a woman?

LIVIA: Well, wait! Just you wait! . . . Quite soon I hope to be able to tell you.

ERNESTINA (*after a shocked silence; in a tone of controlled remonstrance*): What have you got in mind? Whatever are you trying to do! Let it rest, my dear child! Remember this is somebody who has suffered . . . terribly.

LIVIA: Suffered. Yes. You can tell by the hair.

ERNESTINA: You must take it from me . . . (*She gestures comically as she suddenly thinks of her own dyed hair.*) What can you tell by the hair?

LIVIA: Well, we know in what state he brought her here!

ERNESTINA: Well, good gracious! They had known each other . . .

LIVIA (*cutting in*): I know, since before I was born. He had forgotten her. And then she got ill and they sent for him, and he rushed off to save her life . . . (*She breaks off.*) Anyway, you wait! And I shall have something much more definite to tell you!

ERNESTINA: Have you been ferreting out secrets?

LIVIA: Don't you start poking your nose in!

ERNESTINA: Has the parish priest got anything to do with it?

LIVIA: I'll show you just how much my father cares about me! He's already worried stiff . . . he keeps looking nervously round as if he's afraid of something . . . and I know . . . I know what he's afraid of!

ERNESTINA: You don't know anything. It's you he's worried about!

LIVIA: Yes! He worries in case I find out! In the two months he has been away, he has been back here eight times!

ERNESTINA: To see you! To spend a day with you!

LIVIA: No, no! That wasn't it! It was something else! . . . And he no longer does anything! . . . It's pathetic, it's humiliating, quite apart from anything else: at fifty, to see him besotted with a woman like that. And why didn't he marry her before if he has known her for such a long time?

ERNESTINA: Well, perhaps he wasn't able to! What a question!

LIVIA: She wasn't married. He was a widower. Why couldn't he?

ERNESTINA: Well, say he could . . . how do you know that it wasn't for your sake that he didn't?

LIVIA: My sake. It wouldn't have been for my sake! For me it would have been better if he had done it sooner, while I was still too young to understand.

ERNESTINA: Well! There will have been another reason, then! Don't go looking for trouble!

LIVIA: You mean because of my mother? No! Because what makes me most angry about this great love of his is that it obviously goes back to when he was young, to when my mother was alive! This makes the insult to her memory really gross! It's almost as if he were still betraying her: that's how it feels to me: as if my dead mother had come back thirteen years later, alive again and young again, to be made to suffer this posthumous love affair of theirs. That's why I hate this woman more and more, the more I see of her. She'd like to be a mother to me but I find her disgusting. She gives me the horrors! It's as if every time she speaks to me or looks at me she were betraying my real mother.

ERNESTINA: What are you saying? What nonsense is all this? To think of such ideas going through a child's mind! Mercy on us! It's a sin even to think of such things!

LIVIA: Yes. And when you see what I am going to do . . .

ERNESTINA: All I can say is, it's a very good thing your father's coming back tonight!

LIVIA: Bringing my little sister!

ERNESTINA: It was my intention to be gone by then. And now I'm wishing I had. But the minute they get here, I shall go . . . There! My mind is made up!

LIVIA: What! What about the new little life beginning . . .?

ERNESTINA: I was thinking of you when I said that. There's not much time left in my life for beginnings! I am old—it's aches and pains for me!

LIVIA: I suppose so! . . . And life will at last begin for me, too!

ERNESTINA (*with a start*): That's better! Now, just you see that it does! (*Another long pause. She moves out onto the verandah and peers down the garden*.) Look at that! The garden gate's open again!

LIVIA: The gardener must have left it open. He can't have gone far.

ERNESTINA: Yes, but it's almost dark! . . . And it's hardly gardening weather! . . . And why is Betty still out? I'm frightened.

LIVIA: Are you worrying about that man who came that time?

ERNESTINA: He stood just there! Just by the gate. Do you remember?

LIVIA: He was snooping. By the way, how was it you didn't know him?

ERNESTINA: Why should I? What do you mean?

LIVIA: But he told you he knew my mother.

ERNESTINA: Well, now! He must have got mixed up! You were looking out of the window. He said he knew your mamma when what he really meant was that he knew Mrs Gelli.

LIVIA: You really think he meant this Mrs Gelli?

ERNESTINA (*disturbed*): . . . Unless you have found something out . . .?

LIVIA: Oh, no. I wouldn't have given it another thought if you hadn't reminded me of it. And then . . . perhaps he is . . . just one more proof . . . turning up, out of the blue . . . looking for her . . .

ERNESTINA: Well, obviously he has met her somewhere!

LIVIA: But *where* . . . that's the point!

ERNESTINA: Livia! I don't want to hear that kind of talk! In my day, young girls . . .

LIVIA: Come off it, Aunt Ernestina! Young girl? Do you really think I don't know what kind of a woman she must have been? One look at the gentleman friend should tell you! He hadn't even got a coat . . . Did he say he was coming back?

ERNESTINA: He said he would wait until she returned.

LIVIA: Well, that's today! (*To herself.*) I'd like to talk to him!

ERNESTINA (*making up her mind after a moment's thought*): Look, I'll go and shut the garden gate. (*She starts to go.*)

LIVIA: No, Aunt Ernestina, you can't shut the gardener out!

ERNESTINA: He's got his key! (*She goes down into the garden via the verandah. LIVIA remains lost in thought. Aunt ERNESTINA returns quickly, shivering with cold.*) It's really freezing tonight!

LIVIA (*after a pause, still wrapped up in her thoughts*): And don't you think it's odd that Papa should want to move to a dump like this with his brand-new wife? We have been here seven months and we still don't know a soul!

ERNESTINA: Now there I do agree! It was a horrid choice; that I will grant you! A shell of a place and miles from anywhere! (*While she is speaking she is hugging herself against the cold, trying to rub some warmth into her upper arms. She is suddenly startled by a dull thud coming from the direction of the hall.*) Oh God!

LIVIA: What's the matter?

ERNESTINA: Didn't you hear that noise? (*BETTY comes in from the hall, all muffled up in outdoor clothes with a battered old hat on her head.*)

LIVIA (*laughing*): It's Betty!

BETTY (*puzzled by their amazement and by LIVIA's laughter*): What is it?

ERNESTINA: It was the door . . . Goodness, what a fright! (*To BETTY.*) Cold, isn't it?

BETTY: And it's going to rain any minute now . . .

ERNESTINA: I'm perished. I am going upstairs to get a shawl. (*She goes out through the second door, right. BETTY approaches LIVIA conspiratorially.*)

BETTY (*in a whisper, gesticulating wildly*): It's as clear as daylight! We have all the proof we need!

LIVIA (*avidly*): Tell me, quickly!

BETTY: He couldn't come over himself. It would have looked too suspicious.

LIVIA: Has he had an answer?

BETTY: He certainly has had an answer! Two days ago! . . . He wanted to come and tell you himself. But, poor old man . . . He was expecting me.

LIVIA: And did he draw a blank?

BETTY: A complete blank. There have been no banns read out either at Merate or at Lodi. And no application at the Town Hall for the civil status certificate.

LIVIA: So?

BETTY: So no marriage! Clear as daylight! She is not his wife! They can't be married!

LIVIA: And there's no way the death certificate on its own would have done?

BETTY: Not a chance. Banns have to be read out for widowers just like everybody else. I mean, he has had thirteen years! He could have had another wife in that time . . . or even two! But no! There's been no banns and no marriage. You can be quite, quite sure.

LIVIA: Oh, yes! It fits together!

BETTY: Well, I mean, it explains everything . . . why she went so far away to have the baby . . . If she had had it here they would have had to register the birth, and the whole story would have come out: her not being his wife and the brat being just like any other little bastard. We shall know for sure in a day or two!

LIVIA: I don't need to wait for that! This is enough for me!

BETTY: Funny, though! She behaved like a lady!

LIVIA (*her thoughts entirely taken up by the hatred she now feels for her father*). How could he! How could he!

BETTY: These women, they are up to every trick! Once they get their claws in a fellow, it makes no difference how decent he is . . .

LIVIA: Well, he might have had the decency to keep her somewhere else! Bringing her here, under this roof, and getting me to call her Mamma . . . !

BETTY: Yes—I don't know . . .

LIVIA: Well—we'll soon see! (*She whispers.*) Sh! (*Aunt* ERNESTINA *re-enters through the second door, right, with a woollen shawl round her shoulders.*)

ERNESTINA: My word, you need a bit of light here! . . . It's quite dark!

LIVIA (*quickly to* BETTY): Come on, Betty, let's go up-stairs! (LIVIA *and* BETTY *go out through the second door, right.*)

ERNESTINA (*alone, after watching them leave*): What's up with those two? And where has that gossipy Betty been all the afternoon? (*She draws in a deep breath and stands holding it as she ponders these questions. Then, with a big sigh.*) What a business! Now, some light! (*She goes to the main door to switch on the light. Meanwhile* MARCO MAURI, *who was already inside the garden when Aunt* ERNESTINA *went to close the gate, comes in from the verandah. He has aged a great deal in the past year, but his eyes gleam more brightly than ever, with the tragic hilarity peculiar to madness. He has no overcoat; only a shabby light summer jacket. He stands back among the shadows, close to the verandah.*)

MAURI (*as soon as Aunt* ERNESTINA *turns on the light*): May I come in?

ERNESTINA (*turning round in terror, her hand still on the switch*): Oh, my God! Who is it?

MAURI: It's me! Don't be frightened!

ERNESTINA: Do you always come in like that? Like a burglar? How did you get in?

MAURI: I came in through the gate before you shut it.

ERNESTINA: You mean you've been lurking outside all the time?

MAURI: Burglars don't usually ask permission to come in . . . nor do they wait for people to turn on the light.

ERNESTINA: But who are you? What do you want? Why do you keep coming?

MAURI: I asked you last time, if you remember . . .

ERNESTINA: Well, they're not back yet!

MAURI: You said they'd be coming today!

ERNESTINA: Well, they're not here! And we don't know when they are coming, or even if they are coming. So you can go away!

MAURI: Don't worry. It just means I'll have to wait a bit longer. Unless of course you can tell me where I can find her at this moment. I think that might be better, because here . . .

ERNESTINA: They are travelling . . . travelling! (*She peers into his face; her own look is curious, sour and suspicious.*) But what do you want with her? Why do you want to wait for her? What is your name?

MAURI: There is no point in my telling you my name. I have to see her . . . to speak to her! She knows me and so does her husband. Are you a relation?

ERNESTINA: I am an aunt.

MAURI: Hers or his?

ERNESTINA (*warily, trying not to answer*): Well . . . I'm a great-aunt really . . . the little girl's great-aunt.

MAURI: On her father's side?

ERNESTINA (*unnerved, off her guard*): No, her mother's.

MAURI: In that case . . . (*as light dawns.*) Good God! . . . It can't be! She only had one aunt!

ERNESTINA (*overcome by her curiosity, but barely audible, still very much on guard*): That's me! I am her only aunt!

MAURI (*looking at her for a moment with affectionate merriment as he quietly, delightedly, utters her name*): Aunt Ernestina? So you are Aunt Ernestina? . . . Fulvia thought you were dead!

ERNESTINA: Sh! Keep your voice down! . . . For heaven's sake!

MAURI (*even more quietly, in a conspiratorial whisper*): Because *here* . . . she's the one who is dead . . . Right? (*He is clearly overjoyed. Biting the lower lip he raises a finger to his lips and adds, with a triumphant gesture, as if this were a matter of the greatest good fortune.*) She's still dead, is she? Her daughter still thinks she is dead?

(*He heaves a great sigh.*) That's wonderful, wonderful! What a weight off my mind! What a relief! I was horribly afraid the secret might be out . . . (*Impulsively he flings his arms round her.*) So you'll help me, won't you, Aunt Ernestina? You'll help me, because you know what agony . . .

ERNESTINA (*terrified, struggling to extricate herself*): Are you mad? I don't know you from Adam!

MAURI: I was saying, you know what agony . . .

ERNESTINA (*still terrified*): What agony? What are you talking about?

MAURI: Fulvia's agony! Fulvia's agony!

ERNESTINA: Where! . . . Let me go! (*Wriggling free.*) I'll scream!

MAURI: . . . still having to be dead for her daughter!

ERNESTINA: But she has another daughter now! . . . All her own . . . born a month ago!

MAURI (*his voice and gestures breezily jubilant*): It doesn't matter! It doesn't matter!

ERNESTINA: What doesn't matter?

MAURI: I knew it! Even this doesn't matter! It means she wanted to come away with me, even with a new baby! . . . It didn't mean anything! . . . a moment's weakness! So she gave in to him . . . Oh, Aunt Ernestina, if you knew what I had been through! . . . Ah! . . . (*He screws up his whole face and motions with his hands as if to wave away the memory. When he opens his eyes again he has gone pale; he looks dizzy, as if he is about to fall. Aunt ERNESTINA is alarmed.*) No, it's nothing . . . (*He laughs.*) I have been thinking, ever since this morning . . . What was the name of that river in mythology . . . ?

ERNESTINA (*totally bemused*): What river?

MAURI: Lethe, that's it, Lethe . . . (*He gives pompous emphasis to the next words.*) The River of Oblivion.

ERNESTINA: Are you drunk?

MAURI: No, I'm not. Although nowadays if you want Lethe, you have to go to the pub. But I don't drink. And for nights now I have not slept. Shall I tell you what my

eyes feel like, Aunt Ernestina? It's as if each eyelid were
a bridge over a dried up river-bed . . . you know those
places? . . . dusty and parched and full of stones and
crickets? My eyeballs feel like that. And I get cricket
noises in my head, too, a non-stop screeching in each ear
until I am half out of my mind. Oh, I can talk to you!
Here, with you, I can talk quite easily. I'm quite a good
speaker—don't you think? D'you know I used to practise
my speeches wandering about the countryside, in the
days when I hoped I'd be made Public Prosecutor. I'd
take a topic, any topic, and I would improvise out there
in the woods: 'Gentlemen of the Court, Gentlemen of
the Jury . . .' You must forgive me! Talking is something
I just have to do! It's a compulsion, it comes from inside
me . . . I could shout for sheer joy . . . I am going to see
her! . . . Fulvia must have told you something about me.

ERNESTINA: No! Never! I have no idea who you are!

MAURI: But she must have told you about her suicide
attempt, a year ago.

ERNESTINA: Oh, yes, she told me about that.

MAURI: Without mentioning me?

ERNESTINA: She told me about her life and said she
could not bear to go on living it.

MAURI: That isn't true! It was because of me! . . . She
denies it, I know. But it was because of me!

ERNESTINA (*turning to look at him closely, her terror now
tempered with a kind of pity*): Because of you?

MAURI (*with a burst of temper*): And I would thank you
to stop staring at my clothes!

ERNESTINA (*anxious to put things right*): No, no . . . It's
just . . . You look so . . .

MAURI: I am not cold! I'm shivering, but it's not because
I am cold . . . It's nerves! . . . It's nervous trembling! . . .
It doesn't worry me! . . . I could get a job if I wanted one
. . . It doesn't worry me! . . . For a year now, for a year,
I . . . (*He breaks off.*) Oh, hell! The whole thing is quite
impossible! I have simply got to end it, one way or the
other!

ERNESTINA: How can you talk of ending it when it's already over!

MAURI: Oh, no, it isn't! That is just not true. It can't be. Now that I have found her!

ERNESTINA: But I keep telling you—she has got this new baby!

MAURI: But that makes it even better! Just wait . . . you'll see!

ERNESTINA: Is this why you have come? What do you mean to do?

MAURI: I came because I can't go on without her!

ERNESTINA: I can honestly tell you she has forgotten all about you . . . and you can be quite sure that now she is completely taken up with her new baby.

MAURI: If that were true it would be a disaster! A disaster, Aunt Ernestina, because, well, here I am, and I have to be considered. Other people have lives too, Aunt Ernestina, inconvenient though this may sometimes be! So what's to be done! We can't just shut ourselves up inside our own lives as if nobody else existed! And my life is all wrapped up in hers, and without her I am unable to go on living . . .

ERNESTINA: But you can't force people . . .

MAURI: To love another person against their will? I know! And that's the disaster! What happens then, my dear Aunt Ernestina, is that life cannot continue. It has to come to an end, just like that, wherever it may be!

ERNESTINA (*terrified*): Oh dear God! What are you going to do?

MAURI: I don't know . . . I am here. For a year I have been forcing myself to try to live without her. I realize I can't do it. (*At this point the* GARDENER *comes hurrying in from the verandah.*)

GARDENER: Please, Ma'am, the master and missus are here! They are just arriving!

ERNESTINA: Mercy on us! (*To* MAURI.) Please leave now! I beg you, go!

MAURI: I shall stay.

ERNESTINA (*to the* GARDENER): Run and tell them upstairs, John!

GARDENER (*hurrying out of the second door, right*): Yes, Ma'am. Certainly Ma'am.

ERNESTINA: Do you really want to make a scene the moment she arrives, in front of her daughter?

MAURI: Not a scene, no. I shall just speak to her. I shall tell her everything.

ERNESTINA: For pity's sake! You must be mad! Please leave us! Just go!

MAURI: I am not going.

ERNESTINA: I'll speak to her for you! I promise! At least wait until tomorrow.

MAURI: No. Tonight.

ERNESTINA: All right, then, tonight . . . but later, when she is on her own.

MAURI: Do you promise?

ERNESTINA: Yes, yes. Trust me! . . . Now. Your name?

MAURI: Marco Mauri.

ERNESTINA: They're here! They are coming! . . . Off you go . . . out this way! (*She shows him out through the verandah into the garden. Soon after* BETTY *comes in through the second door, right, and at the same time* FULVIA *and* SILVIO *enter from the hall, in travelling clothes, followed by the* NURSE, *who carries the new-born baby in a luxurious baby-carrier, wrapped in a voluminous pink shawl.*)

FULVIA (*her first impulse is to run and embrace Aunt* ERNESTINA, *but she checks herself and offers her her hand*): Aunt Ernestina, dear Miss Galiffi! How are you? How are you? (*She looks round for* LIVIA *and notes her absence.*)

BETTY: Welcome home, Madam! Welcome home, Sir!

FULVIA: Betty, my dear, you too . . . Is everybody well? (*To the* NURSE.) Sit down, sit down. (*She beckons to Aunt* ERNESTINA *and to* BETTY *to gather round the* NURSE *to look at the baby.*) Is she still asleep? (*The* NURSE *sits.* FULVIA *and the other two ladies form a group around her and* FULVIA *gently lifts the shawl to show them the sleeping child.*) There she is!

BETTY: Isn't she lovely!

ERNESTINA: She's a poppet! My word, what a deep sleep!

BETTY: But isn't she like . . . oh! (*To Aunt* ERNESTINA.) Look, look! Isn't she the image of Miss Livia?

ERNESTINA: Yes . . . yes . . .

FULVIA (*to* SILVIO): Didn't I tell you?

BETTY: As like as two peas!

ERNESTINA: As like as two peas! It could be little Livia, couldn't it? That's exactly how I remember her!

BETTY: Me too! Me too!

FULVIA (*with an indescribable smile*): Yes, of course, you too! . . . I, of course, can't say . . . but even I can see a certain likeness . . .

SILVIO: Where *is* Livia?

ERNESTINA: She's upstairs. She has been told . . .

BETTY (*confused*): Yes . . . yes . . . she was with me . . .

SILVIO: Go and tell her to come down!

BETTY: But I think . . .

FULVIA (*to* SILVIO): Let her be, for heaven's sake! . . . If she doesn't want to come down . . .

SILVIO: Oh, no! We're not having this!

FULVIA: Perhaps she's not feeling well.

BETTY: She has shut herself into her room.

FULVIA: There, you see? We'll see her tomorrow.

SILVIO: I'm going up!

FULVIA: All right then, if you must; but don't make her come down if she doesn't want to.

SILVIO: All right . . . all right . . . (*He goes out through the second door, right.*)

FULVIA (*to* BETTY): Be a love, will you, Betty, and show Nurse where her room is?

BETTY: Of course, Madam. (*To the* NURSE.) It's this way!

FULVIA (*to the* NURSE *as she leaves the room, the baby in her arms*): Quiet as you can, won't you? Be sure not to wake her.

BETTY: Now don't you worry, Madam! (*She leaves with the* NURSE, *through the first door, right.*)

FULVIA (*she runs and throws her arms round Aunt* ERNESTINA): Aunt Ernestina! Did you see her? ... I am just so happy!

ERNESTINA (*struggling out of* FULVIA's *embrace*): No ... listen! Listen to me!

FULVIA: Whatever is it?

ERNESTINA: The most awful thing! ... the most awful thing!

FULVIA: Livia? Ouf! Livia can wait!

ERNESTINA: No! A man came looking for you.

FULVIA: Looking for me? Who was it?

ERNESTINA: He did tell me his name ... He's out there in the garden!

FULVIA: In the garden? Out there? Whoever is it? At this time of night?

ERNESTINA: He wants to speak to you.

FULVIA: You mean he's hiding out there?

ERNESTINA: He doesn't come from round here. He wouldn't go away. I promised him I'd tell you.

FULVIA: But what on earth ... ? Now, do you mean?

ERNESTINA: Well, later ... He came before, two days ago.

FULVIA (*under her breath*): Don't tell me it's that madman?

ERNESTINA: Mad? ... Yes, I think he could be mad! He told me that it was because of him, that you ...

FULVIA: Mauri? Was his name Mauri?

ERNESTINA: Yes ... I think it was ...

FULVIA: And what does he want?

ERNESTINA: I think he means to do something dreadful ...

FULVIA: To me?

ERNESTINA: He says that without you he can't go on living ...

FULVIA: Oh, he's not still on about that? ... Did you tell him that I ... ?

ERNESTINA: I told him about the baby, yes!

FULVIA: Well, then!

ERNESTINA: He says it makes no difference.

FULVIA: He's mad! . . . It's a fuss about nothing. You are not to worry, Aunt Ernestina.

ERNESTINA: But he's out there . . . And if . . .

FULVIA: Oh, I know, I know. He could create a big scandal. But how did he get here? How did he know where to come? What did he tell you?

ERNESTINA: Well . . . I'm not sure I understood very much . . . He was talking about crickets at one point . . . and then he started preaching . . . One thing he said though, was that he has got to 'end it'.

FULVIA: Still?

ERNESTINA: I told him . . . but he threatened me! I told him . . .

FULVIA: Never mind, it doesn't matter. My one worry now is for Livia. I don't want her to hear . . . And I mustn't let myself get upset, that I really must not do. (*Happily*) I am breast-feeding, you know! (SILVIO *enters from the second door, right.*) Oh, Silvio . . .

SILVIO: She says she's coming down.

FULVIA: Livia? Oh no, she'd have done better to stay upstairs!

SILVIO: On the contrary! She should be here! If only out of respect for me!

FULVIA: You didn't force her?

SILVIO: I will not have her carrying on like this! She wouldn't even open the door to me! However, she did in the end say she would come down.

FULVIA: Aunt Ernestina, go and see if you can stop her!

SILVIO: Why?

FULVIA: Because that man is out there in the garden . . . that Mauri . . . You know?

SILVIO (*astonished*): Here? . . . How the blazes . . . ?

FULVIA: It seems he has been here for two days.

ERNESTINA: Yes, yes . . . He came looking for . . .

SILVIO (*in a sudden panic*): He hasn't spoken to Livia?

ERNESTINA: No, no . . . He spoke to me!

SILVIO: And what does he want?

FULVIA: Oh, the usual! He's off his head!

SILVIO: Not still? How did he know where to come?

FULVIA: How should I know! Look, do go and get rid of him before Livia comes down. (SILVIO *goes towards the verandah.*)

ERNESTINA: No! Don't go out there alone!

SILVIO: Oh, for heaven's sake! (*He shrugs and goes out.*)

ERNESTINA: Listen, I think you should send John out, too.

FULVIA (*annoyed*): No, Aunt Ernestina! They have to see each other alone . . . Now you're getting me worried . . .

ERNESTINA: He was in such a state when I saw him.

FULVIA: In that case I had better go myself!

ERNESTINA: Oh no, not you! (BETTY *enters from the second door, right.*)

FULVIA (*quickly, to* BETTY): Where's John?

BETTY: John? . . . I don't know . . . In the gardener's cottage, probably.

ERNESTINA: Well, that's a relief! He'll be within reach . . .

BETTY: Miss Livia has given me some instructions, Madam, and I don't really know as how I ought to do as she asks.

FULVIA: What instructions?

BETTY: She has ordered the car . . .

ERNESTINA: I knew it! She wants to run away! She told me.

FULVIA: What's this? Run away? Where?

BETTY: I think she's been packing . . .

FULVIA: To run away? Tonight? I suppose this was planned to coincide with my arrival?

ERNESTINA: I'm afraid, my dear, plots have been hatching here for quite some time. (*She glares at* BETTY *with ill-suppressed fury.*)

BETTY: Are you referring to me, Madam?

ERNESTINA: Indeed I am referring to you! You and that parish priest . . . Heaven knows what you've been getting him to do . . .

FULVIA: But where is she thinking of going? And why?

BETTY: I don't know . . . She just gave me instructions . . .

FULVIA: And where does the parish priest fit into all this?

ERNESTINA: You were over there today, for more than four hours! Don't try and deny it!

FULVIA (*displeased, but determined not to let such obviously cruel and unjust behaviour upset her*): Well! . . . she can sort it out with her father! I'm going to see my baby. (*She makes towards the first door, right, but as she does so* LIVIA *enters through the second door, right, dressed for a journey*.)

FULVIA (*stopping in her tracks, to* LIVIA): What is all this? Livia, What is this silly nonsense?

LIVIA: Where is my father?

FULVIA: You want to leave? Where are you thinking of going?

LIVIA: That's my affair.

FULVIA: Are you serious? At this time of night? And may one ask why? . . . why, suddenly, for no reason?

LIVIA: Oh, I have a very good reason—as you yourself must very well know . . . '*Mrs Gelli*'!

FULVIA (*staring at her*): Is that how you speak to me now? What a welcome home! What on earth has been happening here? What is this 'reason' you're so sure I must know?

LIVIA: I want to talk to my father!—Where is he?

FULVIA: Do you imagine your father will let you go away?

LIVIA: I think my father has forfeited the right to keep me here, under the same roof . . .

FULVIA: . . . the same roof as me, you mean?

LIVIA: No. The same roof as both of you.

FULVIA (*looking at her hand; very controlled*): All right. You may say what you like. But what makes you think your father will let you . . .

LIVIA: I'll sort that out with him.

FULVIA: Will you, now! All right then, you sort it out with him! . . . I'm tired. You haven't even seen yet what I have brought with me. (*She makes towards the door.*)

LIVIA: Go to her, go on! It's all right by me. You've got *her* now to play happy families with.

FULVIA (*suddenly hopeful, thinking that* LIVIA's *decision may have been prompted by jealousy of her sister*): Ah! So that's it! Oh, no, Livia! Livia darling! You can't possibly know how much I have longed to hold you two children, side by side, together in my heart . . . (*She tries to embrace her.*)

LIVIA (*recoiling with immediate, violent revulsion*): Oh, no! Let me go! No thanks! Side by side with that brat . . . No thank you!

FULVIA (*making a superhuman effort to contain herself, preferring to be hurt herself than have her baby be the object of* LIVIA's *disgust*): It's because of me you feel like that, isn't it Livia? You don't feel that about the baby herself?

LIVIA: I feel like that about you *and* your baby!

FULVIA: Oh, no, no! Because . . . whatever you may think of me . . . whether you like it or not . . . she is your sister!

LIVIA: What? Not yet, she isn't! She is not my sister!

FULVIA: How do you work that out?

LIVIA: She is not my sister because you are not married to my father!

FULVIA: Am I not? What am I then?

LIVIA: You should know better than I do what you are!

FULVIA (*hope dawning once again*): So that's it! . . . Well, Livia, if that's what it is . . . oh, no! Oh, Livia, my dear, how could you think it . . .

LIVIA: Where is your marriage certificate?

FULVIA (*turning to Aunt* ERNESTINA *and* BETTY *in turn*): Was that the conspiracy? (*To* BETTY *and* LIVIA.) Is that what you two have been ferreting out?

LIVIA: There is no record of your marriage!

FULVIA (*interrupting in fierce retaliation*): Oh yes, there is! You can't have searched very well! There's a record, all right!

LIVIA: I need more than that! Where is it, then?

FULVIA: For pity's sake, Livia, don't make me say any more. It's for your own sake, not for mine! I beg you not to push me any farther. I am very tired.

LIVIA: No. You don't need to say any more. What you have said is quite enough.

FULVIA: What is enough?

LIVIA: What you have just admitted.

FULVIA: What's that?

LIVIA: That you keep things back from me. You conceal things which you say it's best for me not to know.

FULVIA: I am not concealing anything!

LIVIA: What was it you begged me not to make you say then? Was it something to do with me?

FULVIA: No . . . no . . . I wouldn't say that . . .

LIVIA: Well, then? Something to do with you?

FULVIA: With me . . . yes . . .

LIVIA: It's not hard to guess!

FULVIA: You couldn't possibly guess! Never in a hundred years could you guess! And it's best this way . . . I do assure you this way is best! Now let it rest and let me be.

LIVIA: I'll let you be! I'm leaving!

FULVIA: But you can't! You mustn't! I have crucified myself during this last year trying to keep you and your father together . . . since you won't be friends with me . . . (*She sees* LIVIA's *scowling face and corrects herself.*) . . . All right, since you *can't* be friends with me. I haven't forced myself upon you. All I have done is show you love, as much love as a real mother, until I realized I must hold back, because it just wasn't working . . . you didn't want my love, it made you angry. Well, I don't want anything. Go on being angry with me if you like. But I am legally married to your father. I don't care what you think about me, but I do care about your baby sister.

You don't have to love me, but she is your sister and you do have to love her. A daughter, just like you . . . exactly the same in every way. And the sooner you realize it the better. Exactly the same, do you hear me? I will not have you think that she differs from you in any way whatsoever.

LIVIA: I suppose you will allow that we have different mothers.

FULVIA (*finally losing all control in response to* LIVIA's *stinging sarcasm*): No, not even that!

LIVIA (*even more icily ironic*): What? Not even that? Don't tell me we have the same mother!

FULVIA: But what is it you think I am? What is it you think of me?

LIVIA: Well—the things you hide, the things it's best for me not to know.

FULVIA: And you want these things to blight my baby's life? Well, you shan't have your way!

LIVIA: My own mother . . .

FULVIA: For God's sake shut up about your mother! You never even knew her!

LIVIA: I may not have known her, but I know who she was! And I know who you are!

FULVIA: Who am I, then? (*She takes hold of* LIVIA *and shakes her in her blind fury.*) What can you know about it? You're so very sure, aren't you? You've got it firmly fixed in your mind, haven't you? You'd like to think my daughter has a whore for a mother? That's it, isn't it? Well, let me tell you, you are exactly the same yourself, you too are the daughter of just such a whore, the same one in fact!

LIVIA (*appalled, horrified*): No!

FULVIA: Oh, yes! Oh, yes! The very same one! You are daughters of the same mother. I am your mother! I am your mother! Do you understand? They told you I was dead! It wasn't true! I am here! I am your mother! What I am for her I am for you! Without any difference! Exactly the same! . . . I feel free, now. Set free. I feel alive, now. (*As she speaks* LIVIA *falls in a dead faint into the arms of her father who, alarmed by the sound of raised voices, has come hastily in with* MARCO MAURI *from the verandah.*)

SILVIO (*holding* LIVIA *close to his breast*): You've killed her!

FULVIA: It's your lie that I've killed! Did you really want it to hang over your other daughter for ever and crush her too? Well—it can't do that now.

SILVIO: After this you can't stay here!

FULVIA: I shall leave. I shall go away. Yes! But not like last time. No, this time it will be different! (*To* MAURI.) Get my baby! She's in there! (*She points to the first door, right.*) Please go and get my baby! (MAURI *hastens to do as she asks.*) My baby!

SILVIO (*trying to bring* LIVIA *round from her dead faint*): Livia! Livia!

FULVIA (*standing by the first door, right, impatiently waiting for* MAURI *to return with the baby*): Is that Livia? . . . This time I'm taking Livia with me. You can tell your Livia that when she comes round. My Livia's coming with me—my own child, alive, beside me, mine to live for! We shall have life! . . . Whatever happens, we'll take our chance!

CURTAIN

THE IMBECILE

L'Imbecille

1922

Translated by
Felicity Firth

CHARACTERS

LUCA FAZIO
LEOPOLDO PARONI
THE COMMERCIAL TRAVELLER
ROSA LAVECCHIA
FIRST JOURNALIST
SECOND JOURNALIST
THIRD JOURNALIST
FOURTH JOURNALIST
FIFTH JOURNALIST

A small shabby room in a private house, the personal office of LEOPOLDO PARONI, editor of the 'Republican Gazette' of Costanova. PARONI is the local leader of the Republican party. He lives alone, and has no time for material comfort, or even, it seems, for cleanliness. There is dirt and total confusion everywhere in the room; the floor and the battered old furniture are littered with rubbish. The desk is cluttered with piles of paper; there are papers and books on the chairs, newspapers everywhere. There are books shoved chaotically into the bookcase, and on a broken-down old leather sofa lies a torn and dirty pillow with its stuffing spilling out in several places.

The street door is on the right. Glass doors, centre back, lead into the main newspaper office. A door to the left leads to PARONI's own apartment.

It is evening. As the curtain rises PARONI's office is in darkness, lit only by a dim light from the murky glass doors to the room beyond.

LUCA FAZIO is sitting huddled on the dirty old sofa, his feet drawn up, while his shoulders, wrapped in a grey woollen shawl, are propped against the pillow. He wears a large travelling cap, which is jammed down over his nose. From time to time an emaciated hand emerges from his shawl, clutching a rolled-up handkerchief. When the light goes on he is seen to have a waxen yellowish cadaverous face with a drooping bedraggled fair moustache and a patchy, sick man's growth of beard. Every now and then he stuffs his rolled-up handkerchief into his mouth in an attempt to stifle the deep cough which racks his chest. From the lighted glass doors come the confused raised voices of PARONI and the staff of the 'Gazette'.

PARONI (*offstage*): We'll just have to give him a thorough
     slating!
OTHER VOICES: He's right, you know! Give him the
     works! That's the stuff! Tear him to bits! But you can't!
     You can't do that!
FIRST JOURNALIST (*his voice carrying above the others*):
     If you do that you'll be playing into Cappadona's hands!
OTHER VOICES: That's right! You'll only be helping the
     Monarchists . . . But that's ridiculous! . . . God, no! You
     mustn't do that!
PARONI (*in a voice of thunder*): No one is going to think
     that! No, we are simply following our line and attacking
     him on the basis of our principles. That's all there is to
     it! Now let me get on and write it!

*They fall silent. LUCA FAZIO has not moved. The door
from the street opens and a voice asks, 'May I come in?'
LUCA FAZIO does not answer. The voice repeats, 'May I
come in?' and the COMMERCIAL TRAVELLER enters.
He is about forty, Piedmontese, and wears a puzzled expression.*

COMMERCIAL TRAVELLER: Is anyone in?
LUCA (*without moving, in a cavernous voice*): They are all
     in there.
COMMERCIAL TRAVELLER (*startled*): Oh, I'm sorry.
     Are you Signor Paroni?
LUCA (*still not moving*): In there. In there. (*Nods towards
     glass doors.*)
COMMERCIAL TRAVELLER: Is it all right to go in?
LUCA (*irritated*): Don't ask me. Go in, if you want to.

*The COMMERCIAL TRAVELLER approaches the door at
the back, but another outburst of voices greets him and he
stops in his tracks. This tumult is echoed by another one
which comes from a popular demonstration outside in the
square. It appears to be getting nearer. The TRAVELLER
stands still in amazement.*

VOICES (*from the inner office*): There you are now, you see? It's a demo, a bloody demo! It's Cappadona's men! The bastards!

FIRST JOURNALIST: They're shouting 'We want Cappadona!' What did I tell you?

PARONI (*banging his fist down on the table and yelling*): And I tell you it's Guido Mazzarini's blood we're after! Cappadona's not my problem!

For a moment the din in the square drowns the journalists' argument. The demonstrators can be heard running past in vast numbers, shouting, 'We want Cappadona. Government Inspectors go home!' As the demonstrators move away, cries from the newspaper office can be heard again: 'Pigs! Pigs! Selfish, unpatriotic pigs! Cappadona's put them up to this.' Two of the JOURNALISTS burst through the glass doors, hats on their heads and armed with sticks. They rush for the street door to go to join in the demonstration.

SECOND JOURNALIST (*furiously rushing towards the door*): Bastards! Bastards!

THIRD JOURNALIST (*bumping into the COMMERCIAL TRAVELLER, and yelling in his face*): They've got the nerve to shout for Cappadona! (*Exit*)

PARONI'S VOICE (*still in the inner room*): Go on, get out! Get out the lot of you! I'm staying here to write!

Three more JOURNALISTS burst through the glass doors, dressed for the street, and make for the demonstration, confusedly yelping 'rotten bastards', 'filthy pigs', 'it's a put-up job'. Again one of them bumps into the COMMERCIAL TRAVELLER and shouts in his face, 'They're calling for Cappadona! Don't you understand?' The three JOURNALISTS exeunt.

COMMERCIAL TRAVELLER: I don't understand at all ... (*To* LUCA FAZIO.) What's going on?

LUCA *has a fierce bout of coughing and blocks his mouth with his handkerchief. The* COMMERCIAL TRAVELLER *peers at him sympathetically but to his shame and embarassment cannot quite conceal his repugnance.*

LUCA: Bloody journalists! Stinking of tobacco! Please stand back! Let me have some air! Let me breathe! (*A bit calmer.*) So you don't live here in Costanova?

COMMERCIAL TRAVELLER: No. I'm just passing through.

LUCA: My dear good sir, we are all of us just passing through.

COMMERCIAL TRAVELLER: I travel for the Sangone papermills. I wanted to see Signor Paroni about supplying the 'Gazette'.

LUCA: I don't somehow think this is the right moment.

COMMERCIAL TRAVELLER: Yes, I heard. There's a demonstration going on.

LUCA (*with sombre irony*): The people here are all still fuming at the results of the elections eight months ago. They can't be doing with their Member of Parliament, Guido Mazzarini.

COMMERCIAL TRAVELLER: Is he a Socialist?

LUCA: I don't know. I think so. In Costanova itself he had no support at all. He got in on the votes of the other districts. He's a great man. (*Rubs his finger and thumb together to indicate that Mazzarini has money.*) And now they're cutting up rough because he has hit back at them. He has sent a government inspector down here—do you mind . . . do you mind moving away a bit . . . I can't breathe—a government inspector to look into local politics—thanks—that's quite a thing, a government inspector!

COMMERCIAL TRAVELLER: But they were booing!

LUCA: That's right. They don't want him. Costanova, you see, is a very important place. You have to realize that the entire universe revolves around it. Look out of the window. See those stars? Do you know what they are doing? They are stuck up there for the sole purpose of

squinting down at Costanova. I've heard it suggested
that the stars find Costanova a bit of a joke. Don't you
believe it. The stars are all consumed with one desire, to
have a city just like Costanova. And do you know where
the fate of the Universe is decided? At the meetings of the
Costanova Urban District Council. At the moment the
Council has been dissolved and consequently the
Universe is in total disarray. One look at Paroni's face
will tell you that. Have a look, go on, you can see it
through those glass doors!

COMMERCIAL TRAVELLER (*going up to the doors*):
It's frosted glass!

LUCA: So it is. I forgot.

COMMERCIAL TRAVELLER: You're not on the staff
of the newspaper?

LUCA: No. I'm a sympathised. Or rather, I was. I'm on the
point of leaving altogether. I am suffering from the local
disease. Quite a crowd of us have got it. My two brothers
for instance, they were on the staff of the newspaper before
they copped it. I was a medical student until the day before
yesterday. I got back this morning. I have come home to
die. You sell the paper that newspapers are made of?

COMMERCIAL TRAVELLER: Yes, among other kinds.
We sell at competitive prices.

LUCA: To make people print more and more newspapers?

COMMERCIAL TRAVELLER: Believe me, the price of
paper . . . in the present state of the market . . .

LUCA (*cutting him short*): I'm sure you're right. It's a
comfort to me you know, to think you will be travelling
around in the years to come, going from town to town,
offering the paper you make at your papermill at competitive prices to piddling little weekly local newspapers!
You 'll get back here, say in ten years' time, and see this
same old sofa, though it won't have me sitting on it.
Perhaps Costanova will have settled down by then . . .

Three of the JOURNALISTS *who had run out to the
demonstration burst in through the street door, shouting.*

FIRST JOURNALIST: Paroni! Paroni!

SECOND JOURNALIST: All hell's broken loose out there!

THIRD JOURNALIST: For Christ's sake, come out, Leopoldo!

LEOPOLDO PARONI *comes hurrying through the glass doors, Paroni the proud Republican. He has a dirty oil-lamp in his hand. He is about fifty. He has a lion's mane, a big nose, an upturned moustache, a mephistophelian goatee beard and a red tie.*

PARONI: What is it? Are they fighting? (*He puts the lamp on the desk, shifting some papers to do so.*)

SECOND JOURNALIST: They've gone mad!

FIRST JOURNALIST: It's the Socialists. They have come in hordes from all over the province.

PARONI: Who are they attacking? Cappadona's people?

THIRD JOURNALIST: No, us!

FIRST JOURNALIST: Come on! Let's hurry! (*To* PARONI.) You really are needed out there!

PARONI (*extricating himself*): Hang on a minute. What about the police? What the hell are they doing about it?

FIRST JOURNALIST: The police? It's just what that bloody Inspector wants! He can't wait to see us beaten up! Come on!

PARONI: Let's go! (*To the* THIRD JOURNALIST *who instantly obeys.*) Go and get my hat and stick! Where are Conti and Fabrizi?

SECOND JOURNALIST: Out there. They are doing what they can.

FIRST JOURNALIST: In self-defence!

PARONI: Couldn't Cappadona's chaps have called in the police?

FIRST JOURNALIST: Cappadona's chaps have got the hell out!

PARONI: And did it really need all three of you to come and get me? One would have done.

THIRD JOURNALIST (*re-entering from inner office*): I can't find your stick.

PARONI: Over in the corner by the hat-stand.

FIRST JOURNALIST: Come on, can't you! You can have my stick!

PARONI: You'll need it yourself! They are clubbing each other out there!

Enter Miss ROSA LAVECCHIA, *out of breath and in a state of shock. She is about fifty, red-haired, thin, bespectacled and dressed in a somewhat mannish style.*

ROSA (*exhausted, trying to get her breath*): Oh God ... Oh my God!

PARONI AND THE OTHERS (*with great anxiety*): What is it? What is it? What has happened?

ROSA: Don't you know?

PARONI: Have they killed someone?

ROSA (*staring at them, not understanding*): No ... Where?

FIRST JOURNALIST: What? Don't you know there's a demonstration out there?

ROSA (*still baffled*): A demonstration? Is there? No, no, I have just come from poor Pulino's house.

SECOND JOURNALIST: Why, what's up with him?

ROSA: He has killed himself!

FIRST JOURNALIST: Killed himself?

PARONI: Pulino?

THIRD JOURNALIST: Young Lou Pulino, killed himself?

ROSA: A couple of hours ago. They found him hanging from the light fixture in the kitchen.

FIRST JOURNALIST: He hanged himself?

ROSA: God, what a sight! I went and saw him ... He was black in the face ... his eyes and his tongue were sticking out ... his hands were clenched ... He looked all elongated, dangling there in the middle of the room ...

SECOND JOURNALIST: I say, poor old Pulino!

FIRST JOURNALIST: He was clapped out already, poor old chap! He hadn't long to go anyway.

THIRD JOURNALIST: But what a way to go!

SECOND JOURNALIST: He was putting himself out of his misery, I suppose.

FIRST JOURNALIST: He couldn't even stand . . .

PARONI: But the man's an imbecile! What a waste! There's a bloke, with no further use for his life, and he goes and . . .

FIRST JOURNALIST: What do you mean?

SECOND JOURNALIST: Why shouldn't he kill himself?

THIRD JOURNALIST: Why does that make him an imbecile?

FIRST JOURNALIST: If his time is up anyway! . . .

SECOND JOURNALIST: What kind of a life did he have . . . !

PARONI: That's just it! That's the point! . . . My God, I'd have paid his train fare.

THIRD JOURNALIST: His train fare?

FIRST JOURNALIST: What are you talking about?

SECOND JOURNALIST: His train fare to Heaven?

PARONI: No! His fare to Rome. I'd have paid his fare to Rome. God, yes. My God, I would! When a bloke has no further use for his life . . . When he's made up his mind to kill himself anyway, before he goes he might as well . . . Christ, what a kick I should get out of making my death serve some kind of purpose! Don't you *see*? So I'm ill. I'm going to die tomorrow. And there's this man who has shamefully betrayed my home town; everybody is agreed that he has let them down disgracefully . . . and needs to be removed—Guido Mazzarini. Right: first I kill him and then I kill myself!—That's the way to do it! Anyone who misses a chance like that is an imbecile.

THIRD JOURNALIST: The poor chap won't even have thought of it!

PARONI: He couldn't fail to have thought of it. Living here . . . well until a couple of hours ago . . . he was just as much a victim of the local scandal as we all are. The whole place is disgraced, poisoned with it. I'd have put the gun into his hand myself! Kill the other chap . . . then kill yourself . . . Imbecile! (*At this point the two other* JOURNALISTS *re-enter jubilantly from the street.*)

FOURTH JOURNALIST: All finished! All finished!

FIFTH JOURNALIST: They turned tail like a flock of sheep!

FIRST JOURNALIST (*coldly*): Did the police intervene?

FOURTH JOURNALIST: Yes, but only at the end!

FIFTH JOURNALIST: Our chaps got in first though . . . they were terrific . . . you should have seen them . . . on top of them . . . they were like lions!

FOURTH JOURNALIST: They flayed them! (*Suddenly noticing that his words are not having much effect.*) What's up?

ROSA: It's poor Pulino . . .

FIFTH JOURNALIST: What has Pulino got to do with anything?

FIRST JOURNALIST: He hanged himself two hours ago.

FOURTH JOURNALIST: Did he? Lou Pulino? Hanged himself?

FIFTH JOURNALIST: Poor old Lou! Well, yes, he told me he had had enough of it. Cut short the agony. Well . . . it was a good thing to do.

PARONI: He could have done even better. We were talking about it just now. Okay, he was doing himself a favour by killing himself. He could have gone to Rome first and disposed of that public pest, Guido Mazzarini! It wouldn't have cost him anything. I would have paid his fare. By God, I would! It was the death of an imbecile.

FIRST JOURNALIST: Well, there we are. It's late.

SECOND JOURNALIST: It certainly is. We'll write up tonight's events tomorrow.

THIRD JOURNALIST: After all we've got until Sunday.

SECOND JOURNALIST (*with a sigh*): And we'll put something in about poor Pulino.

ROSA (*to* PARONI): I'll do something if you like, Paroni . . . actually having seen him . . .

FOURTH JOURNALIST: We—ell, we could go and take a look ourselves, couldn't we, lads? We'll be going that way.

ROSA: You may find he is still hanging. They can't take him down till the Coroner gets back from Borgo.

PARONI: What a waste! We could have given over the whole number this Sunday to Pulino and his patriotic gesture!

FIRST JOURNALIST (*suddenly noticing* LUCA FAZIO): But look who's here! It's Fazio! (*They all turn to look.*)

PARONI: Luca!

SECOND JOURNALIST: Have you been sitting there all the time? Why didn't you say?

THIRD JOURNALIST: When did you get here?

LUCA (*impatiently, but not getting up*): This morning.

FOURTH JOURNALIST: Are you ill?

LUCA (*with some hesitation, then pointing to his chest*): Same as Pulino.

PARONI (*noticing the* COMMERCIAL TRAVELLER): And excuse me, who are you?

COMMERCIAL TRAVELLER: Ah, Signor Paroni, I called about supplying you with paper.

PARONI: You must be the traveller from Sangone. Come back tomorrow . . . if you don't mind. It's late now.

COMMERCIAL TRAVELLER: I'll call in the morning, sir. I want to start back in good time.

FIRST JOURNALIST: Let's make tracks. Good-night Leopoldo. (*He exchanges goodnights with* PARONI.)

FOURTH JOURNALIST (*to* LUCA FAZIO): Aren't you coming?

LUCA (*sombrely*): No. I want a word with Paroni.

PARONI (*apprehensively*): With me?

LUCA (*still sombrely*): Just two minutes. (*They all look at him nervously, seeing the obvious connection between his present desperate condition and Pulino's 'imbecile suicide'.*)

PARONI: Can't you say it here in front of everyone?

LUCA: No, I want to see you alone.

PARONI (*to the others*): Well, you'd better go then. I'll wish you all goodnight (*Renewed goodnights.*)

COMMERCIAL TRAVELLER: I'll come at about ten.

PARONI: Earlier, if you like, earlier. Goodbye. (*Exeunt all except* PARONI *and* LUCA FAZIO, *who finally takes his legs off the sofa and sits hunched, staring at the floor.* PARONI *comes up to him solicitously and is about to place a hand on his shoulder.*) My dear old chap! Luca, my friend . . .

LUCA (*getting up, with a gesture of pushing* PARONI *away*): No, keep away from me!

PARONI: Why?

LUCA: You make me cough.

PARONI: You're really ill, aren't you? I can see.

LUCA (*nods affirmatively before replying*): Yes, I'm done to a turn, for your purposes. Shut the door properly. (*Points to street door.*)

PARONI: Yes, of course. (*Shuts the door.*)

LUCA: Turn the lock.

PARONI (*doing so with a laugh*): There's no point. No one will come in here this late. You can speak quite freely. It won't go any further.

LUCA: Shut that door as well. (*He point to the glass door.*)

PARONI: What's the point? You know I live alone. There's nobody in there. In fact I'll switch off that light. (*Goes to do so.*)

LUCA: And then shut the door. That room stinks of tobacco.

PARONI *goes into the newspaper office turns off the light and comes back, closing the door behind him. Meanwhile* LUCA FAZIO *has stood up.*

PARONI: There. Now, what did you want to say?

LUCA: Keep away . . . Keep away . . .

PARONI: Why? For my sake or for yours?

LUCA: Partly for yours.

PARONI: But I'm not afraid.

LUCA: Don't speak too soon.

PARONI: Well, what's it all about, then? Take a seat ... here, sit you down!

LUCA: No, I'd rather stand.

PARONI: So, you've come from Rome?

LUCA: From Rome. (*Coughs*) I got ill, as you see. I had a tidy sum of money, but I got through it all. I just kept enough ... (*brings out a large revolver from his coat pocket*) ... to buy this gun.

PARONI (*growing pale at the sight of this weapon in the hand of such a man in such a state, and raising his hands instinctively*): Oh! ... is it ... is it loaded? (*Watching as LUCA scrutinizes the weapon.*) Luca, I'm asking ... is it loaded?

LUCA (*icily*): It's loaded. (*He looks steadily at PARONI.*) You said you weren't afraid.

PARONI: No, but ... for Christ's sake ... (*Tries to take the gun away from LUCA.*)

LUCA: Keep away ... let me finish telling you. I had shut myself in my room, you see, in my room in Rome. I was going to finish myself off.

PARONI: What a crazy idea!

LUCA: It was a crazy idea. And I was really going to do it. As you said, yes, it was an imbecile idea.

PARONI (*after staring at him for a moment, his eyes suddenly lighting up with joy*): Ah! you mean ... you don't mean ... do you?

LUCA (*quickly*): Wait. You will see what I mean.

PARONI (*gleefully*): You heard what I said about Pulino?

LUCA: Yes. That's what I'm here for.

PARONI: You mean you'd do it?

LUCA: Right now.

PARONI (*jubilant*): But that's terrific!

LUCA: Let me finish my story. I was holding the gun to my temple when there was a knock at my door ...

PARONI: This was in Rome?

LUCA: In Rome. I opened the door. Who do you think it was? Guido Mazzarini.

PARONI: Mazzarini? At your house?

LUCA: He took one look at the gun in my hand and one look at my face and he knew what I was going to do. He ran at me and took hold of my arms and shook me and shouted at me. He said 'For God's sake, Luca, you're not killing yourself just like that? You can do better than that, you imbecile! Come on! If you're going to do that . . . I'll pay your fare . . . just get yourself down to Costanova for me first and wipe out Leopoldo Paroni!

PARONI (*who up to this point has listened in some agitation to* LUCA's *grim and peculiar story, half- expecting to see the young man commit some dire act of violence in his presence, now feels his blood run cold and smiles an inane and ghastly smile*): . . . Is it a joke?

LUCA (*drawing back a pace, his face twitching one-sidedly in a convulsive grimace, and speaking from the side of his mouth*): No. It's not a joke. Mazzarini paid my fare.

PARONI: He paid your fare? What do you mean?

LUCA: And here I am. So, first of all, I kill you. And then I kill myself. (*He raises the gun and aims.*)

PARONI (*terrified, his hand over his face, trying to duck and shouting*): Are you crazy? Luca! Don't do it! . . . Stop playing the fool . . . Are you crazy?

LUCA (*in a voice of fierce authority*): Don't move! If you do, I really shall fire, you know.

PARONI (*petrified*): All right . . . all right.

LUCA: Crazy, eh? You think I'm crazy? You can call me crazy, when just now you called Pulino an imbecile for not going to Rome to kill Mazzarini before he hanged himself.

PARONI (*trying to get up*): But that's completely different! Good God, that's a different thing altogether. I am not Mazzarini!

LUCA: Different? How is it different? What earthly difference do you suppose there is between you and Mazzarini to people like me and Pulino? We're not interested any more in your lives and your pathetic little circus acts!

We don't care whether it's you we kill or somebody else. It's all the same to *us*!

PARONI: You can't say that! How can it be the same! You couldn't commit a totally mindless and gratuitous crime!

LUCA: Whereas you want to use us as the tools of your personal antagonisms and idiotic rivalries, now, when for us it's all over and time is up! And if we refuse, you call us imbeciles. All right, then: I don't wish to be called an imbecile like Pulino; I'm going to kill you (*He raises the gun again to take aim.*)

PARONI (*imploring now, desperately trying to keep out of the line of fire*): For Christ's sake, Luca! What are you doing? Put that thing down! Why, for God's sake! I've always been your friend!

LUCA (*the temptation to pull the trigger flashing in his eyes*): Don't move! Don't move! Now, kneel! Go on, kneel down!

PARONI (*falling to his knees*): All right . . . But for Christ's sake don't do it!

LUCA (*sneering*): You talk about having no more use for one's life! You idiot! . . . Calm down, I shan't kill you. Get up, but don't come any nearer.

PARONI (*getting up*): What a low-down dirty trick! I suppose that gun makes you feel you can do anything.

LUCA: And you are scared out of your mind because you know there's nothing to stop me. I suppose as a true republican you're an atheist, a free-thinker. You must be. Or you wouldn't have called Pulino an imbecile for not killing.

PARONI: I'll tell you why I said that . . . it was . . . well . . . because I'm so mad at the way we have been so shamefully treated.

LUCA: Well, that's fine. But you're still a free-thinker, you can't deny it. You make a thing of it in your newspaper.

PARONI (*muttering*): Free-thinker . . . well . . . what about you? I don't suppose you believe in punishments and rewards in some mythical after-life.

LUCA: I find it an appalling idea . . . to have to drag into yet another life the chance experiences of twenty-six years spent here.

PARONI: Well, then, you see . . .

LUCA (*quickly*): I see I could do it. I could kill you just like that. That is not what's stopping me. But I shan't kill you. Nor do I think I'm an imbecile if I refrain. Frankly, I pity you, I pity *your* imbecility. If only you knew; to me now, you seem so very far away. You look to me like a funny little man, rather sweet, a bit pathetic actually in that silly red tie. And while we are talking about your imbecility, I'd like a signed statement.

PARONI (*still stunned, not hearing properly*): What are you saying?

LUCA: A signed statement. A certificate. It's my right, the privileged right of a man on the brink of death. You're not in a position to say no. Sit down. Sit down there, and write. (*He points with the gun to the desk.*)

PARONI: Write? What shall I write? Are you serious?

LUCA: Oh yes, I'm serious. Sit down there and write.

PARONI: What do you want me to write?

LUCA (*again pointing to the desk, then placing the gun against* PARONI's *ribs*): Get up and sit over there! Go on, do as I say!

PARONI (*at gunpoint, going to the desk*): What now?

LUCA: Sit down. There's the pen. Come on, there's the pen.

PARONI (*picking up the pen*): What must I write?

LUCA: I'll dictate. You're the underdog now, but I know you. Tomorrow when you hear that I, too, have killed myself like Pulino, there will be no holding you down, you'll be shooting your mouth off . . . In here, down at the café, all over the place, calling me an imbecile, this time!

PARONI: Oh, no! You don't think I'd do that? That wasn't supposed to be serious!

LUCA: I know you. I want to avenge Pulino; I'm not doing it for myself. Write!

PARONI (*looks at desk*): What am I supposed to write on?

LUCA: Here, come on, this piece of paper will do.

PARONI: What shall I say?

LUCA: I want a brief statement.

PARONI: A statement . . . who for?

LUCA: Not for anybody. Come on, let's get it down. I'm sparing your life on this condition. If you don't write, I shoot.

PARONI: All right, all right . . . Start dictating.

LUCA (*dictating*): 'I, the undersigned, hereby express heartfelt remorse and repentance . . .'

PARONI (*objecting*): Hey, what's this about repentance?

LUCA (*with a smile, playfully placing the gun's nose against PARONI's temple*): You don't fancy a spot of repentance?

PARONI (*extricating his head and eyeing the gun*): Well, let's see what it is I'm supposed to repent of . . .

LUCA (*continuing the dictation*): 'I, the undersigned, hereby express heartfelt remorse and repentance at having called Pulino an imbecile . . .'

PARONI: Ah, that's it, is it?

LUCA: That's it. Carry on, 'in the presence of my friends and colleagues, on the grounds that Pulino, before committing suicide, did not go to Rome to kill Mazzarini.' So much is pure fact. We'll leave out the bit about your being willing to pay his fare. Have you got that down?

PARONI (*resigned*): I've got it. What next?

LUCA (*dictating*): 'Luca Fazio, before killing himself, . . .'

PARONI: You really are going to kill yourself?

LUCA: That's my business. Go on, 'before killing himself, called on me'—do you want to put in that I had a gun?

PARONI (*at the end of his tether*): Oh yes, oh yes please!

LUCA: Go on, then! . . . 'armed with a revolver.' They will hardly be able to get me for carrying an offensive weapon. Right. Got that? Well, then, 'armed with a revolver, and proceeded to tell me, that to avoid being called an imbecile by Mazzarini or by anybody else, he would have to shoot me like a dog.' (*He waits for PARONI to get it all down.*) Have you got, 'like a dog'?

Good. New paragraph. 'He could have done so, but he did not. He did not do it because he was overwhelmed by disgust. (PARONI *raises his head questioningly*. LUCA *continues inexorably*.) No, wait a minute. Put 'disgust and pity.' That's it. 'Overwhelmed by disgust and pity at my cowardice.'

PARONI: I can't put that . . .

LUCA: It's the truth. Don't forget I am armed.

PARONI: No . . . how could I? . . . Whatever you say, my dear fellow . . .

LUCA: That's right. Whatever I say. Have you got that last bit?

PARONI: I've got that last bit. Will that do now?

LUCA: No, hold on, there's the conclusion! Just a couple of words now, and we're done.

PARONI: What do you want a conclusion for? Isn't that enough?

LUCA: I've got it. Here we are! Put, 'It was enough for Luca Fazio that I declare the true imbecile to be myself, Leopoldo Paroni.'

PARONI (*pushing the paper away*): No, I'm sorry, but that's going too far!

LUCA (*peremptorily, spelling out the syllables*): 'I declare the true imbecile to be myself, Leopoldo Paroni.' It might be more dignified my dear chap if you kept your eyes on the paper and not on this gun. I have told you I intend to avenge Pulino. Now sign it.

PARONI: I've signed it. Is that all now?

LUCA: Give it here.

PARONI (*handing him the paper*): There you are. But what are you going to do with it now? If you're really going to do away with yourself . . .

LUCA (*who does not reply at once but finishes reading what PARONI has written*): Right . . . What am I going to do with it? Nothing. They will simply find it on me, tomorrow. (*He folds it in four and puts it in his pocket.*) Let it be some consolation to you, Leopoldo, to think that I am going off now to do something which is perhaps just a mite more difficult than what you've just done. Open the door. (PARONI *does so*.) Goodnight.

CURTAIN

BIBLIOGRAPHY

The following is a list of Pirandello's plays with the date of the first Italian performance. The English title is given where the play has been translated:

1910 *La morsa* (The Vise)
 Lumie di Sicilia (Limes from Sicily)
1913 *Il dovere del medico* (The Doctor's Duty)
1915 *Se non cosi*
1916 *Pensaci, Giacomino!* (Think it over, Giacomino!)
 Liolà (Liolà)
1917 *Cosi è se vi pare* (Right You Are, If You Think You Are)
 Il berretto a sonagli (Cap and Bells)
 La giara (The Jar)
 Il pacere dell 'onesta' (The Pleasure of Honesty)
 L'Innesto (The Grafting)
1918 *Ma non è una cosa seria*
 Il giuoco delle parti (The Rules of the Game)
1919 *La patente*
 L'Uomo, la bestia, e la virtu'
1920 *Tutto per bene* (All for the Best)
 Come prima, meglio di prima (This Time It Will Be Different)
 Cece' (Chee-Chee)
 La Signora Morli, una e due
1921 *Sei personaggi in cerca d'autore* (Six Characters in Search of an Author)
1922 *Enrico IV* (Henry IV)
 All'uscita (At the Gate)
 L'Imbecille (The Imbecile)
 Vestire gli ignudi (Clothe the Naked)
1923 *L'Uomo dal fiore in bocca* (The Man with a Flower in his Mouth)
 La vita che ti diedi (The Life I gave Thee)
 L'Altra figlio (The Other Son)
1924 *Ciascuno a suo modo* (Each in His Own Way)
1925 *Sagra del signore della nave* (Our Lord of the Ship)

1927 *Diana e la tuda*
L'Amico delle mogli
Bellavita (Bellavita)
1928 *Scamandro*
La nuova colonia
1929 *O di uno ò di nessuno*
Lazzaro (Lazarus)
1930 *Come tu mi vuoi* (As You Desire Me)
Questa sera si recita a soggetto (Tonight We Improvise)
1932 *Trovarsi*
1933 *Quando si e'qualcuno*
1934 *La favola del figlio cambiato*
1935 *Non si sa come*
1936 *Sogno (ma forse no)* (A Dream—Or Is It?)
1937 *I giganti della montagna* (The Mountain Giants)